About the Author

Devanath Thenabadu grew up in Sri Lanka and lived in Paris, France, before leaving for Montreal, Canada, where he currently resides. For most of his adult life, he has been focused on the core themes of this book, namely a quest for meaning, waking up in everyday life and emotional healing. The written word having had a transformative impact on his life, he's now looking to give back in writing what he has received from books, teachings and the world.

Devanath Thenabadu

Journey to the West

One Man's Odyssey into His Own Mind

AIA PUBLISHING

Journey to the West: One Man's Odyssey into His Own Mind
Devanath Thenabadu
Copyright © 2022
Published by AIA Publishing, Australia
ABN: 32736122056
http://www.aiapublishing.com

All rights reserved. No part of this publication may be reproduced, stored in a retrieval system or transmitted in any form or by any means electronic, mechanical, audio, visual or otherwise, without prior permission of the copyright owner. Nor can it be circulated in any form of binding or cover other than that in which it is published and without similar conditions including this condition being imposed on the subsequent purchaser.

ISBN: 978-1-922329-36-3

In order to awaken, first of all one must realize that one is in a state of sleep.

George Ivanovich Gurdjieff

Any reflections, descriptions or statements about characters or events in this book are purely personal opinion.

Interpretations of various texts, teachings and concepts are based on the author's experience. Readers are urged to consult the sources and come to their own understanding.

Contents

Part I Paris ... ix
Chapter 1 *Jardin du Luxembourg* ... 1
Chapter 2 *Rue Descartes* ... 10
Chapter 3 *Rue Rochambeau* ... 18
Chapter 4 *Hôtel d'Alger* ... 29
Chapter 5 *Rue Oberkampf* ... 47
Chapter 6 *Rue Nicolas Charlet* ... 61
Chapter 7 *Bibliothèque Sainte-Geneviève* ... 71
Part II Montreal ... 85
Chapter 8 *Mount Royal* ... 87
Chapter 9 *Boulevard Saint-Laurent* ... 104
Chapter 10 *Pacific Ocean, Vancouver* ... 119
Chapter 11 *Indian Ocean, Mount Lavinia* ... 132
Chapter 12 *Nowy Świat, Warsaw* ... 143
Chapter 13 *People's Cathedral, Moscow* ... 158
Chapter 14 *Mount Royal Revisited* ... 173
Part III Pilgrimages ... 205
Chapter 15 *Bodh Gaya, India* ... 207
Chapter 16 *Boulevard Saint-Laurent Revisited* ... 223
Chapter 17 *Eihei-ji, Japan* ... 233
Chapter 18 *Sherbrooke Street* ... 247
Chapter 19 *Avon, France* ... 255
Chapter 20 *Gyumri, Armenia* ... 265
Chapter 21 *Saint Louis Square* ... 282
A Note from the Author ... 301

Part I
Paris

Chapter 1
Jardin du Luxembourg

The train from Charles de Gaulle airport sped through suburbs of sprawling concrete. Splattered with menacing graffiti, they were so unlike the popular images of lively cobblestoned Parisian street scenes. We made several stops, and the car became crowded. I removed my large red-and-black duffle bag from the seat next to me and squeezed it under my legs. Since then, I've always travelled with a duffle bag. I like the feeling of picking my bag up off the baggage carousel with one hand, slinging it over my left shoulder, and striding ahead of my fellow passengers lugging heavy baggage.

To my surprise, the train dipped underground as it approached Paris. It probably showed in my face that I had just arrived in the country, having left home for the first time. My thoughts went back to the previous night. Reading Ernest Hemingway's *A Moveable Feast* not long before my flight, my heart had quickened when I came across the line "If you are lucky enough to have lived in Paris as a young man, then wherever you go for the rest of your life, it stays with you, for Paris is a moveable feast." But when I'd climbed the boarding stairs of the plane that night, my feet felt heavy.

I remembered waving goodbye to my mother through the glass partition at the airport just outside Colombo. I was too far away to see the expression on her face but as she craned her neck to get a last look and slowly raised her hand, she looked smaller than usual.

We arrived at the Gare du Nord to scenes of chaos. I stood on the platform as people brushed past me on both sides and incomprehensible announcements in French blared from the PA system over the general din. Somehow, I found my way to a youth hostel just south of the Jardin du Luxembourg. I waited at the front desk, leaning back in my chair, elbow on arm rest and chin on palm. The balding receptionist laboriously filled out the information from my passport into an imposing-looking black register. When finally done, he took a key from a drawer and told me how to get to my dormitory. About a dozen beds filled the large room. I dumped my duffle bag next to the bed closest to the exit, took a quick shower and stepped out onto the streets of Paris.

It was a Sunday, the streets empty of cars, and although it was well into the morning, everywhere I wandered, the sweet scent of fresh baked bread followed me. Strangely enough, during my thirteen-year stay in Paris, I never smelled it so strongly again.

I followed Boulevard Saint-Michel past the gold-tipped iron railings of the Jardin du Luxembourg on my left, and the Panthéon with its rather incongruous facade of massive Greek columns on the right. I kept going north and stopped on the bridge over the Seine, leaning over the side on my forearms with my hands clasped together, almost facing the Notre-Dame de Paris cathedral. From my vantage point, I couldn't see any of the gargoyles and flying buttresses I remembered from a film version of *The Hunchback of Notre-Dame*. I turned around and leaned against the side of the bridge with my arms folded.

The previous evening I had been in my family home in Mount Lavinia, a place few people outside of Sri Lanka had heard of. It should have felt extraordinary to be standing there in the heart of iconic Paris. But it didn't. I wasn't really seeing the beauty and rich history all around me. Instead, it was as if I were looking at everything through an impenetrable fog.

I'm not really here!

I continued north and ended up on Rue Saint-Denis, famed for its streetwalkers and the setting for *Irma la Douce*, an old movie I had seen. It was not yet noon, but some women in various stages of undress were already standing together in groups of twos or threes in animated conversation, dragging on cigarettes. Two carried on a loud conversation across the street, uninterested in drumming up any business. A couple of other women leaned wearily against doorways, looking as if they hadn't had any business in a while. Nothing much had changed since Irma's time.

I stood at the intersection of Boulevard de Sébastopol, wondering which way to go, when I was struck by the strange sight of several men coming toward me. Their faces were covered by large sheets of white paper. As they came closer, I saw they were eating large, well-wrapped sandwiches. I tracked the trickle of sandwich eaters to their source: a small restaurant tucked into a side street. As I approached the takeout section in the front, the man behind the counter looked at me questioningly. I pointed at a customer walking away with a white package in his hands and a look of anticipation on his face.

"Merguez frites," the man behind the counter said, nodding.

He threw a handful of frozen french fries and several thin red sausages into a deep fryer, then cut a large loaf of French bread into three pieces and slit one open. He then lifted the steel mesh basket from the fryer, tossed the contents a few times in the air to drain the oil and took out the sausages with a pair of tongs and placed them inside the piece of bread. I watched him as he added a squirt of some red sauce from a thin plastic bottle, then tilted the mesh basket to slide the fries into the sandwich and sprinkled salt all over. Finally, he deftly wrapped the sandwich.

Holding the sandwich in one hand and picking out fries with the other, I took off again. A crowd was milling in front of a cinema complex showing Hollywood blockbusters on Boulevard Poissonnière. As a regular at film festivals organized by embassies of various European countries in Colombo, it was puzzling to see people of a country that had such film directors as Jean-Luc Godard and François Truffaut flocking to see commercial American movies.

Two Black women came toward me. One of them unwrapped an ice cream and let the wrapper fall to the ground. An older White man nearby said something sharply to her. She picked up the wrapper and threw it into a trash can with a gesture of annoyance. The man swaggered past me, a satisfied self-righteous look on his face saying, "We have to teach *these people* how to behave." I walked away unsure whose side I was on.

On my way back to the youth hostel, I came upon Rodin's bronze sculpture of Balzac on Boulevard Raspail. I stepped back to get a better look. This Balzac's massive torso was wrapped in a cloak. His rugged face exuded strength and purpose like a general going out to battle or a captain of industry looking to grind his competitors into the ground. Nothing like the sensitive and fragile artist I'd imagined. But I remembered a quote from Balzac that went something like "I had to write thousands of pages before I could sign my name." I learned later that Rodin was striving for a *psychological* and not a physical likeness. But the patrons who had commissioned the work would have none of it and rejected the sculpture Rodin had worked on for seven years. His Balzac is now considered by some to be the first truly modern sculpture.

Back in my dormitory, I took off my shoes and had a nap. When I woke up, I saw a small man with dark, thinning hair sitting on the bed next to mine. He was writing in a notebook. I stretched my arms and legs in a somewhat exaggerated manner to let him know I was awake.

He looked over at me and introduced himself as Henry, from London. He swung his legs across and sat on the edge of his bed. I sat in the middle of mine with my legs crossed under me and introduced myself.

"So what do you think of Paris?" he asked.

I wanted to say something about Rodin's Balzac, but instead I heard myself saying somewhat sanctimoniously, "I didn't expect to see so many billboards and so much advertising in the streets. I believe consumerism represents a real risk for society."

Henry shrugged. "What's the big deal? Billboards sell products, companies make profits and pay taxes and governments use the money to pay for education and health. Seems like a good system to me."

A couple of years earlier, I had converted to Marxism, a religion that had lost its appeal, and I was trying to think of a suitably crushing response to this infuriatingly reasonable argument when Henry changed the subject.

"Just curious, what were things like in Sri Lanka, for you?" he asked.

I hesitated. I saw my younger self riding his bike in our leafy neighbourhood, the cool morning breeze on his face, reading books and more books, playing street cricket with friends, and attending school at a sprawling campus by the Indian Ocean.

"Not bad. I can't complain."

Henry didn't look satisfied, so I continued, "But I felt stifled. Lots of pressure to conform, you know. I had to leave to figure out what I needed to do with my life."

It was my turn to change the subject. I asked him what had brought him to Paris.

"I come here often," he said. "I'm dating a local girl. I like French girls. They're so feminine," he added.

Up to then I had thought all women were feminine, but Henry seemed to be saying that some women and even an entire nation of them could be more feminine than others. I wondered whether femininity, a much more elusive concept than physical attractiveness, could explain why some women were more appealing than others.

Not long after, when I started taking French classes, I was surprised to learn various parts of French grammar are inflected for gender. It occurred to me then that language could have something to do with femininity. As words are what we all use to explain the world around us, our worldview is undoubtedly conditioned by our own specific linguistic structures. So as soon as French girls start to talk, language is another fact of life that sets them apart from the boys.

Henry told me he had studied at Oxford and dated a Sri Lankan girl there.

"She had an inseparable friend, a Pakistani girl, who discovered sex at some point during her time at Oxford. So we called her Lahore." He threw back his head and laughed.

Noticing I didn't join in the merriment, Henry felt he had some explaining to do. "La . . . whore," he repeated, exaggerating the space between the syllables. "And Lahore is the capital of Pakistan. Get it?"

I was pretty sure Lahore wasn't the capital of Pakistan but that was beside the point. I also wondered why an Oxford man like Henry, who must have been close to thirty, if not older, was staying in a hostel dormitory.

~

The next morning I followed the smell of fresh coffee up the stairs to the kitchen. Sunlight filtered through the open windows as a fresh breeze lifted the lace curtains. Baskets of freshly cut French bread, plates of butter, and jars of jam covered the long table in the middle of the room. A dozen young people sat on two long benches on either side of the table with bowls of steaming coffee in front of them. A chorus of voices in different languages rose above the clatter of cutlery and the hissing of percolating coffee. *A moveable feast*, I thought as I stood at the entrance and took in the scene. My heart quickened again, and I remembered how, after starting to read books in English when I was about seven, I had discovered there was a great big world out there and wanted very much to be part of it.

Dazzled by the sunlight, it took me a while to figure out that the young man I sat next to was blind. Liam from Belfast buttered his bread and told me he was studying at a prestigious school where most of the French political elite studied. Not knowing then that I too was going to study there, I didn't pay much attention; I was looking for the cheese. After some hesitation I asked Liam whether they might have forgotten to put it on the table.

"French people don't eat cheese for breakfast," he replied in a rather professorial tone, holding up his butter-streaked knife.

"Really?" I began to say, but changed it to "Ah, yes," as if I had known all along but it had just slipped my mind. I'd have liked to know at what time during the day French people ate their famous cheese but, of course, I couldn't have asked Liam.

I cradled a warm bowl in my palms, raised it and tilted it toward my face, taking in the smoky aroma and the bitter-sweetness of coffee laced with milk. Drinking coffee from a bowl made the experience much more sensual, I thought, and patted myself on the back for thinking such an interesting thought. I wanted to share it with Liam but he was too busy talking to his neighbour on the other side.

I headed off to do some sightseeing that included standing behind a large group of excited people at the Louvre and trying to catch a glimpse of the *Mona Lisa* from a distance. I crossed the Jardin des Tuileries to the Jeu de Paume museum, which housed important Impressionist works, and gazed at the Van Goghs in relative solitude. He was one of my heroes, not so much for his art but for his quest to find out what he needed to do with his life and subsequent unwavering dedication to his calling, despite continuous hardships.

After a short nap back at my dormitory, I bought a bag of chips, a small carton of milk and a banana from a nearby convenience store, and went to the nearby Jardin du Luxembourg. Close to where I sat, a man was putting the finishing touches to a painting of the park. The large pond glistened in the foreground, with the Luxembourg Palace in the background, while well-tended flower beds provided a splash of colour.

My mind flashed back to an epiphany I'd had about two years earlier. On my way to see a movie, I was walking past a house in our neighbourhood that I had passed countless times before. A typical middle-class house, a car sat in the driveway and a child's bicycle lay on the lawn. But that day, that moment, this ordinary scene took on an extraordinary aspect. The light became brighter, the grass greener and the house, the car, the bicycle and the trees in the garden all came into sharp focus. My body jerked back and I knew with absolute certainty something I hadn't known before: *The typical middle-class life this house represents is not for me.*

I hurried away.

If that's the case, what am I supposed to do?

To find out, I had to go away.

As the light faded around us, I crunched on the salty chips and watched the painter. I had to admit to myself that I had no plan for Paris. Quite naively, I had thought that just walking the streets of Paris would be sufficient to find myself.

Chapter 2
Rue Descartes

Back in the dormitory, I lay in bed looking at the ceiling with my palms crossed behind my head and thought about Siri, my literary-minded friend. Also driven by a compelling need to leave, he had left for the UK about a year earlier but with a solid plan. We had hung out a lot during my last few years in Sri Lanka. He had introduced me to writers like James Joyce, Henry Miller and Samuel Beckett, all self-exiled in Paris. Before he left, Siri gave me his bound volume of the collected works of Oscar Wilde, who had spent the tragic last years of his life in Paris.

I had met Siri through two of my old school pals, Piyal and Aravind, who all lived in Mount Lavinia at a rooming house, formerly a palatial manor house incorporating several architectural styles, from pre-colonial to Dutch.

Although we were about the same age, Siri had a proper job and was already self-sufficient. Generous with his disposable income, he treated us regularly—or "stood us," as we used to say—to dinner at one of the several adjoining eating houses that operated 24/7 at the Bambalapitiya junction, a twenty-minute bus ride from Mount Lavinia. The grand-sounding New World Restaurant was our favourite. Our regular waiter would come bustling forward as soon as he saw us. He'd usher us into a private enclosed area, as Siri usually tipped him generously, and tuck the money away in his shirt pocket, giving a quick nod to acknowledge receipt of his rightful due for the excellent service he was providing. No sooner were we seated than the young busboy, shabbily dressed and looking as if he had stepped out of a Charles Dickens novel, would come along with a pile of plates, utensils, a jug of hot water and a large bowl. We'd each take a plate, pour some hot water on it, swirl the water around and drain it off the into the bowl placed in the middle of the table. We'd repeat the same sterilizing process for the utensils and order kottu roti, one of the most popular street foods in Sri Lanka.

The kottu-maker's open workspace is strategically located in front of the restaurant so pedestrians can see through the glass and, more importantly, hear his handiwork. The base ingredient is roti, a thin paper-like oblong flatbread. The man takes a soft dough ball marinated in oil, flattens it on his large griddle with his palms, and, holding a corner with one hand, flips it in the air and slaps it back on the griddle with the other hand until it is thin enough. He fries it on both sides, takes out two square, shiny steel blades with a flourish and a look in his eyes that says, "You ain't seen anything yet" and chops up the roti into small pieces, making as loud a racket as possible. He squirts some oil into another area of the griddle and throws in the other ingredients, usually cabbages, carrots, leeks, onions, garlic, ginger and some protein—chicken, beef or eggs. He stir-fries everything together for a few minutes before chopping them up with another deafening clatter of steel on steel. Finally, he mixes up the chopped roti with the other ingredients, douses it in a red sauce, chops everything a bit more and, using the edges of his blades, scoops the now ready-to-eat kottu roti onto a plate.

Siri liked to wash down the kottu with cups of sweet milk tea and talk about his plan of going to London, working for a couple of years and saving enough money to enrol in London Film School.

"I'm interested in all the arts, and film is the medium that brings everything together," he said.

Impressed with how he had thought things through, I was convinced I'd see his name on film credits one day. Thanks to Siri, I had discovered vague artistic aspirations in myself. I remember telling him soon after I had finished reading Dostoevsky's *The Brothers Karamazov*, "I think the best thing a man can do is to write."

Once, all four of us went to Siri's family home in Kandy, in the mountainous center of the country—the capital of the last Lankan king before the British took over the whole country. The city is best known for the famed Temple of the Tooth, which houses a tooth of the Buddha, in the former palace complex. We took the bus from Colombo, holding onto the back of the seats in front of us as it navigated hairpin bends up the narrow road. We caught ephemeral glimpses of thick forests, green mountains, lush valleys and tea plantations dotted with rows of women in colourful saris plucking tea. The drive from Colombo to Kandy is undoubtedly one of the most scenic routes in the world. It's one of my top three to date along with the road trip from Lumbini to Kathmandu in Nepal and the train ride from Osaka to Mount Koya in Japan.

We spent a night at Siri's spacious family home in an upscale neighbourhood. His mother wore a white sari, the Buddhist colour of mourning. I sensed a heavy and almost funereal atmosphere even though Siri's father had passed away over a decade earlier.

I lost my father much earlier in my life, but unlike me, Siri had a frosty relationship with his mother and perhaps even harboured some kind of resentment against her, which puzzled us. One day, feeling under the weather, I was on the way to see our family doctor accompanied by my mother when we ran into Siri. The next time we met, he sneered, "So the little boy needed his mother to take him to the doctor? You need to grow up, *machang*!"

~

As I lay in bed in Paris, I wished I had a solid plan like Siri's. My plan was a more outdated one, inspired by George Orwell's *Down and Out in Paris and London*. In it, the writer describes his life of self-imposed poverty in Paris in the 1920s. I planned to trace Orwell's footsteps as he went looking for work. I should have started with the Rungis market but it had long been moved to the suburbs and replaced with a sprawling steel-and-glass structure housing Les Halles shopping mall. Although a popular hangout for youths, it left me a bit cold. But I tracked down the dingy café that served as a temp agency for restaurant workers, where Orwell had once looked for a job as a dishwasher or *plongeur*.[1]

I ordered an espresso and looked around at my fellow job-seekers sitting silently in the damp and dimly lit room. Most of them were more than twice my age, red-faced and drinking wine at ten in the morning, and a few had fallen asleep on the tables. The ringing telephone cut through the silence. The sleeping heads jerked up and the drinkers put down their wineglasses with

---

1 Literally means diver.

an expectant look. The café owner, a stocky woman with dyed red hair, came out of her little office at the back, put down her hands wide on the counter, stretched to her full height of about five feet and yelled, "A *plongeur* for the 5th arrondissement."

A few hands shot up. Others went up more hesitantly. She surveyed the room, savouring the moment, and then pointed dramatically at the chosen one. "*Toi!*"

There seemed little chance her finger would point at me, but Haris, a fellow Sri Lankan I had run into at the Alliance Française, helped me get hired as a part-time *plongeur* at a mid-range restaurant on Rue Descartes. This small cobblestoned street winds down from Place de la Contrescarpe, where the Panthéon looming above casts a shadow on its broad sidewalks, toward the permanent open-air market at Square Saint-Médard. One of the oldest streets in Paris, it's a continuation of the better-known Rue Mouffetard, where I'd live for a couple of years.

I soon came to think of Place de la Contrescarpe as the true heart of the Latin Quarter, rather than, as most tourists supposed, the maze of narrow streets south of the Left Bank and bounded by Boulevard Saint-Michel and Rue Saint-Jacques. On my way to work, I'd cross the cobblestoned square where sprawling café terraces covered the sidewalks, making it popular with both tourists and locals. In the centre, a fountain ringed by trees served as a meeting point. Hemingway, who referred to Place de la Contrescarpe in the opening paragraph of *A Moveable Feast*, did his writing in a room on the top floor of a hotel on the square.

The name of the street where the restaurant was located was a good omen. René Descartes's famous quote, "I think, therefore I am," had made an impression on me, confirming my rationalistic belief that matter preceded mind and consciousness. I thought it was the complexity of the brain, resulting from the evolutionary process as described in Darwin's *On the Origin of Species*, that had given rise to consciousness. I also believed it was the dualistic separation of consciousness from the world outside that had made possible the tremendous material progress achieved by man, especially in recent centuries.

In the following years, I'd hear much about the Cartesian spirit of the French or their logical way of thinking, and learn how to write a dissertation in the proper French way. You start with an introductory paragraph, set out your thesis in the first section, present the antithesis in a second and then conclude with a paragraph synthesizing all the arguments and triumphantly tying in with what you said in the introduction—*et voilà!*

About a decade later, I'd go on to conclude that the dualism between the body and the mind, the separation between the self and others, and the separation between the body-mind identity and the real self were the root causes of our suffering and society's many ills. I'd then paraphrase Descartes as "I am, therefore I think."

On my first day at work in the restaurant, I proudly donned my soiled blue apron. Smelling of dirty dishes, the apron made me feel I had at last become a member of the working class I had been rooting for. The chef, perched on a stool nearby, his starched white jacket open at the neck, was reading *L'Humanité*, the newspaper of the French Communist Party, which still had a substantial following, unlike in other European countries.

Christina, one of the two waitresses, strode into the kitchen. "Ah, the chef is reading his newspaper."

The chef raised a finger in the air. "No, the chef does not read his newspaper. He studies it."

Before the restaurant opened, we'd all sit together, and Christina would serve the meal. When in a good mood, the chef took special requests. I'd ask for mutton cooked in the chef's special sauce. It reminded me of the meat curries I used to eat at home, and it was served in a miniature copper casserole that enhanced the culinary experience. We passed around a baguette, each person breaking off a piece. While we ate, the restaurant door would crack open. A head would poke through, and Christina would yell, rather harshly, "We're not open yet!" The head would hurriedly withdraw.

Over the years following that first taste of sitting around a table and sharing a meal with French people, breaking bread with friends in restaurants, apartments, or in country homes—where we sat around a table under the shade of a tree, eating, drinking and talking until the sun went down—became an important part of the movable feast that was my Paris.

My stomach full, I'd go into the kitchen and start tackling the piles of dirty dishes, plates and pans. The setup, consisting of two huge metal sinks, seemed almost as old as the Panthéon just outside. I now understood why I was called the *plongeur*—I had to dive in. Piped hot water was not yet a thing at Rue Descartes, so I had to manually turn on the small water heater above the sinks. Sometimes the heater broke down and I'd have to boil water in the kettle over and over again to fill them.

Despite the medieval working conditions, I soon developed a liking for dishwashing. I found its rhythmic quality soothing. What's more, it was a mindless job that left me free to ponder the more important things in life. At least, that's what I told myself. Seeing the pile of dirty dishes on my left diminish as the clean pile on my right kept rising gave me a sense of accomplishment. On more serene days the dishes slid into the sink of dirty soapy water, slid out into the clean water and then deposited themselves on my right, without much effort on my part.

I'm in the zone!

When I was in a more philosophical mood, I'd see dirty

dishes I had just washed coming back dirtier than before, making me think about the Buddhist notions of impermanence and samsara, the eternal cycle of life and suffering.

On days when the heater was broken and the pile of dirty dishes on my left climbed impossibly high, I'd ask myself what I was doing there and long for my life back home. There, food appeared on the table like clockwork. Breakfast at seven thirty, lunch at noon, tea at three thirty, and dinner at eight. Nothing much was asked from me and I spent my time at home studying or reading. When I wanted to go out with my friends, I simply took the money I needed from my mother's purse.

But on days at the restaurant when I was in the zone, I tried to prolong my mood by walking at least part of the way home. Looking up at apartment buildings, their windows lit up, I thought warmly about the people inside basking in the golden glow. And when I crossed the bridges over the Seine, I felt connected to the still dark waters, the bluish-black sky and the illuminated buildings all around me.

But it would take me some seven years to understand that feeling of connection and what it meant to be in the zone.

Chapter 3
Rue Rochambeau

I had been living in the suburbs and commuting for work and French classes, but things changed when I met Gord at the Alliance Française. On my way to the job centre in the basement, I saw a young man in blue denim overalls and a white T-shirt sitting on the steps.

He looked up at me and asked, "Hey, are you looking for work?"

He was trying to find someone to take over his job as a cleaner in a daycare while he moved on to somewhat better things—manning the night reception in a small hotel.

We went to have lunch at the nearby Mabillon university restaurant on a small side street off Rue du Four. The meal tickets came in small pink booklets of ten, and standing in line to buy them, we got acquainted. Gord was from South Africa and had just turned twenty-seven.

"I wish I were twenty-one like you," he said, tearing a ticket from his booklet.

We joined another line and pushed our stainless-steel trays along the counter behind which stony-faced, green-aproned restaurant workers ladled out the food.

University restaurants—or restos U, as insiders call them—are a unique but lesser-known Parisian institution. Although officially reserved for card-carrying university students, restos U can be a haven or even a lifeline for the financially strapped, particularly foreigners. More than a dozen such restaurants were scattered across Paris, so I discovered the city by trying out all of them. Weekly menus were displayed at their entrances, and since they never changed, I soon got to know the food on offer each day across the city. My expertise soon became known, and friends and acquaintances leading precarious lives in Paris asked me for advice on which resto U offered the best fare on a particular day.

Amid the loud chatter and the clattering of cutlery on trays, we lunched on green salad, spicy paella and yogurt. Gord had given up his cushy teaching job at the University of Cape Town—out of disgust for apartheid, or so he said—to bum around the world looking for himself. But as it transpired later, the actual reasons were more personal and complex.

"I can find a decent job teaching business English," he said, "but I don't want to get sucked into any kind of career. I need to sort out a few things in my head. I figure I can get by doing dead-end jobs until then."

I put down my fork and looked intently at Gord. Although I hadn't articulated it so clearly at the time, I knew that this was why I had left home as well.

After lunch we went to have an espresso in one of the sidewalk cafés lining nearby Boulevard Saint-Germain. We surveyed the bustling crowd sitting in rows of stylish wood-framed rattan chairs against the backdrop of the medieval Saint-

Germain-des-Près church across the street. Waiters in black trousers, white long-sleeved shirts and black waistcoats weaved in and out of the rows of round tables, arms aloft balancing trays on fingertips.

"Nice chairs. Comfortable too," I commented as we sat.

Gord agreed. "Ideal for people-watching!"

"All cafés in Paris seem to have these chairs. It's like their trademark," I added.

"Those two places are famous." Gord waved in the direction of two nearby cafés on opposite sides of Boulevard Saint-Germain—Les Deux Magots and Café de Flore.

I seized the opportunity to show off my literary knowledge. "I know. Sartre and Hemingway used to hang out there."

"I must suss them out one of these days."

Gord's audacity impressed me. I didn't know then that Parisian cafés are an extremely democratic institution where you'd find the CEO of a nearby company or a local celebrity rubbing elbows with a construction worker on his lunch break.

Before we parted ways, Gord suggested I move into the room he shared with a friend. "We have an extra mattress for you," he offered.

Soon I was pushing through the heavy wooden door to the entrance of 7 Rue Rochambeau, a small, quiet street in the 9th arrondissement behind a leafy square on Rue La Fayette, a long street that cut across the northern part of the city. With my trusty red-and-black duffle bag slung over my left shoulder, I crossed the cobblestoned courtyard under the watchful eye of the concierge—a ubiquitous character on Parisian streets with whom it was important to maintain a cordial relationship, as I'd soon learn—and climbed up the narrow and dusty back staircase to the sixth floor.

The top floors of most Parisian apartment buildings are lined with servant rooms or *chambres de bonne*, tiny, spartan rooms containing a washbasin, a bed, a cheap wooden wardrobe and a small table. As I walked down the musty corridor, thinking these must be the poets' garrets I had read so much about, I felt excited about actually living in one. Built for the servants of the occupants of the spacious apartments on the lower floors, the rooms are now mostly rented out to students. Gord's room was much bigger than the typical *chambre de bonne*. It had floor-to-ceiling windows and a small balcony, whereas most other rooms on our floor only had a skylight. There was even a tiny kitchenette, but no bathroom. Instead, all the occupants of the floor used the same small toilet next to the top of the staircase. Showers were an unheard-of luxury, so we went to the public baths in the Latin Quarter once a week. A tall Black man dressed in spotless white showed us to our respective stalls and wrote the exact time with a piece of chalk on the door. When our allotted twenty minutes were up, he'd come and bang on it.

I soon got to know my neighbours, all living in a state of self-exile. Gord had spent a year in Israel exploring his supposed Jewish roots. I didn't quite get it. He'd been adopted and with his blue eyes and blond hair, he hardly looked the part. He had a French friend named Giselle, a nurse who happened to be a Jehovah's Witness. Gord didn't really fancy her, but one evening in a moment of weakness he had slept with her and found himself in a relationship no-man's land the next morning. Giselle, on the other hand, was very into Gord and considered it her mission to save his confused soul. So Gord dragged me along whenever he had a date, just to keep her at bay. Needless to say, not much love was lost between the two of us.

He even asked me to tag along on a weekend trip with

Giselle to the Normandy coast in her classic Citroën hatchback. Gord had booked a room for three in a small hotel and the elderly receptionist shook her head in disgust when we checked in and climbed up the stairs. The room obviously wasn't meant for three adults. We drove back to Paris in lashing rain. The wipers didn't work so Giselle had to drive with one hand on the wheel, leaning forward and wiping the windscreen with the other.

Gord played the guitar a bit. He'd sit on his bed, strum the strings and sing Joplin's "Me and Bobby McGee." I'd join in the chorus with gusto, feeling uplifted by the reference to freedom.

One day, he said, "I think I'm good enough to busk in the metro. I need you to come along and pass the hat around."

To my relief, he didn't follow through on this plan. But he was always thinking up creative ways to make money. Another idea was to go to the Charles de Gaulle departure lounge and ask people waiting to check in for the French change they no longer needed. That seemed feasible, so off we went to the airport. Once there, though, we got cold feet and ended up drinking overpriced panachés in the airport bar.

Our other roommate, Ariel, had fought in the Israeli army in Lebanon and felt entitled to a lucky break. More specifically, he was looking to make a fast buck and hook up with French girls. He had no patience for the soul-searching conversations Gord and I would have over a bottle of cheap wine.

"Group therapy . . . a waste of time!" he'd snort, and stomp out of the room.

He also took issue with me. "You're such a bloody high-minded idealist! You know nothing about the real world. You need to grow up, man!"

Ariel's grasp of the real world was tested when on an unusually cold day, we decided to try to cook something instead of going to the resto U. He reached into the kitchen cupboard and took out a box of pasta a previous tenant had left behind.

"The instructions are in Norwegian, I think." Ariel looked unsure. "Do we cook it in cold or hot water?"

"Well, rice is always cooked in cold water," I offered.

"But it might not be same for pasta."

"They're both carbohydrates, so I don't see why it should be different for pasta."

Convinced by my very scientific argument, Ariel threw the pasta into a pot of cold water and the whole thing came out a soggy mess. So we grabbed our coats and rushed to the resto U before it closed.

One evening Gord and I were leaning on our balcony looking at the goings-on in the small park below when Ariel rushed in. He had learned from the concierge that a Swedish au pair named Britt had just moved onto our floor. Ariel sang the praises of Swedish women—and their physical attributes—adding that, in his opinion, French women were highly overrated and quite hopeless in bed. Gord and I exchanged a knowing look, but we all agreed that with a name like Britt, she had to be gorgeous. We trooped off to knock on Britt's door. When it opened, we saw that she didn't correspond at all to the prototype of Swedish beauty Ariel had conjured for us. She was less than five feet tall and her weight would have been ideal for someone about two feet taller. We went in and Gord gave her some basic Paris survival tips while Ariel sulked on a stool and I looked on, stifling a smile.

Ariel would walk down Boulevard Saint-Michel, his scissor-like movements probably because his jeans were a size or two too small for him. With his man purse tucked tightly under his arm, his jaw thrust forward and beard bristling, he'd scoured the nubile students passing by. Desperate and frustrated, he ended up "taking some comfort" on Rue Saint-Denis.

Our next-door neighbour was Jay, a blond giant from San Francisco with short-cropped hair. I was impressed by his strict regimen of writing for six hours each day and how he always introduced himself as a writer even though he had not published anything. I told Gord that if a man writes for six hours a day, he has the right to call himself a writer, whether published or not, because that's what he's doing. I should have grilled him for his motivation, process and material, but I didn't. I didn't even bring up my own vague aspirations of writing. One day, he and I were going on a walk up to Montmartre when Jay stopped, whipped out a notebook from his backpack and jotted down something I had just said. I was flattered. He always had a frisbee at hand and would get the urge to throw it regardless of where he was, provoking indignant looks from the locals that said, "These foreigners!"

Ania occupied the room facing ours. Fed up with economic hardships in her native Poland, she had slipped through the Iron Curtain to live the good life in Paris. For the time being, the good life consisted of checking out the window displays of chic boutiques on Rue du Faubourg Saint-Honoré. After several years in the bureaucratic system, her application for political asylum had been rejected. The authorities refused to buy her harrowing account of repeated beatings, rape, solitary confinements and the assassination of several members of her family at the hands of the Polish secret police. Ania just wasn't able to rein in her wild imagination when pitching her story to the refugee board. She might have even come to believe some of the things she had made up.

When she received a package from home, as often happened, she'd invite us over. We'd all cram into her minuscule room, a couple of us sitting on her bed. Ania would pass around saucers with slices of dried Polish sausages and vodka shots. Fuelled by vodka, she'd complain bitterly of the situation back home. That kind of talk made me uncomfortable.

One day, she asked, "Did you know we didn't have bananas and oranges?"

I couldn't resist pointing out that the lack of bananas and oranges were a small price to pay for building an egalitarian society and the lofty goal of creating a new type of human being.

Ania was livid. "If that's what you believe, why did you come here instead of going over there?"

Her next-door neighbours were Abdul and Ali from Tehran. They were struggling to learn French so they could go on to study engineering. Strong supporters of the Iranian Revolution, they disparaged decadent Western civilization. Ariel called them the mujahedeen, and they called him the Zionist. Both parties assured me their respective label wasn't offensive. Faraway geopolitical hostilities are often played out in Paris and our floor was no exception. Sometimes I got caught in the middle. I used to pop over to their room to help myself to Abdul's rudimentary Persian dishes. Despite his professed cultural rigidity, Abdul was an easygoing, gentle soul who called me his brother and treated me so. But Ali disapproved of my Westernized lifestyle. Suspecting he saw in me a potential candidate for conversion to Islam, I plied him with questions on the Koran just to keep him happy.

Not all was fun and games on our floor. The fifth-floor tenant's bedroom was right below ours and according to the all-knowing concierge, he was an insomniac who hadn't had a good night's sleep in more than ten years. One night he banged on our door in his dressing gown, hair dishevelled, and explained to us in a mixture of French, English and improvised sign language that his hearing was so sensitive he could even hear us switching on the light from his apartment. When he said he wanted us to go to sleep by ten, we burst out laughing. He stalked off, growling, "*Attention a la carte de séjour!*"

Since none of us had a *carte de séjour*,[2] we laughed even louder. But he made good his threat, and we soon received a summons from the neighbourhood police station. We promptly stuck it on the wall and showed it off to friends who dropped by. With the French police after us, we felt like a bunch of desperadoes.

A more formidable opponent was the woman living in the room next to the toilet who'd poke a broomstick from her window into the toilet or yell, "*Charogne, charogne!*" from behind her door. We had no idea what she meant, but it didn't sound complimentary. Her son paid her infrequent visits and the longer the period between them, the more aggressive she became, her behaviour peaking during long weekends. We made it a point to give her a wide berth but one day, I was climbing the stairs when she appeared on the landing. Unusually tall and strongly built for a French woman and standing a few steps above me, she seemed like a giant. With straggling white hair and a wild look in her eyes, she brandished her walking stick at me. I threw pride to the wind, bolted down the stairs and waited at the corner of the block, heart racing and laughing until the coast was clear.

⁓

After a few months Ariel's savings ran out, so he packed his backpack and Gord and I saw him off at the Poissonnière metro station. When he gave us a wave and walked down the stairs, his shoulders were stooped, but not just from the weight

---

[2] Resident's card.

of his backpack, I suspected. At twenty-seven, for Ariel, the trip to Paris had been a desperate last attempt to do something different before he resigned himself to a modest life in a Tel Aviv suburb.

"He's so cut up about leaving. He should have tried harder to stay," I said as we walked back home.

"He's broke," Gord said. "What else could he have done?"

In hindsight, I might have been a bit harsh on Ariel. He was carrying around some heavy baggage, which probably didn't have much to do with his time in the army or even with the history of his ancestors.

Not long after, Abdul too announced that he was going back home, citing family reasons. A bunch of Iranian friends and I accompanied him to the airport, Abdul having bought bus tickets for all of us. But in his excitement, he forgot to punch in his own ticket and had to pay a seventy-five-franc fine when we got off the bus. Unfazed, Abdul handed his camera to the ticket inspector and asked him to take a picture of all of us.

The man acquiesced. "This picture costs seventy-five francs!"

Jay's savings ran out as well, so he went back to California to earn more money. Gord had not voiced any doubts about his self-imposed life of poverty, so it surprised me when he decided to accept a respectable English teaching job. I suspected his shrink, paid for by his well-heeled parents in Cape Town, had something to do with the decision.

I had looked up to Gord, so I felt betrayed. But I don't think I told him.

A year had gone by and not only had I survived Paris, but it had been quite the moveable feast and has stayed with me ever since. But I was no way closer to finding my life purpose. With several people around me bailing out—rather prematurely, in my opinion—I knew that I had to hang in there for the long haul. But I needed some kind of structure—or an alibi of sorts—so I signed up for an undergraduate degree. I chose economics over literature or philosophy, which I figured I could learn on my own, partly owing to my interest in Marxism, but also because I thought it would be useful for what I needed to do with my life. As it turned out, I couldn't have been more wrong.

Chapter 4
Hôtel d'Alger

When Gord announced he was moving up in the world, I jumped at the chance of taking over his job as a night receptionist. Sitting behind a desk, answering the phone and handing over keys to hotel guests was the dream dead-end job to me.

Hôtel d'Alger was located on a small side street off Rue de Rivoli, across the Jardin des Tuileries. Weather and time permitting, I'd walk at least part of my way to work and sit for a while on one of those aluminum chairs you find in all Parisian parks. I'd stroll along the Seine on Quai Voltaire, cross the Pont du Carrousel and enter the courtyard of the Louvre, which had yet to get its glass pyramid. With the Louvre on my right, I'd look through the Arc de Triomphe du Carrousel on my left and see cars streaming up Avenue des Champs-Élysées to the much larger Arc de Triomphe de l'Étoile.

Letting out a sigh at the prospect of spending the evening cooped up inside, I'd push through the heavy glass-and-iron doors of the hotel. And if I looked at the mosaic-patterned tiles, I'd notice my shoes were covered in dust from the gravel in the Jardin des Tuileries. Alonso, the day receptionist, acted like he was the manager. He waited for me with a big smile behind the desk at one end of the small L-shaped lobby, flanked by floor-to-ceiling mirrors. Having worked at the hotel twelve hours a day for several decades, Alonso had bought a condo in a Paris suburb and was building a house in his native village in the south of Spain. The other side of the lobby consisted of a sitting area, where I'd read in one of the comfortable armchairs during the many lulls or chat with friends who dropped by. The lobby's small, antique elevator was a minor tourist attraction. People wandered in just to photograph it.

To the right of the reception, next to the winding staircase, the manager and owner of the hotel, who everyone called Mademoiselle, had her small office. I found it ridiculous to call someone in her fifties Mademoiselle, but the name quickly grew on me. It also made sense to me when I learned that Mademoiselle had dropped out of medical school following a serious heartbreak involving a fellow student and had remained chronically single ever since. Always tastefully made up and elegantly dressed, epitomizing the middle-aged BCBG[3] style, she was feminine, courteous and well spoken.

To help her recover from her breakdown, her wealthy lawyer father had bought the hotel for her to manage. Her parents came to the hotel every evening, and in return for their generosity, Mademoiselle prepared a grand dinner for them in the kitchen below. She served it in the dining room located to the right of the lobby. While they ate dinner watching television, hotel guests passing through watched them through the glass doors in hushed awe, counting themselves lucky to see a typical Parisian

---

3   *Bon chic, bon genre* – classy and stylish.

family performing this sacred French ritual. Mademoiselle's father monopolized the dinner table conversation and had the irritating habit of voicing his conservative political views loudly in response to something on the TV and yelling at the images of the socialist president, François Mitterrand.

One evening the news was dominated by the assassination of the Indian Prime Minister, Indira Gandhi. I heard the mother ask, "Is Indira Gandhi the daughter of Mahatma Gandhi?"

"Of course!" the father bellowed. "They have the same surname! *Voyons donc!*"

I smiled to myself. *You know-it-all, Indira Gandhi is the daughter of Nehru, India's first Prime Minister. She just happens to have married someone named Gandhi.*

My dinner was prepared by Sancho, the cook, whose culinary skills left much to be desired. Mademoiselle would poke her well-groomed head through the doorway between the dining room and the lobby, flash a dazzling smile, and say, "You can go and have your dinner now," as if I were in for the treat of my life.

Eating the frugal meal in the bleak basement while the family feasted in the dining room upstairs was a source of resentment for the night receptionists. From time to time Mademoiselle brought me tasty morsels from their table, adding insult to injury, or a glass of vintage wine that didn't really agree with my palate, used to a strict regime of the cheapest wines convenience stores had to offer.

Like Alonso, Sancho was Spanish, gay and single, but older. Though he had spent most of his adult life at the hotel, he could hardly speak French and communicated with me in a mixture of Spanish, French and miming. He was obsessed with the idea that Alonso might be cheating him of his fair share of tips and often hung around the reception, fawning over guests about to leave.

Alonso would then hiss at him, "Go down to the kitchen! Don't you have work to do?"

Lucie, the chambermaid, the sole French employee and a God-fearing middle-aged spinster, shuffled around the lobby with a dazed look on her face, her mouth half-open, holding a duster in one hand and adjusting her thick black-rimmed glasses with the other. The night receptionists, all students simply passing through, considered themselves a cut above these three long-serving employees.

"They're like domesticated animals eating out of Mademoiselle's hands," said Manuel, who worked the weekday night shift. "She treats Olaf better than them."

Olaf was Mademoiselle's black-and-tan English cocker spaniel, and her faithful male companion. He flopped like a rug at the entrance to her office or waddled behind her everywhere she went, his long ears almost brushing the floor. Part of my duties included taking the overfed and overweight dog on his nocturnal walk. We despised each other. Olaf figured out right away I was one of the hired help and wasted no time on pleasantries. Fortunately, it was still the Wild West in Paris when it came to dog poop; it would have been too humiliating to pick up after a dog who ignored your existence. When my brother and his family came over from London to visit Paris and stayed at the hotel, my little nephew saw me taking out Olaf for a walk. Dressed in a red sweater that said *Kids Rule, OK?*, he asked ever so sweetly, "Uncle, is Olaf your boss?"

I spent about six years at the hotel, all through my forever-student days. When I moved on, I handed over the reins to a friend of mine, but a couple of weeks later, Mademoiselle called me to complain about his work. Something snapped in me, and all the pent-up resentment against her finally broke through the barrier of excessive politeness between us. I can't remember everything I said but the gist was that considering the conditions at her hotel, she should consider herself lucky to have my friend working for her. Mademoiselle also dropped her mask of superficial gentility and said, "I'm very hurt by what you said. I believe I always treated you well."

Five years later, after moving to Montreal, I couldn't remember what I was so angry about. Barring some minor irritations, Mademoiselle had indeed treated me well. She might have even created work for me, like asking me to do the bookkeeping for her, just so I could earn some extra money. Not to mention her many acts of kindness, such as visiting me and feeding me dinner when I ended up in hospital for two weeks, paying for a private medical consultation with her doctor to get a second opinion, and gifting me expensive books.

One evening she placed leading French publisher Gallimard's book catalogue on the reception counter and asked me to select a book. I chose the collected works of Albert Camus. Her nose wrinkled at my choice of a writer with leftist leanings, but when I turned up for work a few days later, I found a beautifully wrapped package waiting for me. I opened it carefully and held the book in my hand. Its delicate paper and fine print alone were a work of art.

After arriving in Montreal I sent Mademoiselle a picture postcard informing her of my move, and on my first trip back to Paris, I went to see her to make amends. But it was too little, too late. She was cold and aloof.

Thinking back to my time at the hotel, it had been a dream dead-end job for me while I tried to figure out what to do with my life. Although my job title was *veilleur de nuit*, which implies keeping watch throughout the night, I'd lock the doors around midnight and sleep for a good six hours on the couch in the lounge to the left of the lobby. The hotel had only about twenty rooms. Most of our guests were older and would generally turn in early. And even when I was sitting at my desk, there was usually little to do, so I'd spend my time studying or reading.

I have painful memories of ploughing my way through the three volumes of *Critique of Pure Reason*, *Critique of Practical Reason* and *Critique of Judgment* by Immanuel Kant, a man who supposedly travelled no further than sixteen kilometres from his place of birth. I had started to think of myself an intellectual—and might have even come to think that was my life purpose—and an intellectual needed to be familiar with Kant's ideas. I had no idea of the implications of what I was reading; my intention was to memorize Kant's arguments so I could throw them out casually at parties or during discussions with friends. But decades later, I'd see the connection between Kant's central doctrine of transcendental idealism and the teachings of Advaita Vedanta.[4]

A much more inspiring read was Robert M. Pirsig's *Zen and the Art of Motorcycle Maintenance*, which became an unlikely bestseller in the '70s after being rejected by 126 publishers. The unnamed narrator goes on a motorcycle trip through Midwestern America and in the process rediscovers a truer part of himself that society had tried to destroy. The narrator also carries on a monologue on reconciling two opposing attitudes to life—rational and romantic. The book was given to me at the hotel by Govinda, a friend from London. I didn't even know he was in town; he just walked up to the reception and handed it to me as if he had come all the way from London solely for that purpose. It immediately made my list of all-time favourites—books I'd read again and again over the years.

Gord gave me J. D. Salinger's *The Catcher in the Rye*, another book on that list, and I read it mostly at the hotel. Unlike Pirsig's

---

[4] Non-dualistic Vedanta, Vedanta being one of the six traditional Indian schools of thought.

middle-aged narrator, Salinger's main protagonist, Holden Caulfield, is a teenager. He wanders around New York for one day looking for something without really knowing what he is looking for. Both characters have breakdowns during their respective quests and spend time in a mental institution, something I'd narrowly avoid. Of course, I had no inkling of that at the time.

Mona from New York came to see me at the hotel while I was sitting in the lobby, reading about Holden's journey. She looked at the book disapprovingly.

"Isn't it about teen angst? And aren't you too old to be reading a book like that?"

Her tone irritated me. "Not at all. It's about general human existentialist angst. I think Holden Caulfield's quest for authenticity is relevant for any age."

Mona and I had hit it off right from the day we sat next to each other in class, and we soon became inseparable, seeing each other every day, or if that wasn't possible, having long phone conversations. Early on she asked me, "Do you want a relationship with me or do you want to be just friends?"

My strong connection to her was more mental than anything else, so she moved on. One day, I met up with her at the Beaubourg, officially known as the Centre Pompidou and a favourite haunt of ours. The futuristic glass-and-steel structure was designed inside-out, optimizing six floors of column-free space for collections of modern and contemporary art, books, audio-visual materials, reading rooms, films, discussions, activities for children and so on. After finishing our respective studies, we went to drink kirs at a sidewalk café in adjoining Les Halles.

At one point, Mona put down her glass. "When I see you, I ask myself, is this a man or a boy?"

I laughed, shamefaced.

Another time, she told me, "When I'm attracted to a guy, I know it right away, or at the latest, the second time I see him. I don't get people who first start off as friends and then become lovers."

I didn't agree with her then, but I now see things her way.

I knew Mona was dating guys during the time we were close. But when she fell in love and moved in with someone, I felt betrayed and decided I couldn't see her anymore, even though I knew my feelings were irrational and unjustified. It took me a few years to get over the "betrayal." She told me then that although she was deeply in love, what I did had hurt her and she wanted to know why. I told her I didn't know, which was mostly true. I'm still quite perplexed. We moved on and grew closer again, but things were never the same.

~

A couple of years into my stint at the hotel, I spent a summer on an extended vacation in Sri Lanka. There I caught up with Piyal, the friend who had introduced me to Siri. He had gotten married in the meantime. In my honour, he organized a safari to Yala National Park, a wildlife sanctuary in southeastern Sri Lanka and home to a variety of wildlife, including leopards and elephants. The trip started badly: our jeep broke down as soon as we got out of Colombo. When we reached Yala, we saw more jeeps than wildlife. On our way to the lodge Piyal had booked for the night, I was sitting in the back facing Sarojini, his sister-in-law. As we rattled down a long stretch of dusty road with shrub land on either side, she pointed in my direction and said, "Look, there's a deer."

I turned around but it was gone.

"It hopped and ran away in a flash." She raised her forearms and made a swift forward movement with her fists, mimicking the deer hopping away.

I found the gesture cute and looked at her with new interest.

The lodge turned out to be something of a shack. I had been expecting a sprawling bungalow, like the one my brother, a plantation manager, lived in. Flustered, Piyal kept saying, "This can't be the place," and then "There must be some mistake," while his wife repeated, "There's no way I'm going to sleep in this shed."

But it was getting late, so we resigned ourselves, and when we came back after a refreshing soak in the nearby river, the shack looked more like a proper lodge. Our steps quickened when we caught whiffs of frying fish and heard the clatter of pots and pans coming from the small kitchen at the back, where the caretaker was preparing our dinner. Piyal opened a bottle of arrack, the popular local spirit distilled from coconut flowers, and Sarojini joined us for a drink. I was impressed. Most Sri Lankan women don't drink and certainly not arrack. The caretaker brought us plates of halmasso, a type of sprat, caught in the local river and fried in a batter as a bite to accompany our drinks. Soon the shack was looking more like the comfortable and spacious bungalow I had envisioned. I can't remember how it happened or whose idea it was, but after dinner, Sarojini and I went for a stroll in the moonlight. I experienced an unusual, delicious feeling, and when we got back to Mount Lavinia where she happened to live as well, we started seeing each other every day.

She introduced me to her parents as Piyal's friend, but her mother caught wind of something more and asked Piyal what kind of person I was.

"He's a nice guy," he said, "but not very stable."

I still like to remind him that he stabbed me in the back.

I became a persona non grata at Sarojini's place, so she started visiting me. I thought Sarojini was quite the catch—attractive, articulate and bright, and above all, from a "good" family—so I was surprised my mother didn't seem impressed. Soon after she left after her first visit, my mother muttered under her breath, "What a forward girl!"

When Sarojini called, my mother didn't tell me or take any messages. And when I asked her whether someone had called, she'd say, as if she'd just remembered, "Ah, yes, someone did call." I'd then ask whether it was a male or female, and she'd reply that she couldn't tell. I found my mother's attitude odd but didn't read too much into it.

We'd often meet in the second-floor lounge of the Venus Café, a fancy ice cream parlour and café in an upscale and leafy area in the heart of Colombo, filled with cuddling young couples. As young people in Sri Lanka usually live with their parents until marriage and even afterwards, their opportunities for intimacy are limited. So couples huddled together under large black umbrellas are a frequent sight on beaches, in parks and in other public places.

One day, I met up with Sarojini in the gardens of the Colombo Public Library. We were sitting close together on a bench, quite far from the library building, when a library employee came running toward us with an embarrassed look on his face and said, "I was told to tell you to sit further apart."

Sarojini looked humiliated and frustrated. "Can't you find a friend's place we can use during the day while they're at work?"

After about a month of dating, my initial feelings of excitement waned. The tipping point came when I returned home one late afternoon after spending a good part of the day with Sarojini, and she called me to ask me to go for a walk. I complied with heavy feet. Our relationship was becoming a burden. I thought things would get easier when I went back to Paris. We wrote to each other, but after a few months, even writing was a chore. Knowing someone out there had expectations from me was something I wasn't ready for. I can't remember how I put it to her but I did and she took it badly, especially since I couldn't properly explain why I wanted to break up. When I went back to Sri Lanka the next summer, she came to see me and we sat together in our living room. I kept looking at the garden to avoid making eye contact and eventually she stumbled out in tears. My little nephew who was staying with us at the time looked at me wide-eyed.

A couple of years later we met up again, and I apologized for what happened.

Sarojini was gracious. "Yes, you hurt me badly, but I got over it. So don't worry about it."

I had fallen into a mild depression after the breakup, followed by a bout of hypochondria over recurring headaches, so it might well have taken me longer to get over hurting her.

~

Not long after the breakup with Sarojini, I started hanging out with Alexandra, or rather, she started hanging out with me. We first got acquainted when she sat next to me in class. She didn't think too much of her fellow students.

"They take themselves so seriously! I just put up with this crap because I want to get a job with a decent salary that will allow me to enjoy life as much as possible."

I might have become one of them, even though initially, I was biding my time until I figured out what I wanted to do. But somewhere along the way, I had come to consider studying an end in itself.

Alexandra kept asking me to have lunch with her, so I wondered whether she fancied me. One day, we lunched on miso soup, marinated bean sprout salad and yakitori with steamed rice at a popular Japanese place off Rue de Rennes.

"For me, to go out with a guy, he has to be cute." She held up a chicken skewer in one hand with the palm of the other hand outstretched toward me in a stop sign.

Not considering myself at all as cute, I figured she was trying to tell me she wanted to just be friends. My hopes, or perhaps my fears, about her intent were unfounded. She then asked me if I was free to go to the movies the next evening, muddying the waters again.

As a teenager, given my looks or lack thereof, I'd despaired of ever getting together with a beautiful young thing—or a "byt," as we used to say. But in later years, I comforted myself with the thought I could win over girls with my intellect, wit and book knowledge.

As if reading my thoughts, Alexandra said, "I know some girls are seduced by intelligence. I just don't get it. What has that got to do with anything? What I want from a guy is simple." She waved her chopsticks in the air. "Be tender and fuck me well. Is that too much to ask?"

I made a sign with my head to imply I agreed with her, though I thought the two asks might be mutually exclusive. I considered Alexandra to be an outlier, but I wonder now whether that is what many women really want but don't get from their men.

She then told me the last guy she'd dated was her contemporary dance teacher. He also happened to be a male model. "When we were going out, one of his ads was plastered on billboards across Paris. Talk about pressure!"

I gave a mental nod. *Talk about pressure!*

The next evening, we went to see a romantic movie Alexandra had picked. During a climactic scene she turned to me and hissed, "Take my hand, damn it!"

I took her hand, but rather unconvincingly, I think. She soon snatched it back.

As we left the cinema, I avoided making eye contact with Alexandra. I don't know whether this is just me, but when walking out of a movie theatre, I feel strangely embarrassed and avoid making eye contact. Perhaps the sense of shame comes from allowing myself to get caught up in a collective illusion. That conclusion made even more sense, several years afterward, when I delved deeper into Buddhism and Vedanta. According to which, the whole world is *maya* or illusion and not real as we believe it to be.

Wanting to break the awkward silence, but having nothing better to say, I commented, "Not terribly authentic."

Authentic was a word I liked to use often back then. Alexandra looked away, not deigning to reply. She took a dim view of my existential angst. We were having coffee one day at the sidewalk café at the corner of Rue des Saints-Pères and Boulevard Saint-Germain, when she pouted her lips and said, "What's there to search for? The meaning of life is right here," pointing her outstretched hand downward.

Again, a couple of years later, I remembered her hand movement when I learned about the Buddha's sacred hand gestures, or *mudras*, and what he did when confronted by Mara, the god of delusion, who challenged him, saying, "Who says you're enlightened?"

The Buddha pointed to the ground with his outstretched hand and fingers. "The earth is my witness."

It also occurred to me that the previous hand gesture she'd made, at the Japanese restaurant, with her raised palm facing outward was similar to the Buddha's *abhaya* mudra, which signifies "Be not afraid."

Driving me home after the movie, Alexandra became chatty, forgetting or forgiving me for the whole hand-holding debacle. When I was about to get out, she leaned over me and peered up through the car window, "So which floor do you live on?"

As I climbed the stairs, it struck me that she'd wanted me to ask her up. I didn't know then, but the lag between the expression of a woman's intent and my understanding of it would create a disproportionate amount of grief in later years.

But not so much in the case of Alexandra. A couple of days later, we had lunch at the Necker resto U across the street from my place, and afterwards we went to my seventh-floor room for tea. After pushing some books aside and putting her mug on the coffee table, she lay down on my bed, her back propped against the headrest, took the latest *Cosmopolitan* from her bag and flipped through it.

Feeling a bit left out, I said, "You're always carrying that big bag around. What's in it?"

She kept turning pages without looking up. "Girl stuff." She stopped flipping and exclaimed, "Short legs! That's my problem."

She turned it toward me and tapped her fingers on the page. Alexandra was petite but I didn't know she had a short legs problem, or that such a problem even existed, but figured it must be quite widespread for *Cosmo* to run a whole article on it.

The next time I met Alexandra at her studio apartment in Barbès-Rochechouart, in northeastern Paris. With her long blond hair and blue eyes, she stood out in the largely African neighbourhood. When I pointed it out to her, she responded, "I like my neighbourhood. It's colourful."

I took off my jacket and sat on the couch next to her, and she said, "I wrote you a letter."

"When? I didn't get it."

"I didn't send it," she added coyly. She walked over to her desk, took a crumpled ball of paper from her wastepaper basket and held it up.

"Can I see it?" I asked.

She smoothed out the letter on her table and gave it to me. The letter began, "Despite all appearances to the contrary, you're actually unavailable." It went on to say our expectations of each other were mismatched. It was a sweet letter. Alexandra came across as vulnerable, quite unlike her usually feisty self. My resistance melted.

Her enthusiasm for me soon waned, but her final words to me served as an insightful teaching at critical moments on my journey.

"I feel your mind is completely cut off from your body. Sometimes, when I look at you, all I see is a talking head."

I didn't understand what she meant. I might have even taken her comment as a compliment confirming my opinion of myself as an intellectual holding himself aloof from the carnal needs that mere mortals are subject to.

Neither did I understand what she meant by "You're unavailable." I was going through a highly extroverted period of my life and believed I was very available.

Although Alexandra was what guys today would call a hottie, I wasn't attracted to her at first, but when we went back to being just friends, my enthusiasm for her waxed. I felt a sense of loss, albeit short-lived, perhaps for the first time.

~

During my Hôtel d'Alger years, I'd often go to London to see my elder brother and an old school friend, Sami, and to browse in independent bookstores. On one such visit I caught up with Siri, the aspiring filmmaker—or at least, that's what I thought—in a pub in the city. Siri was wearing a pinstriped suit like pretty much everyone else in the place. He confessed he hadn't followed through on his plan to go to London Film School. I felt betrayed and told him so.

"I got married. We had a kid. I had to support my family," he said defensively. "But I'm glad you haven't sold out. You've got to carry on, for all of us."

He seemed sincere. Mollified, I took a swig of beer. But I wasn't sure what exactly I was supposed to carry on.

~

Toward the end of my Hôtel d'Alger period, I got somewhat obsessed over Delphine, one of those BCBG types Alexandra would have disapproved of. She also had long legs, another good reason for Alexandra to dislike her. I met Delphine through a friend and although still in her early twenties, she had recently divorced her wealthy German husband.

"During all the years I was with him in Berlin, he never bought me a French-language magazine," she complained.

"Did you ask him to?" I ventured, showing my practical masculine side.

"No," she replied indignantly. "A woman doesn't have to tell her man what she needs. He has to figure that out on his own."

I tilted my head diplomatically, implying my agreement. I did agree in principle. *But a need for a French magazine? What kind of man would be able to figure that out?* A pretty flimsy reason to divorce a guy, especially since Delphine wasn't doing much in Berlin and could easily have gone out and bought a magazine herself. I met her ex-husband later when he came to visit her in

Paris. The three of us went to a jazz club and he seemed like a perfectly decent guy to me.

Delphine was living with her parents in their upscale 16th arrondissement apartment, and she asked me over to have tea with her mother one day. Holding a dainty porcelain teacup in one hand and balancing a matching saucer in the other, I sat in their spacious living room. It was filled with Louis XIV furniture. Her mother was elegantly dressed and wore a pearl necklace. It felt like having an audience with royalty. Afterwards, Delphine and I went for a walk in the neighbourhood. We stopped in front of a shop window displaying stylish Canadian parkas with fur-lined collars.

"You'd look good in that," she said. "Let's go in."

"Buy it!" she urged after I had tried it on.

I didn't have enough cash on me, so she whipped out her chequebook and said, "You can pay me back later."

I realized later she probably didn't like the thrift store jacket I was wearing and had planned the whole thing.

Soon after meeting her, I invited Delphine to dinner at a cozy Sri Lankan restaurant near the Cardinal Lemoine metro. We ordered rice with dhal, chicken curry, fried eggplant and stir-fried spinach.

She leaned forward with her forearms crossed on the table. "How come you don't have a girlfriend?"

"Women don't like me," I said rather coyly.

She laughed. "Do you expect me to believe that?"

"Is it so hard to believe?" I countered.

"*I* like you."

"*Why* do you like me?" I asked, sensing an opportunity.

She shrugged as if annoyed at the question. "Because you're cute."

I was expecting her to say something more substantial.

She leant forward again. "Seriously, why are you single?"

I took a sip of red wine and settled back in my chair to gather my thoughts.

"I'm afraid that if I'm in a relationship, I'll get sucked in and lose my individuality and won't be able to follow my calling. I've seen it happen to friends." I told her about Siri's "betrayal."

"No." She shook her head vehemently. "It's with the right person at your side that you can follow your dreams."

I shook my head in turn. But decades later, I had an epiphany that she was right, and tracked her down. Delphine had walked her talk. She and her husband had uprooted themselves from their life in Paris to go and live in a utopian community. I was impressed. I told her about my road to Damascus moment and asked whether she remembered me.

"Yes," she said. "I remember an idealistic and tortured young man."

Chapter 5
Rue Oberkampf

About a year after I moved on from the Hôtel d'Alger, I met Bibi in the tiny but colourful kitchen of my new workplace, a not-for-profit organization providing information and assistance to political refugees and immigrants. While not exactly dead-end, my new job wasn't a career either.

A petite young woman with thick reddish-black hair cut shoulder-length sat at one of the round red tables. Dressed in a light beige cashmere pullover, a darker matching skirt and topped off with a gold chain, she had come to see one of our colleagues regarding her application for political asylum. Her high cheekbones, dimpled cheeks and the cleft in her chin caught my attention.

Without much small talk, Bibi looked straight into my eyes. "Do you have a dream?"

I felt uneasy. We didn't know each other and no one had ever asked me such a question, and I couldn't put my finger on the answer. With hindsight, any dream I had would have been buried under my self-constructed intellectual persona. Not that I had any real intellectual accomplishments to speak of. I walked around town wearing a brown tweed jacket with patched elbows, the latest edition of *Le Monde* tucked prominently into the front pocket. *Le Monde* offered analysis and opinions and carried no pictures. Some of the newspaper's articles had long footnotes like research papers. I also kept Kant's hefty three-volume *Critique* set conspicuously displayed on my coffee table—even though reading it had given me no pleasure or real insights—and liked to talk about my favourite existentialist philosophers, such as Sartre, Camus and Kierkegaard.

Bibi kept looking at me expectantly, intensely, with her big brown eyes. To cover up my uneasiness, I rambled on about how unrealistic dreams could prevent us from having practical accomplishments. She looked away, saying almost to herself that she didn't like intellectual men. But Bibi's question continued to reverberate in me like a Zen koan,[5] working through various levels of my mind.

Despite Bibi's disappointment in me, telephone numbers were exchanged and a few days later, she woke me up with a call, looking for information on the political asylum process. We met in a café near the Rennes metro, and I learned she had spent time in the notorious Evin prison in Tehran for participating in school protests against the strict discipline of Ayatollah Khomeini's Islamic Revolution. I told her I knew someone at the OFPRA, the French government body in charge of processing political asylum applications, who might be able to help her. When we parted ways in front of the metro, I invited her to have lunch with me at a small Cambodian restaurant at the corner of Rue de Vaugirard and Boulevard Montparnasse, just up the

---

5   A paradoxical statement or enigmatic question used in Zen Buddhism to demonstrate the inadequacy of logical reasoning and to provoke enlightenment.

street from my place.

The restaurant was run by a middle-aged couple who had fled the killing fields of the Khmer Rouge. Tren, a tall, soft-spoken man with glasses, and a university professor in his previous life, had been driving a taxi, but since his wife was a good cook, they had decided to start their own restaurant. His wife passed the dishes through a small window in the partition that separated the kitchen and dining room, and Tren served them. Tren's long shirt must have been white at some point. The wall paint was also discoloured in some places. The furniture, a couple of long tables with benches and a motley collection of smaller rickety tables of different shapes and sizes, was apparently scavenged off the street. But as I have seen it happen elsewhere, the place had become trendy with a certain crowd—in this case, young, artsy types. They relished the grungy, unpretentious and amateurish feel of the place, not to mention the flavourful, inexpensive dishes. But then, as it happens sometimes with such restaurants, the owners—blissfully unaware of the secret of their success—get ambitious and move into larger premises with freshly painted walls, proper furniture, cheap tablecloths, shining cutlery and glistening glassware. They then stand in front of their empty restaurant, wringing their hands, a bewildered look on their faces.

Tren brought our steaming soups, spreading a tangy aroma of lemongrass throughout the restaurant. Bibi tried a spoonful and nodded her approval. The sweetness of coconut milk tempered the soup's distinctively spicy taste. She told me about her passion for skydiving and swimming and invited me to hear her sing with a choir at the Saint-Germain-des-Prés church. Opening up more, she talked about growing up in Tehran, about Prince, the pet rabbit she had as a child, and her love for her father.

"He used to take me on his lap and braid my hair, which I wore long when I was small. Then one day he just stopped doing it." Bibi's face crumpled.

"When I got older, he taught me all about cocktails," she continued, brightening up. "He taught me what a young lady should drink."

She told me about learning to fly light airplanes in Tehran, about her skiing holidays in Switzerland and shopping trips to Milan. Clearly she had been living a highly privileged lifestyle. I asked her what her father did for a living but she remained mysteriously coy. She even let out that as a young girl, she had met President Nixon, but again she refused to elaborate on the circumstances. Bibi had a veil of mystery about her I was never able to penetrate.

Her closeness to her father made her life difficult. Her mother was resentful, and her older brother bullied her, driving her to rebellion. "When things got rough, I'd lock myself up in my room, put on some loud music and dance my blues away."

I wanted to tell her about my own mother, who had given me a strong sense of security while allowing me the freedom to explore the world outside, but decided the timing wasn't right. Instead, I talked to her about my own childhood—losing my father very early in life, growing up as the youngest in a family of six, voraciously reading books and forming a secret society to solve mysteries with a few close friends. I told her about my school's sprawling campus by the Indian Ocean with two large playing fields, a swimming pool, tennis courts and even a chapel.

"I loved everything about school. But it's a strange thing, you know—I felt somewhat different from the other kids."

Bibi raised an eyebrow and took a spoonful of soup.

"Maybe because I didn't have a father," I continued. "There was only one other kid without a father."

On the first day of school every year, the class teacher called up each boy to his desk and wrote down their father's contact information. I anxiously waited for my turn and when it came, I'd stand close to the teacher, my heart beating fast and my throat dry. He'd ask for my father's name, and I'd lean forward and say in a hoarse whisper, "My father's dead, sir!"

The teacher's pen would hover.

And sometimes, when chatting in small groups during the lunch interval, one boy would start talking about his father, and another one would say something about his own dad, and I'd feel my body getting unpleasantly hot.

Bibi then told me about how she had run away from her girls' boarding school at the age of sixteen, about her admiration for Michael Jackson and about her desire to move to the United States. She looked up from her bowl of soup and pointed her chopsticks at me.

"You should go to Canada."

"Canada? But why? It's too cold there. Besides, I love it here. Isn't this"—I waved in the direction of Boulevard Montparnasse—"the centre of the universe?"

I tipped my bowl and scooped out the last spoonful of the now cold soup. A woman with grey hair, sitting alone next to us on the bench and looking quite out of place, had been throwing sideways glances at us. She said she was a psychic and offered to tell my fortune for fifty francs. I shook my head, but Bibi nodded vigorously.

The woman took out a pack of Tarot cards, shuffled them several times and then laid a few cards face down on the table, uncovering them one by one. With her elbow on the table and her chin cradled in her palm, Bibi looked on expectantly. I watched the pedestrians outside, feigning indifference.

The fortune teller opened up the cards and made some general observations that could have applied to anyone. I gave Bibi an "I thought as much" look.

Then she warmed up. "You'll be leaving France soon. I see you living in a place close to the US–Canada border."

That's too easy. She must have overheard our conversation.

I asked, "What about work? What will I be doing in the future?"

"You have the gift to heal people."

I must have had a look of disbelief on my face, so she looked down at her cards again.

"I see you working in a large, structured organization, maybe a consulting company or something like a hospital. That place will be important for your development and your understanding of yourself."

The woman's voice got louder, more confident. "You have an important mission to fulfill."

I sat up straight and turned toward her.

"You have a role to play in the transformation of human consciousness." The psychic had a triumphant gleam in her eyes, or so I thought.

This must be the boldest and most outrageous prediction she has ever made.

Time stood still. Tren was cleaning a table behind us, and the dirty rag in his hand froze in mid-air. Two large beads of sweat formed in my armpits, growing and then dripping in slow motion.

"And how am I supposed to carry out this mission?" I asked with all the haughtiness I could muster.

She consulted her cards again. "You have the tools. You'll learn to use them in due course."

I took out my wallet, gave her fifty francs and went to the cash register to pay our bill.

"Isn't she the best?" Tren's wife gushed. "She's a friend of mine."

We walked to the No. 96 bus stop in front of Gare Montparnasse.

Bibi broke the silence. "Why did you get angry?"

Yes, why was I angry? Here was someone finally recognizing my true potential and telling me what I needed to do with my life.

"Because it was so preposterous. C'mon, how can anyone tell the future?"

~

I had gone out with Bibi three times but thought she wasn't my type. Back then, my type was someone cerebral like me. Bibi seemed to be into me, which was a good reason to hold back, intriguing and drawing her in even more. For our next date, she suggested a *salon de thé* at the top of Rue Mouffetard. Bibi scanned the daunting menu as if she knew more than a thing or two about tea and picked out a pot of white *Thé de Ceylan*. "For you," she said. I ordered tiramisu to go with the tea. She behaved differently that day, rather distant and cold, which was annoying and yet somewhat compelling.

Bibi leaned back in her chair, folding her arms across her chest.

"Sooo?" Her mouth formed an O.

I settled back in my chair and looked around. Red checked curtains on the windows, shining silver teapots on white tablecloths, waitresses dressed in identical black dresses moving swiftly and noiselessly, cups clinking on saucers and conversations in low voices.

"This is a nice place. I've never been here before, even though I've lived on this street for a couple of years. I must come again."

Bibi raised one hand, showing me her palm. "Ah, but you

must get my permission first."

She giggled mischievously, seeming pleased with what she said.

Seeing her little raised hand and hearing her giggle, something shifted in me. One moment, I was sitting across a table from a woman I found attractive and intriguing but for whom I didn't have any feelings. The next moment, I felt I really cared about her and wanted to form a special bond with her. An emotional quantum shift.

Later, as we walked out, I took her hand and kissed her. Or rather, I was kissed—well and truly kissed. I felt my lower lip being sucked in and a warm, throbbing tongue pulsing in and out. I was speechless, but I shouldn't have been too surprised, knowing that even a kiss on the cheek from Bibi was memorable. Unlike the usual delicate brushing of cheeks, Bibi's cheek slammed into mine. I hardly had time to recover before the other cheek received the same treatment. It was a rather overwhelming experience. Still, it felt like the proper way to greet or part from someone: with gusto.

We walked hand in hand down Rue Mouffetard, winding down from Place de Contrescarpe. Bibi's heels clicked on the cobblestones as we passed Greek restaurants displaying skewers of meat interspersed with red, green and yellow peppers. Black-trousered, white-aproned waiters with their dark hair slicked back waved menu cards and hustled for customers on the sidewalk. We gazed at the tempting and tasteful displays in front of the *fromagerie* and the *poissonnerie* and paused at the farmers' market at the bottom of the street.

A look of childish delight lit Bibi's face as vegetables and fruits of varying colours, shapes and sizes were taken in hand, sniffed, tapped or shaken, handed back to the blue-aproned stall attendants, weighed, wrapped and tucked into bags with a swift exchange of banknotes and coins, and sometimes a few words about the weather, politics, soccer or the previous evening's television.

We went over to Square Saint-Médard and listened to the three-man band playing a medley of jazz favourites in front of the medieval church. Bibi tapped her heels and bobbed her head. When the music stopped, she stepped forward, put a coin in the hat, picked it up and went around, presenting the hat with a flourish to the circle of onlookers.

~

That summer, we went for long walks, biked in the Bois de Vincennes and attended classical music concerts in dark churches. Bibi tried to teach me to swim, threatened to take me fishing and introduced me to a range of restaurants, from greasy soup joints in Belleville's Chinatown to upscale places in Le Marais, where she worked. Although a connoisseur of gourmet food, she also loved to picnic on bread, cheese and wine. Once, while picnicking on the banks of the Seine, she was so enthralled by the sight of a mother duck leading her brood of tiny ducklings in single file out of the water that she talked about it for days afterward. My detached and observer-like attitude to life irritated Bibi and perhaps also intrigued her.

She lived in a spacious *chambre de bonne* on Rue Oberkampf in the 11th arrondissement—a street that soon became trendy, especially the eastern part close to Ménilmontant. She had decorated the room herself and transformed it into what I called a doll's house, with bright pastel colours and wallpaper with flower motifs everywhere. One day, when cooking lunch for us, she asked me to get the vial of saffron for her from the top shelf of her kitchen cupboard.

"I have short legs," she said with an apologetic look, reminding me of Alexandra's problem.

Bibi had the habit of suddenly changing the subject and asking open-ended questions in a childlike but urgent voice, as if her life depended on the answer. It was endearing yet irritating, as I often floundered and said something without thinking too much, and invariably she looked disappointed. I continued thinking about what I should have actually said while trying to keep up my end of the conversation.

One day, we were sitting and chatting on her couch when she turned to me and asked, "What's Buddhism?"

I told her what I remembered about Buddhism's Four Noble Truths—the truth of suffering, the truth of the cause of suffering, the truth of the end of suffering, and the truth of the path that leads to the end of suffering. Of course, Bibi was disappointed with this abstract explanation.

I then thought about how I could have responded better. I could have told her how I had learned about Buddha's journey as a five-year-old sitting next to my grandmother on her bed, my legs swinging, and listening to Buddhist monks giving talks on the radio. They'd often repeat the well-known story of Siddhartha Gautama growing up in a sheltered environment before discovering the existence of suffering when he was in his late twenties. He then took the radical decision to leave behind his home, family, wife and newborn baby, to search for an answer to his burning question: *What is the solution to the problem of suffering?* After spending seven years wandering in forests practising various meditation techniques, he finally achieved his goal. I could have told her that what drew me to the Buddha was Siddhartha's heroic journey from unawakened to awakened, from darkness to light. I could have also added that while I was growing up without a father, the Buddha had filled the void, serving as my role model.

Mona was out of the country on a journalistic assignment, and I was cat sitting for her in her apartment near the Place de la Bastille. Bibi came over, and we bought provisions in the Sunday farmers' market in the square just outside. Bibi grilled two salmon steaks and made a fruit salad while I made Sri Lankan fried rice—basmati rice tempered in butter with finely chopped leeks and grated carrots.

"See, I didn't chop any onions today," I said rather triumphantly.

Bibi gave a suppressed smile.

I was referring to a comment she had made on a previous day. *"You're so funny. When you're cooking, you always start by chopping onions."*

"What's so funny about it? Doesn't everyone?"

"No, other people don't."

After lunch Bibi watched TV while I washed the dishes in the kitchen. She called out to me, looking over her shoulder and beckoning me with her hand. "Come watch."

I went over and stood behind the couch.

She pointed at the screen. "Woman-child. That's my problem. They're talking about it."

I stood there for a few minutes and went back to the kitchen. Bibi was often childlike, an endearing trait, but the woman-child concept was new to me. The amateur psychologist I prided myself to be showed no interest in learning more about it, and it wasn't until much later that I understood why.

That summer, I didn't have much time for my usual activities, like hanging around with friends in cafés, bars and restaurants. I took Bibi to a dinner with some friends at the boisterous *La Coupole* on Boulevard Montparnasse, but she wasn't impressed.

"You and your friends know how to fix all of the world's problems, but how come you don't seem to have much money?" she asked.

It should have been a glorious summer, but it wasn't. A sense of impending doom had been growing in me ever since I discovered Bibi's dark side. Although I had seen signs before, it sank in one day as we sipped kirs on Boulevard Montparnasse, watching the world go by.

Seeing my eyes roving, she frowned. "I notice you're a gourmand."

I knew she wasn't referring to food and tried to maintain my focus on her. But seeing me looking away again, she called out my name, and when I turned my head around, she stuck out a finger, like a child in play. When my cheek hit her pointed finger, she broke into peals of laughter.

I couldn't help smiling. "You're so childish, Bibi."

Though my tone was warm, I had touched a raw nerve. Bibi's face went dark and she brooded for the rest of the date. It was a relief when we finally parted ways.

She was subject to wild shifts in mood, and I never knew who would turn up at our date—the exuberant Bibi full of generosity and tenderness, always ready to break into peals of laughter, or the brooding, paranoid and smouldering Bibi waiting for a spark to erupt into a fire. The plasticity of her face could range from extremely alluring to downright plain, depending on how she felt inside. She was probably bipolar—though I hadn't heard of that condition yet.

One evening we had plans to have dinner in Montparnasse

and met up in front of the train station.

Bibi had other ideas. "Let's buy some food and eat at your place."

We bought cheese, bread, wine, nuts and grapes at my local convenience store and climbed the seven floors to my room. Bibi bumped me with her hips from time to time, laughing gaily. She was in high spirits, which was both exciting and ominous. When she was on a high, a low was never far away.

Bibi was particularly coquettish that evening, asking me to feed her the succulent purple grapes and then eating them with exaggerated relish, gently biting my fingertips in the process and laughing as she mopped away the grape juice dribbling from her mouth with a white napkin. Several times she threw her arms around my neck, gave me a big smack on the cheek and then drew away, smiling at the red imprint left on my cheek before brushing it away with the back of her hand. After we had finished our last glasses of red wine, Bibi lay down on my bed and closed her eyes.

Later, as we lay together under my orange bedcover, she turned her face to me abruptly.

"Do you love me?"

I froze. I was getting attached to her, but I didn't think I could honestly say I loved her. I didn't know what love was. I'd experienced some crushes, pined for a few women, but those were simply mental states. Over the years, I had given quite a bit of thought to this issue of professing one's love to someone and concluded it's not as easy as it looks in movies. As a follower of the Buddha and a believer in the notion of *anicca* or impermanence, how could I say "I love you" to someone, knowing very well that, like all things, love wouldn't last? Plus, although I'm no stickler for grammar, there seemed something wrong about the words themselves. It would be more correct to say "I will love you," or "I want to give you love" or "I'm in love with you." All these thoughts were racing through my mind as Bibi waited, first expectantly and then sulkily.

She looked up at the ceiling, and then turned toward me again and said fiercely, "Say you love me."

I complied, but hearing the words coming out of my mouth, I knew they lacked conviction. Bibi looked away, and the next morning it was the dark and brooding Bibi who left and never came back. But her scent lingered for days.

During the brief time that we dated, Bibi had initiated several separations, but this time it felt real. A deep sense of loss engulfed me. With hindsight, I'd say an old wound had reopened for the first time. My phone calls and messages went unanswered. I took to sitting in the café on Rue Oberkampf, in front of her building, drinking countless espressos and writing long letters she'd never read. Several weeks went by and one day, I saw her coming out of the building. I tried to catch up with her but she ran away. I went back to the café feeling shaken and tore up the letter I was writing. There was nothing more I could do.

I surrendered.

Sitting in the bustling café terrace with cars roaring up Rue Oberkampf, my mind let go of wanting her to come back. And perhaps of a part of myself too.

Something shifted in my chest. My heart opened and expanded. It was palpable.

Now I know what love is.

Chapter 6
Rue Nicolas Charlet

On the evening of my seventh winter solstice in Paris, I lay in bed in my seventh-floor room on Rue Nicolas Charlet. I had moved to this small side street near Boulevard Pasteur in the 15th arrondissement, just south of Montparnasse, after living on Rue Mouffetard for several years. Propped up against the headrest with a warm mug of tea cradled in my hands, I sensed the onset of a winter of discontent. I still had no sense of purpose. The world was empty and devoid of meaning. This feeling of emptiness, which had dogged me with varying degrees of intensity since my teenage years, was heightened by the loss of Bibi.

So I had been doing a lot of lying around in bed under the orange bedcover, staring at the matching curtains and the wallpaper's garish orange-and-black tropical beach scene. But then again, the room was so small and the bed took up so much space that there wasn't much else I could do but lie in it. Books took up a lot of space as well, piled up on my desk, the small coffee table, the solitary chair, and the floor. I liked clutter back then. I thought clutter was a fitting environment for me, a self-professed intellectual preoccupied with the loftier things in life.

The radio was tuned to the *Radio France* station jubilantly reporting on the fall of the Berlin Wall, which only increased my sense of gloom. I felt I was on the losing side, having clung through all of my adult life to a somewhat half-hearted but necessary belief in Marxism. I needed to believe in something, something big and universal, and the Marxist ideal of transforming man by changing his material conditions fit the bill. I went on believing in it, even in the face of irrefutable evidence that the actual implementation of that ideal was an unmitigated disaster.

I leaned over and turned the radio dial to *Ici et Maintenant*,[6] aptly named, as it turned out. I wasn't really listening to the discussion, but a strange yet familiar name penetrated the fog in my mind, once, twice, several times—Gurdjieff. I felt a sense of urgency to find out more about this Gurdjieff.

Where have I heard that name before? It finally came to me. It was in *The Outsider* by Colin Wilson. This book had leaped into my hands a few years earlier when I was browsing in an alternative bookstore on Charing Cross Road during a visit to London.

I got out of bed, rummaged in the clutter and found *The Outsider*. Published in the 1950s in Britain when Wilson, a school dropout, was still in his early twenties, the book became an instant and unlikely bestseller. It deals with the theme of the outsider in literature—literary anti-heroes alienated by the lack of meaning in life. Although haunted by the sense of a special destiny and life's potential, they also know they have no special skills or talents. Enthralled, I identified with Wilson's anti-hero. The book also featured a number of my

---

6   Here and Now.

literary heroes and anti-heroes, including Herman Hesse's Steppenwolf, Sartre's Roquentin, and Dostoevsky's Raskolnikov and Dmitri Karamazov.

In the later chapters of *The Outsider*, Gurdjieff appears and proposes a solution to the problem of alienation. Since I had been more interested in the outsider than solutions, Gurdjieff did not stand out for me when I first read it. Born in Armenia, Gurdjieff was some kind of guru, perhaps even one of the first to come to the West, during the interwar period. He had travelled extensively in central Asia, India and Tibet in search of an answer to the question that had preoccupied him from a young age: *What is the meaning of life on Earth?* After over twenty years of travel and learning, he shared his findings, first in St. Petersburg and Moscow, then in Istanbul and finally in Paris.

I went to sleep with a sense of anticipation. The next morning I marched down the seven flights of stairs into the crisp winter air, walked along the Montparnasse Tower, negotiated the treacherous crossing between Rue de l'Arrivée and Boulevard Montparnasse and dropped into the boulangerie at the corner of Rue de Rennes. Biting into a still warm pain au chocolat and brushing away pastry flakes from my mouth with the back of my hand, I walked on past the cheerfully familiar blue-and-yellow *La Poste* sign, stepping aside to make way for anxious-looking Christmas shoppers on the crowded sidewalk. After climbing the stairs to the Bibliothèque André Malraux on Rue de Rennes, I flipped through the card catalogue and found a single entry under Gurdjieff—*In Search of the Miraculous: Fragments of an Unknown Teaching* by P. D. Ouspensky. Not a terribly promising title, as I had no interest in the miraculous, but I eagerly grabbed the book from the shelf.

Back in my room, under the orange bedcover, I learned that Ouspensky was to Gurdjieff what Plato had been to Socrates.

Several themes ran through the book but what made me stop, flick back the pages and read over several times were the teachings on consciousness.

Gurdjieff talked about four states of consciousness. The first state is sleep, when we are mostly immersed in dreams. The second, the waking state, is not much different from the sleep state, as we are subject to a constant flow of thoughts and go through life as if it's a dream. It's a state of waking sleep. In the third state of consciousness, we wake up from the state of waking sleep and become conscious of being conscious. Gurdjieff called it the state of self-remembering, but it's still a state of subjective consciousness. The fourth state is objective consciousness, where reality is seen as it is. It's the enlightened state.

Self-remembering was a core concept in Gurdjieff's teachings—it's the third state of consciousness and also the means by which to wake up from the second state of waking sleep. As Gurdjieff pointed out, we think we're conscious when we're not. We all have a potential for consciousness and to realize that potential, we have to remember ourselves. Self-observation is an associated concept. If we observed ourselves, we'd realize we don't remember ourselves. But to really observe oneself, we need to remember ourselves!

I wondered whether self-remembering could be equated with mindfulness, one of the Buddha's core teachings. I had heard much about it growing up in Sri Lanka but without any real understanding. While mindfulness was an abstract concept, the notions of remembering oneself and waking up from sleep were more evocative. "Buddha" means "the awakened one," which further confirmed my line of reasoning. *The Buddha had realized the fourth state of consciousness!*

Gurdjieff also pointed out that the Gospels mentioned sleep and waking up several times and that Christ's disciples slept while he was praying in the Garden of Gethsemane for the last time.

For Ouspensky, in our usual state of waking sleep or the second stage of consciousness, our attention is directed toward and captured by the object of attention. In the third stage of self-remembering, the attention is divided. One part is directed toward the object of attention and the other to the sense of self. For instance, when looking at a tree, you'd also notice yourself looking at the tree.

Ouspensky goes on to give a vivid account of his attempts at self-remembering. Walking around St. Petersburg one day, trying hard to "remember himself," he did succeed, but to his dismay he fell back into a state of sleep and woke up far away in the city two hours later. "The sensation of awakening was extraordinarily vivid," he says. "I can almost say that I *came to*."

Reading Ouspenky's account, I remembered a similar experience I had when I was eight. I was in my second year in primary school and the day started off like any other day. In my navy-blue school shorts and white short-sleeved shirt, I made it to the main school gate as the bell was ringing. I hurried past the chapel, the quadrangle with the well-manicured lawn and the assembly hall and entered my classroom as the teacher was starting the roll call. It was during the afternoon session, when the heat and humidity hit their almost palpable peak, that it happened.

I had a surreal experience of waking up. *Did I fall asleep?* I looked around quickly to see whether any of my classmates were nudging each other and laughing at me as they were wont to do in such situations. But no one was paying any attention to me. I looked around again, this time with wonder, as if I were seeing everything for the first time, almost surprised to find myself there. Everything felt so vivid. The sound of the teacher's chalk on the blackboard made me jump, and the whiteness of the boys' shirts in the front rows blinded me. I heard, as if for the first time, the sound of ocean waves crashing against the rocks on the nearby beach. And when a train went past on the tracks just outside the school walls, it rumbled through my body. An unusual sense of well-being spread through my body and mind. I thought back to what had happened just before I "woke up" and it was like I had been listening to the teacher, taking notes, chatting surreptitiously with my neighbour, all in a dreamlike state. For the rest of the afternoon, I was able to alternate between the dreamlike state and the wakeful state at will. It was like a thrilling game I could play while paying attention to the teacher. But when I tried it again the next day, I found I could no longer do it.

I had similar but much less intense waking up experiences accompanied by a sense of well-being from time to time during my school-going days. It happened again when walking home after my dishwashing gig on Rue Descartes, possibly triggered by the tactile and physical nature of the work.

Coming back to Colin Wilson and *The Outsider*, he wrote in his preface that when he sketched the outline for the book on Christmas Day 1954, he felt he had at last ceased to waste his time; he was starting to do what he'd always intended to do. "There was a feeling like leaving harbour."

I felt something similar when I went to bed on a different Christmas night. I remembered the burning question I had formulated some ten years earlier—*What do I need to do with my life?* Could this be what I had to do? To wake up?

The next morning I rose unusually early.

I put water to boil on the hot plate and draw the orange blind. Feeling my bare feet on the carpet, I see the greenish-blue sky rising above the roof of the apartment building on the opposite side of the street. Hearing the water gurgle, I open one of the large windows and take a carton of milk from the plastic grocery bag hanging from the window latch. A pigeon perched on my balcony rail takes off, its wings fluttering in my heart. I return to the hot plate, put a tea bag in a mug and pour hot water over it, tugging at the string to expedite the steeping process. I dribble in the milk until the tea reaches a creamy chocolate colour and use a teaspoon to squeeze the tea bag against the rim of the mug before throwing it into the trash can. I walk back to my bed, mug of steaming tea in hand.

I noticed I was aware of everything I was doing and my movements were fluid. But it was when I got back into bed and tried to prop my back up against the headrest I knew something unusual had happened. I couldn't slouch as usual. Something like a rod up my back was forcing me to sit bolt upright. My skin, usually dry, especially in the winter, had turned glossy. I felt the blood coursing through my veins and a pleasurable, tingling sensation all over my skin. I sensed the bedsheets touching my body and the rhythmic inhalation and exhalation of breath.

In the shower, with the warm water cascading from the top of my head, I noted my mental state had also changed. The heaviness of recent days had given way to a sense of lightness and quiet joy.

There's absolutely nothing to worry about. Everything's fine with my life and the world.

I was filled with gratitude and goodwill toward everyone and everything. Tears ran down my cheeks. They mingled with the water, leaving a salty taste on my lips.

I had been leading a mostly sedentary life in Paris except during the interlude with Bibi, but after a breakfast of baguette and *Comté* cheese, I felt the urge to go for a walk. I marched up Rue Vaugirard, turned right on Boulevard Montparnasse, then up Rue de Rennes and right again on Boulevard Saint-Germain, clearly hearing the ebb and flow of traffic, usually a dull sound at the back of my mind. On Boulevard Saint-Michel the smell of frying buckwheat crepes wafted toward me from the outdoor stand on Place Saint-Michel. I stopped to take in the scene on the Pont Saint-Michel, at the very same spot where I had stood some seven years earlier on my first day in Paris.

I sensed my feet on the sidewalk and the hardness of the bridge against my back and saw greyish-white clouds change form as they drifted across the clear blue sky. The waters of the Seine flowed underneath, breaking into an endless series of triangular ripples flecked with foam around the prow of a passing *bateau-mouche*. Tourists on the top deck clicked away at their cameras. On the bridge cars roared past and Parisians hurried by, impervious to the beauty and history around them. Tourists meandered, pointing out sights, talking in loud voices and stopping to take pictures of Notre-Dame. To my right was the Palais de Justice with the top of the Sainte-Chapelle spire rising just above it, and to my left I could see the usual hustle and bustle of Place Saint-Michel. I saw and heard everything at the same time, as if my mind had become a very spacious container. And although I had walked across this bridge so many times, I looked around in wonder as if it were the first time.

I'm really here!

Later, feeling hungry on my way back home, I thought of my favourite takeout, poulet-frites. But when I neared the place, I couldn't see myself eating roast chicken covered with greasy fries. Instead, I dropped by the nearby Félix Potin minimarket on my way home and made myself a salad of soft green lettuce, grated carrots and sliced radishes, doused in olive oil and lemon. I crunched through my salad, savouring the flavours combined with the pungent olive oil and thinking about how unusual the day had been.

Did something happen during the night? And when I woke

up, did I also wake up from my usual state of waking sleep like I did that day in school? Was this waking up triggered by reading Gurdjieff's teaching on self-remembering?

After finishing the salad I cleared up the clutter in my room to harmonize my living environment with the feeling of spaciousness in my body and mind. I stored some books in closets and packed others to be sold or donated to the Shakespeare and Company bookstore, the publisher of James Joyce's *Ulysses*. Located on the Left Bank, across from Notre-Dame, its upper-floor library had been a favourite hangout of mine and an English-language haven during my first year in Paris.

During the days that followed, I kept getting up with the sunrise. I could not eat anything other than bread, cheese, salads and fruits. But most after-effects of the waking up experience faded. I returned to slouching in bed, my skin turned dry again, my mind lost the sensation of spaciousness and I fell back into the state of waking sleep.

I've been expelled from the Garden of Eden.

But, as the weeks and months went by, I noticed some after-effects were permanent. My personality had been partly deconstructed. I gave up my rigidly rational attitude to life and became more open, accepting that reason couldn't explain everything.

I let go of a narrative I had absorbed from my family—that we were hard done by because of our father's sudden and premature death. Instead, I saw that life had always given me what I needed, and everywhere I'd been, people had been welcoming, kind and generous with me.

The cynical and pessimistic attitude I had adopted along the way as part of my public persona also dropped away.

Remembering Gurdjieff's teaching on personality and essence, these changes made sense to me. We're born with essence, but we acquire personality. When we get older, as a result of environmental influences, our personality grows while our essence shrinks.

Did the waking up experience consist in letting go of my personality and connecting with my essence?

Looking back, that magical Christmas season marked the end of an era of my life. Something essential in me turned inward. It's laughable that for all these years, I had been searching for something outside of myself when the answer was within. Previously, whatever I did, whether buying a book or going to see a movie or an exhibition, I'd hoped something in it would help me put the finger on what my purpose might be. On my way to meet up with a couple of friends just for a drink and a meal, I'd expected someone to say something in a moment of alcohol-fuelled inspiration that would serve as a eureka moment for me.

I finally knew with certainty what I needed to do: permanently regain the awakened state I had briefly experienced and then lost.

But now I had a new quest.

How to wake up permanently?

Chapter 7
Bibliothèque Sainte-Geneviève

I had been neglecting my friends, not returning calls, so I picked up the phone again. Soon I was sitting at our favourite table in the café at the corner of Rue du Bac and Boulevard Saint-Germain with Mathieu, Grushka, Marcelle, Daniel and Boris, ordering demis, kirs and panachés.

Félix, the waiter, gave me an exaggerated bow. "Look who's here."

Grushka berated me for my anti-social behaviour but a smile played at the corner of her mouth. I leaned back in my chair holding a cool glass of panaché. It was peak hour. Waiters rushed around barking orders, patrons chattered in loud voices, crockery and cutlery clattered on counters and cars honked outside. It felt good to be with friends but something had changed. I didn't feel the need to talk and was conscious of the space between them and me.

As expected, the talk revolved around the fall of the Berlin Wall. It occurred to me then that the walls in my mind had crumbled at about the same time.

Grushka in particular was jubilant. "I cried when I saw people climbing over the wall and tasting freedom for the first time."

"But what is freedom? Isn't true freedom inner freedom?" I heard myself saying.

Five pairs of eyes turned to focus on me.

I walked back home along Rue de Rennes, feeling disconnected from everything and everyone I had felt connected to before. The meeting confirmed something I had known all along. I had no one to talk to about what had happened. Not that I knew what happened or how to talk about it.

I urgently needed to find answers to my new question— *How to wake up permanently?* And since academic research was the only thing I had learned to do over the previous seven years, a library seemed the right place to look.

The next morning I took the No. 82 bus past the Jardin de Luxembourg. It turned north on Boulevard Saint-Michel, and dropped me off at the terminus just behind the Panthéon. I crossed the street to the Sainte-Geneviève library. The oblong building looked relatively plain compared to the monumental neoclassical Panthéon and even the nearby apartment buildings with their ornate Haussmannian facades.

But inside, crossing the marble floor with its geometric squares of dark and light colours and in the long, dim hallway guarded by heavy square columns, I felt I was entering a temple of knowledge. Above the broad staircase loomed a mural of Raphael's *The School of Athens*, hinting at the prospect of access to ancient knowledge.

I remembered a similar sense of excitement when I was seven years old. I had nervously climbed the stairs to the library of my school, which was still new to me, approached the teacher sitting behind a desk near the entrance and said, "I'd like to join the library, sir." He had a stern, penetrating look and a handlebar moustache, which now reminds me of Gurdjieff. I can't remember who gave me the idea to join the library or how I found my way across our campus to the library building. The teacher didn't seem surprised by my request; as if he was expecting me. He asked for my name and class and filled out my library cards. Cards in hand, I walked inside and looked around.

All these books? I can read all these books?

At the top of the stairs of the Sainte-Geneviève library, I flashed my student card at the thin and sad-looking man in faded blue overalls sitting at a desk behind an iron railing. A vast reading room stretched from one end of the building to the other, bathed in sunlight that flooded in through the large windows lining each side, contrasting with the dimness in the hall below. I had literally moved from darkness to light. The library was more like a cathedral, with soaring arches and a long line of slender cast-iron columns dividing the monumental space into twin aisles of solid wooden tables. When the sun set, the green table lamps, lined up like the helmets of an army of marching soldiers, gave an eerie glow, illuminating the bowed heads, arms and hands of students against the pervasive darkness. The hushed silence was broken only by sounds of shuffling paper, dragging chairs and light footsteps.

I read until the library closed at ten. The next day I went back in the morning, again staying until the close, and again the next day, pretty much every day for about six months, ending up with a large pile of notes.

At the same time I borrowed Ouspensky's book from the neighbourhood library, I also took out *The Crisis of the Modern World* by a French thinker named René Guénon who I had also heard about on *Ici et Maintenant*. Writing in 1927, he was well ahead of his time, debunking the notions of evolution and never-ending progress. He diagnosed the root of the modern crisis as rampant individualism in the West and the lack of authentic spirituality. Not simply an academic exercise, his book was a call to action, urging readers to take up a spiritual practice within one of the world's traditional religions. Guénon belonged to the Traditionalist school, whose main premise is the existence of universal truths shared by all the major world religions, popularized as perennial philosophy by Aldous Huxley and others.

Although the teachings of both were from traditional sources, Gurdjieff's practical, hands-on approach contrasted with the intellectual breadth and Cartesian precision of Guénon's thinking. They also happened to be contemporaries in Paris but despised each other. Convinced that Gurdjieff was a charlatan, Guénon warned people to stay away from him. I wondered why I was drawn to the thinking of two very different men at the same time. I pondered this question like a koan until many years later, the answer revealed itself.

Of course! Gurdjieff's self-remembering is the solution to Guénon's crisis of the modern world! If a sufficient number of people can remember themselves and wake up, the modern world's ills would resolve themselves naturally, organically.

Like Gurdjieff, Guénon pointed out that religions have exoteric and esoteric aspects. As the term suggests, exoteric refers to the external forms of religion available to everyone such as rituals and public ceremonies, and is characterized by dependence on an external source for salvation. While esotericism includes notions such as hidden knowledge, secret organizations, mysterious ceremonies and initiation, what appealed to me most was the idea of self-transformation, of reliance on one's own efforts. Just when the Marxist ideal of transformation from without was literally crumbling, I encountered a teaching that called for transformation from within. I also understood why I was so drawn to the Buddha's own transformative journey while being turned off by institutionalized Buddhism.

I read most of Guénon's books at the library. In his intriguingly titled *The Reign of Quantity and the Signs of the Times*, Guénon sets out a cosmic view for the increasing preponderance of materialism as well as a cyclical conception of time.

In Guénon's *Introduction to the Study of the Hindu Doctrines*, I learned about the six schools of Indian thought. The school of Vedanta appealed to me the most as it was most relevant to what I was looking for. Vedanta literally means end of the Vedas—the earliest Hindu teachings covering exoteric topics such as rituals, ceremonies and sacrifices. The Vedanta texts include the Upanishads, which are esoteric texts on meditation, ontological knowledge and the goal of *moksha*, or liberation from the illusion of a separate self. Vedanta comprises several sub-schools, including the well-known Advaita or non-dual Vedanta. According to Advaita Vedanta, the phenomenal world is an illusion and there is no difference between the ultimate reality and one's true self. I don't think I realized all the implications of what I was reading but Advaita Vedanta appealed to me, especially the concept of a *jivanmukta*, someone who has achieved liberation in this life as opposed to liberation after death, as taught in other schools.

Vedanta also includes the Bhagavad Gita, which is part of the epic poem Mahabharata, and distills the wisdom and teachings of the Vedas and the Upanishads. A dialogue occurs between Arjuna and his charioteer, Krishna, the action taking place on a battlefield. Arjuna is reluctant to go to battle against his own cousins and asks for Krishna's advice. Krishna urges him to fulfill his warrior's duty through selfless action. This key teaching of the Bhagavad Gita—taking action without attachment to the outcome—is the essence of *karma yoga*, or yoga of action, one of the three paths to liberation as synthesized by the Bhagavad Gita. The other two are *bhakti yoga*, or yoga of devotion, and *jnana yoga*, or yoga of knowledge. I thought jnana yoga referred to book knowledge. Later, I realized it meant knowledge of ultimate reality and of the true self as opposed to the false belief in a separate self.

I also learned about Tantra, a group of teachings that spread through northern India around about the eighth century, consisting of various practices offering a fast-tracked path to liberation, influencing both Buddhism and Hinduism. Pre-Tantric teachings require withdrawal from the world, as human desires are considered to be a major obstacle to achieving the goal of *moksha*. In Tantra, practitioners carry on the life of householders and can even use desires as means to liberate themselves.

Non-dual Tantra is a subschool, and like Advaita Vedanta, holds the view that consciousness and the material world are one, or more correctly, not two. Although these two schools share an identical worldview, the means for realizing that view are strikingly different. In Advaita Vedanta, practitioners go inward and realize the world is an illusion. In non-dual Tantra, they go outward, embrace the world and become one with it.

Tantra also includes esoteric teachings on the nebulous concept of kundalini, considered to be a feminine energy coiled at the base of the spine. When awakened, this energy rises up, activating the chakras, which are energy centres located along the spine. I remembered the feeling of something akin to a rod going up my spine at the time of my awakening.

Was that kundalini rising up?

This question gave rise to more questions.

Was the shift in my chest when I felt love for Bibi the opening of the heart chakra? And did that opening facilitate the rising of the kundalini?

Shaktipat is an associated concept that refers to the transfer of energy from the teacher to the student.

Did reading about Gurdjieff's teachings have the effect of shaktipat on me?

I had just come back to my seat at the library with a new book, *The Metaphysics of Sex* by Julius Evola, another thinker of the Traditionalist school, when I heard the sound of high heels approaching. I looked up and saw a girl with short dark blond hair taking off her fur coat, folding it and placing it over the back of her chair. She sat down, pulled up the sleeves of her pink top and took her things out of her bag, placing them on the table and occasionally brushing back a wave of hair from her forehead. Her movements were precise and graceful. She touched her silk Hermès scarf—a must-have item for a Parisian BCBG woman—tied casually around her neck, and looked around with her chin tilted up, as if she was trying to determine whether the temperature warranted her taking it off. She decided it didn't, but she caught me watching her and stared boldly into my eyes. I looked quickly away.

I had gotten into the habit of always sitting in the same area of the library. Over the next few weeks, the girl in the fur coat came later in the morning and chose a seat more or less facing me. One day, I went to the vending machine in the basement and was straightening up with a cup of coffee in my hand when I saw her standing close behind me.

She wore a slightly triumphant smile. "Are you done?" she asked, rather unnecessarily.

"Yes, it's all yours," I said, equally unnecessarily.

I froze for a moment and then returned to my seat, this innocuous scene playing over and over again in my mind. *Why did I walk away like that?* It was unlike me to pass up on an opportunity to chat up an alluring girl. I was concerned she'd ask me what I was working on and I wouldn't know what to say. That seems now like a flimsy excuse. Her seating preferences changed after that, and I only had glimpses of her from afar.

I delved deeper into Buddhism. More specifically, the Buddha's Noble Eightfold Path to enlightenment, which I had heard much about growing up. But what previously felt abstract, dry and not relevant to the modern world came alive to me now as an actual path with a set of practical instructions for awaking permanently, handed down from one generation to another since the Buddha's time. The path is broken neatly into three stages: *Sila*, or right conduct, comprises right speech, right action and right livelihood; *samadhi*, or meditation, is made up of right effort, right mindfulness and right concentration; and *prajna*, or wisdom, is broken into right view and right resolve. A Buddhist practitioner starts by observing right conduct and then practices meditation, which leads to wisdom and eventually to liberation from suffering.

When I learned that *sati*, the Pali[7] word for mindfulness, literally meant remembering, it vindicated my previous insight that self-remembering and mindfulness were the same. This had important practical consequences for me. Though Gurdjieff and Ouspenky discussed self-remembering at great length, they did not set out a clear path to achieving it. The 2,500-year-old Buddhist meditation tradition, on the other hand, did have a roadmap for awakening.

I had found the answer to the question I had posed some months earlier—*how to wake up permanently?* What I needed to do was practise mindfulness within a Buddhist tradition.

Several months had gone by and despite having found what I was looking for, I kept taking the No. 82 bus to the library every morning and spending the whole day reading. I read like

---

7   The language in which Buddhist texts were originally written.

a detective, pursuing one lead after another until they went cold or turned up trumps. One such lead led to *The Hero with a Thousand Faces* by Joseph Campbell. Like the thinkers of the Traditionalist school, Campbell was looking for connections between cultures over the ages. But he focused on mythology, not religion. His premise was that all the important historical myths have a common structure:

> *A hero ventures forth from the world of common day into a region of supernatural wonder: fabulous forces are there encountered and a decisive victory is won: the hero comes back from this mysterious adventure with the power to bestow boons on his fellow man.*

While the Buddha, Moses, Mohammed and Jesus are iconic examples of this monomyth, the quest for meaning is fundamental to the human psyche. The hero's journey has three stages: departure, initiation and return. When I read that one of the substages in the initiation stage is the meeting with the goddess, I thought of Bibi.

Did she initiate me? Am I on a hero's journey? An anti-hero on a hero's journey? Is that even possible?

I also studied the Krishnamurti books I had first read in my late teens. Originally from South India, Krishnamurti had been "discovered" at a young age by the Theosophical Society as a future "world teacher" and educated in London. He later rejected this title but went on to travel the world and teach, attracting a large group of followers. Unlike other teachers from India, he did not rely on traditional teachings or lineages.

Around about the same time, I was having an espresso in a café with a horseshoe-shaped bar when I noticed a woman with grey hair on the opposite side looking at me intently. On her way out she came to me and told me I reminded her of Krishnamurti. Just before I left Sri Lanka for Paris, I had gone to hear Krishnamurti speak at the Colombo Public Library, not long before his passing, and saw from far a frail figure dressed in white on the podium.

I figured that Krishnamurti's core teaching of choiceless awareness probably referred to awareness of awareness. We can safely assume that unlike animals, human beings have awareness of ourselves as separate beings, which is the second stage of consciousness as taught by Gurdjieff. And if we achieve the third stage of consciousness, we're not only aware of ourselves but we also become aware of our awareness. I had probably experienced awareness of awareness for the first time when I awakened at school when I was eight. Three years earlier, another significant event might have made me fully aware of myself as a separate entity for the first time.

I was five, and my eldest brother was taking me to Montessori school on his bicycle, on the way to his school. Wearing his short-sleeved white school shirt and long white pants, he snapped black clips onto the bottoms of the legs to keep them away from the greasy bicycle chain. Before we came to my school, we had to go up a hill, so we got off the bike and walked. Two ladies dressed in housecoats stood on opposite sides of the street having a conversation.

"Oh dear, it was so sudden! What did he die of?" asked the first lady loudly.

"A heart attack. I feel so sorry for the family,"

I sensed something shifting in my brother's body. Our father too had died of a heart attack when I was one and a half years old. I wonder now how I knew that, since we never talked about our father in our home. No pictures of him could be found anywhere, not even the traditional wedding photograph.

My school was actually the teacher's home. She liked me, as I had learned quickly to read and write both English and Sinhalese. After school was over, the children would sit on the veranda chairs, our feet dangling, waiting for someone to come and take us home. Tissa, who lived close to our house, was sitting next to me. He had once given me a pencil sharpener in the shape of a rifle but took it back a few days later. That day his mother came to pick him up and I waited alone. Not long after, I saw Tissa's father opening the garden gate and coming up the driveway.

He put his briefcase on one of the steps leading up to the veranda, took off his glasses with one hand and wiped his face with a white handkerchief. "Has Tissa gone home?"

I was about to say "yes" when I heard myself saying, "No, he's in the toilet."

I can't remember anything that happened afterward. Tissa's father, who I later learned was a Christian missionary, probably lectured me on the perils of the sin of lying. My teacher would have told me that she had been wrong to think I was a good boy because actually I was a very bad boy. And as we walked home together, my mother probably told me, "You've brought shame on me."

But along with shame and the uncomfortable feeling of knowing I'd done something wrong, I must have also felt the wonder and exhilaration of trying to look inside myself for the first time.

Where did that lying voice come from?

~

During my library research period, I also read a few books on hatha yoga. One day, I was taking the bus home when I overheard two people talking about the best place to learn yoga in Paris. I made a mental note of the studio, found its telephone number in the phone book and signed up for a beginner's course. The next Saturday morning, I took the bus to Boulevard de Sébastopol and entered the Sivananda yoga studio, feeling embarrassed about learning yoga from Westerners. But the sunlight streaming in through the sixth-floor windows, the soothing light blue carpeting and the smell of freshly baked carrot cake made me feel I was in the right place.

The class was uneventful and the last posture of *savasana* or simply lying on our backs and letting go of tension was surprisingly the most difficult to do. But later, in the bus going home, I felt an alarming tingling sensation in my body, as if hundreds of tiny worms were squirming inside my flesh. Then I began to enjoy the feeling.

My body is coming alive!

I looked with childlike wonder at the shops, the pedestrians, the lampposts, the trees lining the street and even the trash cans.

What, I'm really here?

Not wanting to go home in such a state of heightened awareness, I got off the bus at Odéon and walked down Rue de Médicis towards the Jardin du Luxembourg. As I entered the park, I saw people dressed in dark coats passing each other on the nearby crosswalk. My heart fluttered, and to this day, when I see people passing each other at a road crossing, I feel touched.

Feeling joyous for no particular reason, I sat on a bench, still enjoying the tingling sensations in my body, and took in the panoramic scene. Young boys sailed model boats in the large pond, poodles strained at leashes, mothers ran after squealing toddlers, and a couple stopped in front of the bust of Charles

Baudelaire. Senior citizens read *Le Figaro* in aluminum chairs, groups of young people sprawled on the grass and a pair of tourists photographed a painter at his easel. Pigeons strutted around, pecked hopefully in the gravel and took off with an almost unbearable fluttering of wings. The Luxembourg Palace reflected the sunshine, and cars roared past on Boulevard Saint-Michel. I saw and heard everything and sensed my body at the same time as if my mind had become a spacious container. And what's more, I also saw myself in the scene as if I were out of my body!

After that I did less reading and more yoga, ending up with a daily practice of two hours in the morning and two in the evening. One day I was doing my *pranayama* breathing exercises when I heard a voice coming from inside. *What are you doing? Go back to the real world!*

The voice was compelling, so I did just that. I signed up for a master's degree, worked more, moved out of my student digs and dated a couple of Bibi look-alikes. Both were unavailable—one was in a long-distance relationship and the other still hadn't recovered from a previous painful breakup.

Like before, I spent much time in restaurants and cafés with colleagues and friends, all in a state of waking sleep, but without experiencing the existentialist angst that had dogged me since my late teens. I knew what my purpose was and how to achieve it, but the timing didn't seem right to follow through on my intention to take up a formal mindfulness practice.

~

A couple of years went by and one evening, I was listening to a BBC program on Canada in my apartment on Rue de Dessous-des-Berges in the 13th arrondissement. It was all doom and gloom: Canada was in the grip of several simultaneous crises—economic, social and constitutional. The host's voice was drowned out by a voice coming from my gut. *Go to Canada.*

I froze. The voice sounded similar to the one I'd heard before, telling me to go back to the real world. I also remembered how Bibi had urged me to go to Canada.

The voice from the radio came back into the foreground. I stood up and took out my Minitel terminal, the precursor to the internet in France, and applied for immigration to Canada, half hoping my application would be rejected. It wasn't, and more paperwork and several months later, I found myself sitting in front of the visa officer at the Quebec delegation office in Paris.

"I'm signing off on your file, but are you sure you want to go to Montreal? You have a good job here. Did you know that the unemployment rate in Quebec is over twelve percent? What's more, you don't know anyone there," she added with a half-skeptical, half-amused look, as if she had never seen anyone like me in her office before.

I said yes, although I wasn't at all sure of what I was doing.

Part II
Montreal

Chapter 8
Mount Royal

I arrived in Montreal on a breezy afternoon in early May, at the Mirabel airport—now a white elephant slated for demolishing—armed with an impressive document with embossed lettering stating I was a landed immigrant, which I handed to the immigration officer.

Immigration formalities completed, I went to the baggage carousel to pick up my bags. I loaded a cart with my portable computer, printer and my usual duffle bag, and pushed it along the moving walkway. Perhaps because I was not used to handling baggage carts, I bumped into the ankles of a woman ahead of me. Twice. The first time, she gave me a look of irritation and the second time, of anger. I wondered whether this could be some kind of omen.

By this time the airport was quite deserted. I stood outside with my bags, feeling all alone on the continent.

I'm a landed immigrant in Montreal!

A few months later, in a café on Saint Denis Street with

my new-found friend Antoine, I symbolically renounced my immigrant status.

"I'm not an immigrant," I said, "I'm a pilgrim. An immigrant travels to better his external circumstances, so his journey is essentially an outward one. A pilgrim is going outward and inward at the same time and his ultimate destination is himself."

~

I checked into the downtown YMCA on Stanley Street. The staff was surly and the fellow residents I met in gloomy corridors gave me a wide berth and avoided eye contact. In the following days, I went from one government office to another with heavy feet, missing the City of Light, its narrow cobblestoned streets, bustling sidewalk cafés and chic women.

After my last official appointment, I headed back, taking the No. 80 bus down Park Avenue. This long street runs parallel to Boulevard Saint-Laurent, which splits Montreal into the English-speaking west and the French-speaking east. The bus swayed and a girl in a sleeveless top in front of my seat grabbed the overhead pole, exposing a surprising tuft of black armpit hair. We emerged from the storefronts and restaurant terraces lining Park Avenue into a wide, open space.

Ahead of us, the tall buildings of downtown Montreal rose against the sky. On our left Jeanne-Mance Park sloped downward into tennis courts and a soccer field. On our right a rolling green field, partially covered by a silky carpet of golden daffodils, sloped upwards, morphing itself into a wood yet to reach its full summer splendour before forming an oblong hill. This was Mount Royal, which gives Montreal its name and distinctive landscape. My energy shifted, dispelling my sense of gloom.

I'm in the right place!

I went looking for an apartment in the McGill Ghetto, which, despite its name, is a pleasant neighbourhood of crisscrossing leafy streets lined with stately nineteenth-century residences. It's bordered by McGill University on one side and a commercial strip of Boulevard Saint-Laurent on the other, and by Sherbrooke Street and Pine Avenue to the south and north, respectively. Vacancy signs abounded, presenting me with a dizzying choice. Walking down Durocher Street, I saw a young blond woman polishing the glass door of a building. We made eye contact, so I went and spoke to her.

We went up to the fourth floor, which had a long balcony with an unobstructed view of Mount Royal and she showed me a spacious studio apartment. It had an alcove for the bed and was sparsely furnished with two portable chairs and a wooden table with a single chair. For someone coming from Paris, the rent was too good to be true, so I signed a lease right away. A friend who came to visit me later told me the place looked like an ascetic monk's cell.

In my new apartment, I read up on local history. Montreal was founded in 1642 as a centre for the fur trade called Ville Marie, which is now part of downtown. But the area had been inhabited for thousands of years by First Nations people. The oldest artifact found in Montreal dates back some two thousand years—or four thousand years, depending on which source you want to believe. In 1535, French explorer Jacques Cartier encountered a village of over a thousand people now called the Hochelaga Iroquoians, on the slopes and at the foot of Mount Royal. With hindsight, it's satisfying to know that Mount Royal, which played a key role during my life in Montreal, had been inhabited for thousands of years by First Nations people.

Montreal is mostly an island, surrounded by the confluent waters of the St. Lawrence and Ottawa rivers. Although water has a calming effect on some people, I found out some years later that living close to large bodies of water can destabilize some minds, perhaps those that are ripe for disruption. Mount Royal was a perfect foil for the water, providing a soothing, grounding effect. Water breaks you down while the mountain holds you together, forming a perfect yin-yang balance.

As I walked around downtown Montreal and the adjacent Plateau, Mont-Royal towered in the distance. It soon became an important ritual for me to gaze at the mountain from the balcony outside my apartment. The mountain was a mecca that I could actually behold and to which I'd pay my respects several times a week. Unlike the manicured parks in Paris, Mount Royal Park was quite wild, although designed by Frederick Law Olmsted, who also co-designed New York's Central Park. In the late afternoons, as summer transitioned into fall, I watched the sun disappearing behind the mountain now bedecked in crimson, yellow and orange. It surprised and even alarmed me to see how quickly the sun's trajectory shifted every day behind the mountain.

Has nature gone haywire?

Having always lived in places burdened by thousands of years of human history and suffering, Montreal, where wilderness was never far away, was a breath of fresh air. Up until then my life had been mostly sedentary, but in my new home, I soon discovered the pleasures of walking in nature. I'd climb the trails on one side of Mount Royal, cut across the mountain along the path overlooking downtown and then take the stairs from the Belvedere at the top. On the way I'd stop to lie on large black rocks and watch the sun filtering through the trees that rose proudly into the sky.

I got even closer to nature and went for long walks in forests when I started spending weekends at the Sivananda yoga ashram in Val-Morin in the Laurentian mountains, just an hour and a half's drive from Montreal. It was there I met Antoine, tall and thin with a pronounced stoop. He'd caught my attention as he was constantly arguing with the ashram's management. Like Gord in Paris, he was six years my senior, but looked much older. We got acquainted over a satisfying dinner of spinach and mushroom lasagne with garlic bread.

Antoine impressed me with his sharp intelligence and encyclopedic mind. I asked him what had brought him to yoga. The short answer was that a book on yoga by the Sivananda yoga ashram's founder literally fell into his hands while he was browsing in a second-hand bookstore. The long answer was that his father was abusive. Antoine had left home at sixteen, drifted on and off the streets of Europe for a number of years, tried his hand unsuccessfully at painting, then descended into a drug-induced hell after meeting a silver-tongued Englishman, who discoursed on Sufism, recited Rumi and T. S. Eliot, and introduced him to crack cocaine. After three years in an Italian prison for drug possession, Antoine now eked out a meagre living buying and selling second-hand books. Not to mention a string of unsatisfactory relationships. The twelve-step Cocaine Anonymous program had helped him with his addiction, but only to an extent, as he kept relapsing. Overwhelmed by despair, and although not a religious man, he fell to his knees and prayed to the Virgin Mary to deliver him from his suffering. And she did. Antoine got up from the floor and walked away from crack cocaine for good. In short, a miracle!

As we met over the weeks and months that followed, I noticed that Antoine talked often about his abusive father. I was shocked and full of empathy, as he was the first person with a difficult childhood I had encountered. Then the amateur psychologist I prided myself to be diagnosed Antoine as having a classic case of the Oedipus complex—it was his attachment to his mother that created a conflict with his father. I put across my theory to him tentatively.

"You have no idea what you're talking about," he said. "My father was a brute, period. You're the guy with mother issues."

It was my turn to protest. "I have an excellent relationship with my mother."

"Maybe too good," he muttered.

~

Before leaving Paris, I had rationalized my move to Montreal by telling friends and family I wanted to finally establish myself in a career, something I could do now that I had a clearer idea of my life purpose. Both the Gurdjieff and Tantric approaches saw no obstacle to the simultaneous pursuit of worldly success and authentic consciousness. In any case, I hadn't actually started working toward my stated goal of achieving permanent awakening.

Not sure of how to set about looking for work in a brand new country, I signed up for a three-week job search workshop for new immigrants. After the participants had introduced themselves, the facilitator, Brigitte, asked us to talk about our biggest achievement to date. I said it was surviving Paris after going there totally unprepared, with few resources, no knowledge of French and no experience living on my own. Frank, from San Diego, said his greatest achievement was getting through a one-month silent meditation retreat at the Shambhala centre in Vermont.

During lunch I told Frank that I had read *Shambhala: The Sacred Path of the Warrior* by Chogyam Trungpa, founder of the Shambhala centre. Frank was involved in running the local

Shambhala meditation centre, so he invited me to come and check it out. I might have responded somewhat haughtily with something like, "I don't really feel the need for that, since I've already received meditation instructions according to our own Theravada[8] tradition."

At the end of the workshop, we filled in the customary evaluation forms. Afterward, Brigitte called me up, saying she had found my feedback constructive and would like to discuss my ideas further over lunch with me. We met for lunch, at the end of which Brigitte suggested we meet again, for dinner this time.

She wanted to go to an Indian restaurant on Saint Denis Street, and I waited for her at a café close by. But when I saw her striding toward me with a big smile, I knew something was wrong. Wearing a short skirt and high heels, she was dressed for a night out, with makeup and jewellery. She projected a different kind of energy from the workshop facilitator I knew.

I'm on a date!

Needless to say, the dinner was a disaster. I kept looking at my plate, our fellow diners or at passers-by on the sidewalk and found it difficult to hold up my end of the conversation.

~

While preparing my move to Montreal, I decided to look for work in the investment industry, a field I had been drawn to in my late teens, perhaps by the fanciful prospect of making a killing on the stock market. During the third week of the job search workshop, I was hired by one of the first investment companies

---

[8] Theravada, also known as the Southern school, is the oldest Buddhist school and is practised mainly in Sri Lanka, Myanmar, Cambodia, Thailand and Laos.

I contacted. Six months into my new job, my boss took me out to lunch in an upscale French restaurant and told me he had performed an evaluation of all his employees. Apparently, I had come out on top. This came as a surprise to me. I was a rookie, while some of my colleagues were highly experienced, and I told him so.

My boss replied, "You do what you're supposed to do. Your colleagues might be experienced, but they don't always do that, and sometimes they spend time doing things they're not expected to do."

He followed by saying he'd like to see me become the manager of our branch. My lack of enthusiasm for the offer must have shown, because he looked disappointed and even bemused. I couldn't tell him that I wanted to keep my options open in case something better came along. Becoming the manager of a small branch didn't seem like an appealing career prospect.

~

About a year after my move to Montreal, I went back to Sri Lanka on vacation. I was finishing my first meal at home when my mother got up from the dining table, went into her bedroom and came back with a piece of paper in her hand.

"Have you heard from Aravind recently?"

"No, but I will soon."

Aravind was a close friend from school who had lived at the same rooming house with Siri and Piyal.

"He might have died."

I went on eating my dessert of ice cream and fruit salad, unconcerned. My mother handed me the piece of paper she was holding in her hand, which turned out to be a press cutting of an obituary notice. I looked at it almost disinterestedly. There it was, in black and white, an irrefutable fact.

Aravind was gone.

I scooped up the last spoonful of ice cream, got up from the table, put the bowl in the sink and sat in my favourite chair overlooking the green lawn and the flower bed of red and white anthuriums. The lawn was freshly mowed, no doubt ahead of my arrival. Something shifted in the pit of my stomach, moved through my chest and welled up in my throat.

My mother came to console me.

I went into my room and lay on my bed.

Aravind had died in a car crash. When I learned the date and time of his death, I found it coincided with a day trip to Ottawa about two weeks earlier. I was strolling around the ByWard Market, a bustling square with an outdoor farmers' market in the middle, fringed by restaurants and cafés, when I suddenly felt as if I were walking through thick mud, each step requiring a monumental effort. I staggered onto the terrace of the Château Laurier hotel restaurant and sat at a table. A buff young man in a white T-shirt, navy blue shorts and white sneakers, bursting with life and vitality, came up to me and asked cheerily, "How's your day, sir?"

I wonder now whether my energy had sensed Aravind's passing. And when I headed back to the train station, a violent storm broke with gusting winds howling and threatening to topple trees and blow away rooftops. Knowing that Aravind was special, I wouldn't be surprised if nature had gotten wind of his passing and wanted to give him a fitting send-off.

Like Antoine, Aravind had been exceptionally intelligent and curious. He had strong analytical abilities but was also interested in the arts. Back then, I liked to think of him as a renaissance teenager. I was convinced he'd do something special like write a masterpiece or direct a critically acclaimed film. Or even win a Nobel Prize, possibly for physics, since he claimed he was one of the select few in the world who understood the theory of relativity.

We used to go to late-night movies and then spend the rest of the night drinking tea in roadside cafés, talking about a range of topics—Marx, Dostoevsky, Fellini, D. T. Suzuki's books on Zen. Anything seemed possible for us.

We'd also sit on our garden wall and chat as people and cars passed by. Aravind had a certain air about him that makes me now think that he might have even experienced awareness of awareness. Krishnamurti's ideas came up often in our conversations, especially choiceless awareness, which we both recognized as a key concept although we didn't know what it meant. We liked that Krishnamurti discouraged people from following any teachings, or a guru, or from even practising meditation, because doing so would reinforce the sense of a "doer" or the ego. I remember Aravind throwing his arms wide open one day and quoting Krishnamurti: "Truth is a pathless land."[9]

Aravind and I embraced this radical approach of non-doing not necessarily because we thought it was the right approach but rather because we weren't ready to commit ourselves to a teaching, guru or meditation practice.

The last time we met, about a year before his passing, I gave Aravind *In Search of the Miraculous* by Ouspensky, hoping it would trigger something in him as well, but he returned it a few weeks later.

"I can't read anymore. It's too late for me, *machang*."

His wife had given birth a few days before. Several years earlier, he had confided in me his rationale for getting married.

---

9   The full quote is: "I maintain that Truth is a pathless land, and you cannot approach it by any path whatsoever, by any religion, by any sect." *J. Krishnamurti Online Archive.*

"She loves me and I don't want to lose her love."

The last time I saw him, we had lunch at a Chinese restaurant in Slave Island, a commercial district in Colombo.

He inquired about my life in Paris and later asked, "Are you too ambitious?"

Taken aback, I denied the charge without asking him what he meant. He might have wanted to say that I should settle for less.

An engineer by profession, Aravind discovered he had a knack for picking winning stocks and ended up becoming a vice-president of an international investment firm, a position worthy of his talents as he seemed to think.

"My boss thinks I have the Midas touch," he told me.

At the end of a lunch of Sri Lankan fried rice, sweet and sour shrimps and stir-fried kankun washed down with a bottle of Lion Lager, Aravind leaned back in his chair. He looked around slowly, as if to say, "What, I'm really here?" He pulled on his cigarette, and we both watched the smoke swirl up, thin and dissipate.

"My life's going well. The only problem I have now is that I have this need to talk. And to talk, I need to drink."

He had become somewhat of a high-functioning alcoholic, drinking heavily with his buddies in the evenings. His death was an accident, but I always wondered about that. In any case, I'd like to think that he'd have raised his last glass of arrack and downed it with his usual sense of awareness before he got into his car and crashed it into that giant tree at midnight. It was a relief to know he hadn't hurt anyone else.

Back in Montreal after my vacation, I slipped into a semi-depressed state for several months. My grief was aggravated by a sense of guilt. Aravind had given me a lot, but I hadn't been able to give anything back in return. As an independent thinker,

Aravind stood out in a culture that encouraged rote learning. He'd inspired me to think for myself. And if he did experience awareness of awareness, it might have rubbed off on me as well. I regretted not giving him Ouspensky's book on my first trip home after my awakening experience, and I regretted not telling him about it. If anyone could have understood, it was probably him.

I took up creative writing as a self-healing therapy and wrote a long poem about Aravind. Not long after, I was walking down Sherbrooke Street with the spring sun on my face when a thought popped into my mind.

It's time to take action to wake up permanently. If anything, I have to do it for him. For Aravind.

The path of non-doing hadn't really worked for him.

The next day I came across an advertisement in the *Montreal Gazette* offering fifty free lessons on true knowledge at a Gnostic centre. I smiled inwardly, wondering what kind of gullible person would be taken in by such an offer. It was clearly some kind of scam. But a few days later, I felt an urgent need to take another look at that advertisement and rummaged through the pile of newspapers on the floor.

The next week I found myself walking up the steps to the Gnostic centre, near the Lionel-Groulx metro. A sheet of paper pinned to the wall near the entrance listed the free lessons, and reassuringly, some topics seemed similar to Gurdjieff's teachings.

The centre taught three key principles: self-remembering, the transmutation of sexual energy and service to humanity. As Gurdjieff said, to wake up from the dreamlike state we call consciousness, we have to remember ourselves. The continual stream of discursive thoughts in our mind prevents us from remembering ourselves, keeping us trapped in the state of waking sleep. That's where the second key teaching of the centre— transmutation of sexual energy—comes into play. Cutting through the stream of discursive thoughts and achieving self-remembering requires a vast amount of energy. If we harness our sexual energy instead of simply releasing it, we'll have sufficient energy to remember ourselves. Far from advocating celibacy, the centre encouraged conscious lovemaking and the exchange of refined sexual energy with a compatible partner. True celibacy or *brahmacharya*,[10] I realized, had nothing to do with renouncing sexual intimacy.

I first learned about this notion of the transmutation of sexual energy at around age sixteen, when my interest in self-help books—a prelude to my interest in self-transformation—led me to read Napoleon Hill's *Think and Grow Rich*. One of the later chapters was titled "The Mystery of Sex Transmutation," which piqued my curiosity, although at sixteen I wasn't quite sure what transmutation entailed. For Hill, the purpose of transmuting sexual energy was to achieve material success.

Some years later, I read a book on Tantra that advocated the transmutation of sexual energy to attain a higher state of consciousness. According to the non-dual Tantric teachings on sex, which form only a small part of the broader teachings of Tantra, sexual energy is a powerful force that should not be used purely for pleasure or procreation. Instead, it should be harnessed to let go of the identification with the individual self and realize that the material world and consciousness are one, or more accurately, not two.

But I wasn't fully convinced about the Scrooge-like hoarding of semen until I had a direct experience of what Tantra was talking about. This happened during my friends-with-benefits relationship with Simone a few years before I moved to Montreal. We'd get intimate episodically and I'd wake the morning after

---

10   Literally speaking, this means "staying true to one's self" and not chastity as it is commonly understood.

feeling depleted, with a foggy mind. One night, for some reason, we just slept together without any sexual activity. The next morning I felt rejuvenated and my mind was clear.

Aha! Those ancient Tantric yogis were onto something.

After learning about Tantric sexuality, I had tried at various points in my life to give up on ejaculations, but abstinence had never lasted more than a month or so. However, soon after frequenting the Gnostic centre, something shifted in my mind and I dropped my attachment to ejaculating just like Antoine had let go of his addiction to crack cocaine.

Previously, I hadn't tried to do anything with the conserved sexual energy, so it had to be released at some point. By tapping into my unused energy to break through the discursive thoughts in my mind, nothing much was left to release. I discovered the first law of sexual energy—it had to go up or out!

Initially, I had to make almost superhuman efforts to create a brief gap in my discursive thoughts. It seemed like a thousand horses were trying to pull my attention back into my thoughts. The gap would be accompanied by a glimpse of clarity, as the world around me became vivid. At the end of a few months of effort, the gaps in the stream of discursive thoughts and moments of light became more frequent. I thought of these breakthroughs as moments of wakefulness.

One day at the Gnostic centre, during the time that I was struggling to break through discursive thoughts, I saw an alluring young girl with short reddish-brown hair. She wore a white summer dress, and sat languidly in a chair, thighs crossed and a red slipper dangling from her small foot. She was out of place, especially since most of the people at the centre were older. Our eyes locked and I felt a subtle energy flowing between us. That same night, I had a vivid dream of making love to the girl, so real and so unlike my typical erotic dreams, which were usually a confusing blur of faces and bodies.

At the Gnostic centre, astral travel was an important topic, but I'd never taken it seriously. Now, I couldn't help thinking that we had met in the astral plane to make love. I only saw the girl a couple of times at the centre and the next time, I was too embarrassed to even look at her. It was perhaps after that initial wordless encounter and the subsequent erotic dream that the process of transforming sexual energy into moments of wakefulness became easier. But it would take decades for me to grasp the full significance of the encounter with the girl.

About a month into my semen retention practice, I noticed a surge in my level of energy. I got up earlier and earlier. One day, feeling the urge to see the sun rising, I put on my dark navy blue track suit and walked west on Milton Street, toward the McGill campus. I climbed the steps to Rutherford Field, a public park built on the underground reservoir, to get the first glimpse of the sun, although I couldn't actually see the horizon. This became my dawn ritual. During this period I'd feel such high energy that I'd want to run and dance, especially when I was in Mount Royal Park. I also got the urge to listen to *kirtans*, Hindu devotional chants, especially the *Shiva Shiva Mahadeva* mantra.

During that time, Antoine and I went for a walk up Mount Royal. Our conversation came around to Tantra and my solo tantric sexual practice. We also talked about the two paths in Tantra. The right-hand path encompasses the orthodox Tantric practices, while the left-hand path refers, among other things, to the tantric sexual practices.

"Giving up on ejaculating would be such a sad thing," Antoine said, with a worried look on his face, as if he was expecting me to ask him to do so.

"Actually, it's just the opposite. By giving up on my puny orgasm, my whole existence has become orgasmic. I'm overflowing with energy. When I walk outside, it feels like I'm making love with the world." I swept my left arm towards the woods around us.

Thinking I might have oversold it, I continued, "According to Joseph Campbell, the right-hand path is about conformity, following the rules and becoming a respectable, successful member of society. By taking the left-hand path, you opt out and embark on a hero's journey. But it's fraught with danger and uncertainty because you don't know where you're heading. So semen retention is not for everyone. It could be dangerous for physical and mental health."

I gave Antoine a pointed look.

"Don't worry," he said with a laugh. "I've no intention of trying anything of the sort. I'm no hero."

~

Also around this time, I had an important epiphany, possibly triggered by the disruption to my habitual thought patterns caused by the moments of wakefulness. It occurred at the end of a long walk on Mount Royal. I watched the drummers setting themselves up near the foot of the monument for the Sunday Tam-Tam. Initially a spontaneous gathering, the Tam-Tams had become a regular event, drawing hundreds of people.

It happened in a flash. One moment, I was sitting there feeling good about myself, and the next, a thought popped into my mind.

I have a fear of intimacy.

One moment, I was a man in the pink of mental health, with a tendency to look down on people with issues. *Why can't they get their act together?* Then suddenly, I was a man with a serious unresolved emotional issue of my own.

It troubles me now to think that I could have got to my thirties blissfully unaware of this problem. After taking a few minutes to digest this unpalatable epiphany, I decided I wasn't ready to deal with the issue and, in the meantime, I'd avoid getting into any relationships. Again, it baffles me how I could have failed to see that avoiding relationships was exactly what I had been doing up to then.

Chapter 9
Boulevard Saint-Laurent

While acknowledging my debt to the Gnostic centre's teaching of transmuting sexual energy for my sporadic moments of wakefulness, I became increasingly irritated by its focus on astral travel and other occult phenomena. I too had been drawn to esoteric knowledge, but when I saw the same desire mirrored in some people at the centre, it turned me off. I could clearly see they were driven by a need for power and a feeling of superiority.

I concluded that to further establish wakefulness in my daily life, I needed to take up a mindfulness practice within a Buddhist tradition—the intention I had set for myself during my period of academic research in Paris. This conclusion led me to reconsider what I'd said to Frank at the job search workshop two years earlier, when he suggested I check out the Shambhala centre.

Passages I had read in Chogyam Trungpa's *Shambhala: The Sacred Path of the Warrior* kept coming to mind. Chogyam Trungpa, a Tibetan Buddhist monk, came to the West in the

'60s, gave up his monastic vows and became a lay teacher. He moved to the United States in the early '70s and set up a network of Buddhist meditation and affiliated centres and institutions across the world over a relatively short period of about fifteen years. After introducing the traditional Tibetan Vajrayana[11] Buddhism, Trungpa taught the Shambhala vision. This secular approach rooted in meditation aims not only to achieve individual enlightenment but also to create an enlightened society, epitomized by the mythical Kingdom of Shambhala. This ambition of creating an enlightened society impressed me greatly, since in the Theravada Buddhist tradition, the aim is to liberate oneself from suffering, or in other words, individual salvation. I had a flash of inspiration.

If a critical mass of people embark on the path, individual liberation could become collective salvation. Transformation from within could lead to transformation without!

Among Chogyam Trungpa's many books, *Cutting Through Spiritual Materialism* stood out for me. The book sets out the dilemma of the spiritual path, that the ego can co-opt anything to its own use, even spirituality. So meditation and other techniques can be seen as a form of self-improvement and used to protect or even develop the ego instead of letting go of it. For some, Buddhism has become yet another product to consume in the spiritual marketplace.

On my way to Bibi's place on Rue Oberkampf, I had often walked past the Paris Shambhala centre, but it never occurred to me drop in and check it out. Perhaps I knew that I wasn't ready. About six months into my association with the Gnostic centre, I felt the timing was finally right and signed up for an

---

11   Literally, thunderbolt. Also known as the Diamond Vehicle, Vajrayana is another school of Buddhism that developed mainly in Tibet, consisting of tantric teachings.

introductory Shambhala weekend.

And so one Friday evening, I walked east on Milton Street, turned north on Park Avenue, crossed the bottom part of Jeanne-Mance Park, took Duluth Street and stood in front of the building housing the Montreal Shambhala centre on Boulevard Saint-Laurent.

Boulevard Saint-Laurent, or the Main as the locals call it, runs through Montreal from north to south, effectively dividing the city into east and west, with street numbers beginning at its intersections. Successive waves of immigrants—Jewish, Chinese, Italian, Portuguese, Greek and Haitian—settled along the Main and the adjoining parallel Park Avenue, with Chinatown occupying the bottom part. The Shambhala centre was located on the trendy strip of the Main with cafés, chic restaurants, clubs and bars, including the Samsara Lounge, a favourite haunt of mine in later years.

As I stood on the Main, the same embarrassment I felt when I had gone for my first yoga class in Paris came back even stronger. More than yoga, Buddhist meditation was "our thing." Following the Buddha's death, his teachings had been handed down orally through generations for five hundred years before they were written down during the fourth Buddhist council held in Sri Lanka. As a result, those belonging to the Theravada or the Southern school of Buddhism think of themselves as the true guardians of unadulterated Buddhism. They tend to look down on followers of a northern school, such as Tibetan Buddhism, that rely at least partly on texts written subsequently. My resistance subsided somewhat when I walked into the spacious, minimally decorated, high-ceilinged meditation hall. Neatly arranged rows of blue square cushions sat on a larger square blue mat of the same colour on the tan hardwood floor.

The actual meditation practice was no different from

what I had learned as a kid in our local Buddhist temple, simply consisting in following or trying to follow the breath. Theravada Buddhists call it *ana pana sati*, which literally means "remembering the inhalation and exhalation." Tibetans refer to it as *shamatha*, or calming the mind. There was one striking difference. While I had learned to keep my eyes shut, in the Tibetan *shamatha* practice, the eyes are open but downcast, letting the world in. This approach was more conducive to my intent of making wakefulness an integral part of my daily life.

Having thought of meditation as a solitary practice, I was also surprised by all the talking and socializing that went on during the weekend—evening talks by the teacher, one-on-one interviews with a meditation instructor, discussions in small groups, group breakfast of bagels and cheese with eye-catching platters of grapes, pineapples and mangoes. All rounded off by a reception at the end of the weekend with wine and succulent, aesthetically arranged dishes. Although distracting from the sitting practice, the socializing was intended to favour the integration of meditation into ordinary life.

Following that weekend, I bought a meditation cushion and started a formal sitting practice of one hour first thing in the morning and last thing at night—a practice I kept up for over two decades. During my time at the Gnostic centre, I had grappled with the continual stream of discursive thoughts while going about my daily activities. To my surprise, sitting on a meditation cushion and following the breath didn't make it easier to achieve moments of wakefulness. But it did provide me with opportunities to observe my thoughts more closely. They turned out to be embarrassingly trivial. Most of the time, I carried on an internal dialogue with myself interrupted from time to time by repetitions or more satisfying versions of dialogues I'd had with other people. The speed at which my mind jumped from one thought to another also surprised me. I'd often find myself thinking about something and wondering how I got there. So I'd do some mental detective work and try to track the train of thoughts to the last thought I remembered thinking before completely losing it.

Over that first Shambhala weekend, my resistance increased, triggered partly by the teacher. In hindsight, my resistance was perhaps a sign that my ego or the sense of a separate self was feeling threatened. I wasn't planning to go back, however, after a couple of months of my sitting practice, I signed up for another weekend retreat. This time, something shifted and my resistance melted.

During subsequent Shambhala workshops I learned that *shamatha* was a concentration practice, the first stage of meditation that prepares you for *vipashyana*, or awareness. *Shamatha* focuses your mind, slowing the stream of discursive thoughts, while *vipashyana* opens your mind, making it spacious. The progression from *shamatha* to *vipashyana* should be gradual and natural. Over the weeks and months, during my sitting practice, I found my initially downcast gaze beginning to rise gradually and taking in more and more of the world around while staying rooted in my sense of self. What I had been calling "wakefulness" might well be the union of *shamatha* and *vipashyana*. Or the combination of *samma samadhi* (right concentration) and *samma sati* (right mindfulness) in the Theravada tradition. Or self-remembering, according to Gurdjieff.

As I sat on my meditation cushion, I'd notice my mind shifting from its focused, contracted state during *shamatha* to the spaciousness of *vipashyana*. While I struggled with the concentration practice, I moved dangerously easily, as I realized later, into spaciousness, having already worked on achieving wakefulness during my previous six months at the Gnostic centre.

During sitting sessions, with my new-found mental spaciousness, I registered more and more sounds—the humming of my fridge, doors being closed in my building, the wind rustling through leaves on trees outside my windows, and cars passing on Durocher Street. To my spacious mind, no sound was irritating; all were manifestations of life and worthy of attention. It was only when my mind contracted and resisted a sound that it became irritating. The ebb and flow of traffic can sound like an orchestra, and on rainy days I loved listening to the rich sound of tires on wet tar. One day, when walking past city workers in orange overalls drilling a hole in the sidewalk, instead of resisting, I let my body and mind open up and welcome the deafening sounds and the reverberations. As I moved more and more into the practice of *vipashyana*, the frequency of wakeful moments in my daily life increased.

Nothing much happened as I sat on my cushion; only irritation and boredom came up. A Shambhala teacher had told me, "Let the world come to you." So when I got off the cushion, went outside, and stilled the stream of discursive thoughts, the world did come to me. It came to me as sacred, as a place of beauty and wonder with endless potential to delight. Without the filter of thoughts, my perceptions of the world became direct, vivid. Colours were brighter; sounds louder, richer.

Once, when I got off the meditation cushion and walked over to the window, I saw a majestic tree growing in the backyard of our building that I had hardly noticed before. As Ouspensky had described in his book, while seeing the tree, I saw myself looking at the tree. The way I perceived changed—when I looked at the world, I could see myself looking. It didn't matter what I was looking at—a majestic tree, an iconic building or just a crack in the sidewalk or a trash can—everything and anything became charged with meaning and worthy of interest.

The ordinary has become extraordinary!

I remember walking through the McGill Ghetto with childlike delight on my way to Mount Royal. I'd linger on sidewalks, gazing at the wrought-iron balconies and the facades with decorative stonework. I stopped in front of a building on Durocher, north of Milton, to admire its intricate top-floor facade. As I noticed more and more details, the facade seemed to be moving toward me.

I'm disappearing into the building!

My heart and mind contracted. I stepped back and the facade receded to a safe distance.

More than ever, walks on Mount Royal became a sacred ritual. Seeing a tree branch waving gracefully in the wind brought tears to my eyes. When I looked at the trees, I saw each leaf clearly delineated and nestling in its own separate space but at the same time connected to a vibrant, intricate network of leaves, branches and trees.

As my practice moved further into *vipashyana*, I noticed that when walking down a road, my gaze lifted naturally as it did on the meditation cushion and I'd see far into the horizon, even though I was short-sighted. I'd notice street lamps, rooftops and building fronts forming captivating patterns and stretching into the distance. Crossing René Lévesque Boulevard, the double-arched streetlamps in the middle formed a canopy covering the street, as if they were performing an honour guard for the cars passing underneath. My awareness also shifted from a narrow focus to a wide-angle vision, allowing me to perceive more sounds, sights and smells, all at the same time.

One of the weekend Shambhala workshops happened to take place during the annual street fair, when the Main is closed off for traffic, with businesses pitching tents outside to sell their wares and restaurants setting up seating space on the sidewalk.

As I walked up the Main, the smell of frying sausages wafted toward me and I saw throngs of people jostling in the middle of the street as far off as Rachel Street, flanked by white tent tops and trees on either side. And I saw myself in the scene as if I were out of my body, similarly to the panoramic scene I had witnessed at the Jardin du Luxembourg after my first yoga class. While that had been a one-off experience, seeing my body in space increasingly became a part of my day-to-day life.

On another such occasion, on Mount Royal, I was sitting on one of the benches that form a semicircle around the monument honouring George-Étienne Cartier, one of the founding fathers of Canada—a column topped by a giant soaring winged female guarded by four bronze sphinx-like lions gazing into the horizon, *vipashyana*-like. It was a Sunday and the Tam-Tam was not yet in full swing, but groups of hand drummers sitting on the steps of the monument were warming up, drowning out the dull drone of the steady stream of cars and buses on nearby Park Avenue. Vendors, a relatively recent addition to the event, had already laid out their trinkets, necklaces, bracelets and incense on brightly coloured cloths around the base of the monument. I always expected to see one of the drummers get up, stomp toward the vendors, jerk the cloths from the ground and send their wares scattering in all directions, like Jesus in the Temple of Jerusalem. Several large dogs were barking, rushing around and kicking up small clouds of dust in their eternal quest to catch a squirrel. A couple of amateur jugglers were practising their moves among the people sprawled over the uneven lawn on one side of the monument, picnicking, reading, chatting in groups or having naps. To my right, medieval reenactors were unpacking their foam-padded weapons. To my left, groups of people walked across the lawn, flitting in and out of the tall trees. They made me think of the Buddha and his monks in saffron-coloured robes strolling in the Jetavana forest, discussing the path to liberation. Or Jesus Christ and his disciples in the Garden of Gethsemane. Or indigenous people going about their daily business while a few sat cross-legged on the ground, backs straight, hands on knees, and gazing straight ahead. And I saw myself in the scene, sitting on a bench with my arms spread over the backrest, and I felt my feet flat on the ground, the drumming throbbing in my chest and the crisp morning air caressing my face.

~

There was much talk at the Shambhala centre about emotions, a topic largely ignored in the Theravada Buddhist tradition. Fear is a key emotion and for Chogyam Trungpa, the essence of cowardice is not fear but rather not acknowledging fear. A warrior is not someone without fear but someone who is unafraid to face their fear. I also learned that dealing with emotions involved first acknowledging them, then observing them with as much detachment as possible and finally letting them go.

It wasn't spelled out, but it became clear to me over time that the continual stream of thoughts and internal dialogue has an important psychological function—to keep a lid on deeply buried negative emotions. Only much later did I see that spaciousness had created a vacuum in my mind, allowing unresolved emotions to bubble to the surface. So, amid the euphoria and sensual joy created by my spacious mind, I also felt pangs of anxiety.

~

During this time I got a call from my eldest brother in London. About to undergo major surgery, he wanted me at his side. Being cooped up with hundreds of people in a small space with no chance of getting out is never a comfortable experience, but given the anxiety that had started coming up, the prospect of taking a transatlantic flight was particularly daunting. Still, I couldn't say no to my brother at his time of need, so I found myself sitting in an aisle seat as usual, on an Air Canada flight to London, next to a sweet-looking older couple.

They were part of a group, and the tour leader came to speak to them. "So how are you doing, Mr. and Mrs. Death?"

I couldn't believe what I'd heard.

No one could possibly have a name like that. But I had distinctly heard the woman say "Mr. and Mrs. Death."

After the tour leader moved on to speak to her other clients, the woman, who was occupying the window seat, turned toward me as if she knew what I was thinking and gave me a sadistic smile that said, "Yes, I'm Mrs. Death, and I'm coming for you." She reminded me of the satanic old lady in Roman Polanski's movie *Rosemary's Baby*. I shuddered and shrank in my seat.

There's no way I'm going to survive this flight!

I did survive it, though, and looking out of the train windows on my way to Epsom, where my brother lived, I felt somewhat surprised to find myself still alive. My brother's surgery had been given priority as he had private insurance, so he was recovering at home by the time I arrived. As we sat chatting, my sister-in-law came along and gave me a book to read—*The Art of Living*.

The author, S. N. Goenka, a lay meditation teacher in the Burmese Buddhist tradition, had set up meditation centres across the world to conduct ten-day meditation retreats. During my most recent trip to Sri Lanka, I had read a newspaper article about a new Goenka centre near Kandy and thought I should check it out. The book was mainly a compilation of the daily evening discourses given by Goenka over a ten-day retreat. He claimed that the main meditation technique used during his retreats—which he called vipassana, consisting of sweeping the body mentally and observing bodily sensations without reacting—could be traced back to the Buddha.

While reading Goenka's book, I felt strange bodily sensations that can only be described as tiny worms wriggling inside my flesh. I became anxious, thinking that something was wrong with me. Then it occurred to me that I might be feeling the sensations that Goenka talked about, triggered simply by reading his book. The ten days I spent pretty much restricted to my brother's house were like a ten-day vipassana retreat.

A few weeks after coming back to Montreal, and about six months into my sitting practice, I noticed one day that I no longer had to make an effort to bring about moments of wakefulness. They arose automatically and frequently, making wakefulness an integral and quasi-permanent part of my day-to-day life. I wondered whether the experience I'd had while reading Goenka's book had something to do with my new state of awareness.

~

My wakefulness practice has always been inspired and supported by my understanding of the *Satipatthana Sutta*, a discourse by the Buddha widely studied by Buddhist meditation practitioners. Translated as "The Discourse on the Four Foundations of Mindfulness," it's a step-by-step guide for the sitting practice. The interpretations vary but I find it useful to think of the four foundations of mindfulness as awareness of the body and awareness of the body's contents (perceptions arising through the five senses of the body), and awareness of the mind and awareness of the mind's contents (thoughts and emotions arising in the mind).

A key term that comes up a number of times in the *Satipatthana Sutta* is *sampajanna*, often translated as "clear comprehension" and for which various learned scholars and serious Buddhist meditation practitioners have proposed different interpretations. Drawing on my own experience, I came to think that clear comprehension is what happens when a gap arises in the stream of discursive thoughts. The habitual fogginess of the typically contracted state of mind is dispelled, bringing about clarity, spaciousness and awareness of awareness.

During my academic research in Paris and subsequently, I read many books on mindfulness, but most authors seemed evasive or even confused about what the word actually meant. Often in psychology, as well as in some Buddhist meditation circles, mindfulness seems to be conflated with concentration or *shamatha*.

One way to resolve this confusion is to consider mindfulness and related terms such as presence, here and now, self-remembering, wakefulness and awareness as referring to a spectrum of experiences. At one end of the spectrum, mindfulness in its most mundane sense is the opposite of absent-mindedness or daydreaming. Near the beginning of the spectrum, mindfulness can be equated with *shamatha*; however, too much concentration could be an obstacle to advancing on the path, as it keeps the mind too narrowly focused and prevents it from opening up.

As we practise mindfulness and become established in one or more of its four foundations, we can move further along the spectrum. If we're well established in all four foundations and gaps in the stream of discursive thoughts occur effortlessly on a quasi-permanent basis and we experience awareness of awareness, we'll be near the further end of the spectrum. I believe most of us experience these gaps at some point in our lives, but we don't recognize them as such because they are few and far between, and we haven't given sufficient thought to their underlying mechanics. When authentic mindfulness arises frequently and spontaneously, it becomes integrated into daily life. However, as long as we still experience awareness of awareness through the sense of an individual and separate self, we're unable to move to the furthest end of the spectrum.

At the other end of the spectrum—here I'm simply speculating, since I don't have an actual experience of it—an ultimate form of mindfulness arises where we let go not only of the stream of discursive thoughts but also of all the underlying thoughts that make up our belief in a separate identity. If we think of mindfulness as a surgical knife, it keeps cutting through various levels of mind as it works its way along the spectrum until there's nothing left to cut. And in my view, when ultimate mindfulness arises frequently and spontaneously, becoming an integral part of daily life, it can be equated with enlightenment, the ultimate goal of Buddhist meditation practice.

~

During one of the weekend workshops at the Shambhala centre, I invited Antoine to have lunch with me at the Mexican restaurant on Boulevard Saint-Laurent in front of Parc du Portugal, where Leonard Cohen's house is located. In later years, I'd practise sitting meditation at his house according to the Zen tradition. The restaurant's wooden tables, gaily painted in yellow, blue, green and red, reminded me of our office kitchen in Paris, where I had met Bibi. Antoine and I sat at the round table near the street front and ordered burritos with green salad, guacamole and nachos. Part of my plan for inviting Antoine was to persuade him to take up mindfulness meditation.

"Meditation is not just one thing, you know. Most people seem to think that meditation is about keeping your eyes closed, concentrating and trying to go inward. The Buddha created a revolution by introducing the concept of *samma sati*, or mindfulness, which is about being present and awake in the world. But he didn't invent anything. He simply rediscovered an age-old practice. Who knows? Even indigenous people right here in Montreal might have practised it thousands of years ago. Up until the Buddha's time, the foundational teaching for meditation practice was Patanjali's *Yoga Sutras*, which sets out the eight steps of the path. But it doesn't mention mindfulness, only concentration, and the aim of meditation is to achieve the transcendent state of *samadhi*. Even if you do achieve *samadhi*, when you come out of the state, your sense of a separate self remains intact, whereas mindfulness has a transformative impact and can take you all the way to enlightenment."

Having made what I thought was a convincing sales pitch, I got to my point. "You should try out an introductory Shambhala weekend."

Antoine, who had been diligently tucking into his burrito, looked up. "What makes you think I have money to spend on meditation workshops?"

Having expected such a rebuttal, I offered to pay for him.

He shook his head. "I'm satisfied with my yoga practice. I don't feel the need for anything else."

Feeling I had done my duty and tried, I laid down my fork and knife, leaned back in my chair and gazed at the people passing by against the backdrop of Parc du Portugal. "I'm stuffed. I might fall asleep on my cushion."

Antoine looked disgruntled. "Not me. I'm still hungry."

I wonder now how things would have turned out had Antoine taken me up on the offer. As I learned later, if authentic mindfulness becomes an integral part of daily life, it will trigger a process of deep self-transformation and emotional healing. However, if this disruptive process is not properly managed, it could have undesirable consequences, as I found out much later.

Chapter 10
Pacific Ocean, Vancouver

I can't remember when or why I decided to move to Vancouver. It might well have been one of those insidious decisions.

When wakefulness became integrated into my daily life, Montreal was at its wintry best. Having lived through thirteen humid and grey European winters in poorly insulated, sparingly heated and damp interiors, the prospect of my first Canadian winter terrified me. Locals didn't help with comments such as "There's no real winter in Europe," or "You've no idea what you're getting into." I bought a top-of-the-range Kanuk winter coat guaranteed to protect me from temperatures as low as minus twenty-five degrees Celsius and waited with trepidation.

But when the winter came, I loved it. I loved the crisp, cold and dry air. I loved that my building was so well heated that I could wear shorts and t-shirts inside. I loved walking around a city blanketed in white snow. I had planned to hibernate during winter, barring a ten-minute walk to my office and back, but soon I started going on long walks to discover and enjoy winter.

With the added dimension of wakefulness, Montreal became magical. On my way to Mount Royal, majestic pine trees, their branches laden with blinding white snow, undulating in the wind, brought me tears of joy and gratitude. My anxiety subsided.

But many months later, as the trees shed their leaves and chilly winds swept through the city, the anxiety returned. It was perhaps then that the idea of a move took shape.

Along with my new-found wakefulness in daily life, the concept of right livelihood—which falls under right conduct, one of the three stages of the Buddha's Noble Eightfold Path—became a concern for me. Similarly to how my enthusiasm for the esoteric waned when I saw myself mirrored in people at the Gnostic centre, the avidity of some clients to make a killing on the stock market turned me off the investment field. Coming to believe that the stock market's focus on short-term results was an underlying factor of several current ills of society, I concluded that I wasn't abiding by the principle of right livelihood.

In Paris I had become interested in environmental protection, buying organic produce and recycling what I could before any of that became a trend. Having taken a Sustainable Development course in the last year of my MBA program—which I had signed up for in the hopes of making up for my late entry into the business world and bolstering my chances of career success—I figured working in sustainability would constitute right livelihood.

Without carrying out any research or talking to anyone, I decided that Vancouver was the ideal place in Canada to look for a job in sustainability, simply because it was home to Greenpeace. But I suspect my decision was more influenced by the memory of a chance meeting in Paris some four years earlier with Roy, from Seattle, an acquaintance from my student years. When I told him about my imminent departure to Canada, he said, "Go to Vancouver! I've heard a lot of good things about it."

Not untypically for me, I decided to do it the hard way and take a train to Vancouver rather than flying, which was much faster and cheaper to boot. The train felt like the proper Canadian way to travel across the country. Forgetting the rigours of a previous epic train journey from Venice to Istanbul about ten years earlier, the camaraderie among fellow passengers and the overall romantic appeal of a long train journey appealed to me.

Antoine came to see me off. When he arrived, I was on my knees on the floor trying to pack my bag.

"That's no way to pack a bag," he said, putting down his backpack and looking critically at my overflowing bag. "I'm an expert packer. When you've lived on the streets like me, you have to be really good at it."

He took my place in front of my bag, emptied it and then methodically put back the items. Since my train was leaving early, Antoine slept over. When I woke him the next morning, he was grumpy.

"I was having such an interesting dream."

He took a notebook and pen from his backpack and started writing. "I write down all my dreams," he said. "I keep a notebook on my bedside table and wake up in the night to write them down. And sometimes, after I go back to sleep, my dream continues from where it stopped."

As we walked down Sherbrooke Street to the train station, Antoine told me something he had heard from a local Mohawk elder. "Because it's located at the confluence of two mighty rivers, Montreal has a special kind of watery energy. It can be disruptive for some people and bring up emotional stuff from their subconscious."

Turning his head toward me with his customary stoop,

he continued, "I figure it's a Shiva-like destructive energy. Shiva destroys what needs to be destroyed so that creation can begin afresh."

I don't remember much of my journey. From my seat in a regular compartment, which was still more expensive than flying, I saw people, mostly First Nations, getting in and out of places with imagination-igniting names like Sioux Lookout and Medicine Hat. I spent most of the trip in the observatory car, looking at the landscape shifting from rocky to forests and lakes to the flatness and vast openness of the prairies, and finally to the majestic stillness of the Rockies.

Things started to fall apart once I got to Vancouver. It's difficult to put my finger on exactly when things began to unravel. Falling apart is a subtle, stealthy process; you can keep going with a business-as-usual attitude until something quite insignificant happens, resulting in a shift in awareness. You then have to admit that things have gone awry.

That happened to me on the second day of my three-day train trip. Every morning, a waiter walked through the compartments handing out the day's menu, and I let myself be persuaded by the moderately priced lunch to head for the dining car.

That day after finishing the excellent main dish of baked Pacific salmon with wild rice and steamed spinach, I wiped my mouth with the white linen napkin and was gazing at the brown prairie stretching flat to the horizon when the solicitous waiter came by.

"Are you ready for dessert?" he asked.

To my surprise, I heard myself saying, "No, thank you, I won't be having dessert today."

The waiter looked disappointed, almost hurt, at missing out seeing another satisfied customer relishing the dessert he considered to be the meal's *coup de grâce*. As I sipped a cup of Earl Grey tea generously laced with milk, I pondered why, with my sweet tooth, I had refused a dessert I was going to pay for anyway. It was then I admitted to myself that I had been feeling anxious and thought that eating something sugary could aggravate my state.

~

I spent the first few days in Vancouver in a sleazy hotel in the East End patronized by prostitutes, pimps, junkies and dealers. I then moved quickly up the ranks of Vancouver society by renting a spacious, tastefully furnished apartment in a trendy part of the West End, at the corner of Bidwell and Haro. From my balcony window, I could see pedestrians passing by on bustling Denman Street with its wide range of restaurants and sushi joints between English Bay and Robson Street.

During the days that followed, I went for many walks along the Vancouver Seawall that shelters Stanley Park from the encroaching ocean and noticed that the state of the water had an effect on my mental state. When the sea was rough and waves lashed the stone seawall, I felt agitated. As I stood at the edge of a cliff in Stanley Park and gazed over English Bay to the great Pacific Ocean beyond, I could see that my new home was located on a peninsula, just a ten-minute walk from the beach. Remembering what Antoine said about Montreal, I wondered whether he had been implying I was running away from its watery energy. If that was the case, I couldn't have chosen a worse destination, as an even greater body of water surrounded my new neighbourhood.

While still in Montreal, my anxiety arose intermittently; however, in Vancouver it soon became a default undercurrent state. I tried to pin down the negative emotions that had intensified since my move. Ostensibly, anxiety was linked to a fear of death triggered by high blood pressure. But I couldn't explain the feelings of dread I was experiencing, presentiments of impending doom, especially when I'd wake up at three in the morning in a cold sweat and unable to get back to sleep.

I remember standing on my balcony and surveying my delightful new neighbourhood. With the bluish-grey Rockies in the distance on my right, the densely green Stanley Park ahead of me and the reddish-orange sun sinking into English Bay, I wondered how I could feel anxiety and dread amid so much beauty. I took heart from a quote by Don Juan Matus, Castaneda's real or fictitious shaman teacher: "The true art of a warrior is to balance terror and wonder.[12]"

I realized then that while wakefulness magnifies the wonder of the world, it can also heighten the terror of being alive. With hindsight, my saving grace might have been the ability of my mind, even in its anxious state, to acknowledge and even appreciate the beauty around me.

~

For most of my adult life, I had avoided doctors as much as possible, waiting for my ailments to go away without any outside intervention. But in Vancouver I became a hypochondriac, making frequent visits to a nearby clinic and even spending one night in the ER following a panic attack. So it's no coincidence I became good friends with Dino, a fellow hypochondriac. Banned from a couple of medical clinics in the West End, Dino had to strike out further and further away from home base to get the medical attention he was convinced he needed.

I met Dino at the Vancouver Gurdjieff centre. I'm surprised

---

12   Carlos Castaneda, *Tales of Power*.

now that despite Gurdjieff's impact on my life, I had made no attempts to reach out to a local centre in either Paris or Montreal. Gurdjieff centres are almost secret societies that fly under the radar. You can't just walk in the door and sign up. I had two interviews with two different senior Gurdjieff people in downtown cafés before I was admitted to a reading group.

I told them about my experience of wakefulness, which I considered to be equivalent to self-remembering. They were respectful but skeptical. I understood then that despite "doing the Gurdjieff work," as they called it, during their entire adult lives, their experiences of self-remembering were fleeting. To address their skepticism, I explained how following the strong impetus provided by my spontaneous awakening, I had worked hard to conserve and transmute my sexual energy into moments of self-remembering. To test me, they asked me to describe my experience.

I said something like, "When the discursive thoughts in the mind subside, the mind shifts from a contracted, claustrophobic state to spaciousness. It's like night and day, like moving from darkness to light. The world becomes more vivid. I become an observer, a witness. At the same time, I'm aware of myself and also see myself in the scene. It's a bit scary to think that if I'm crossing a busy street in a state of waking sleep, I don't really see my body in space."

I was hoping they'd invite me to join an inner circle as recognition for my state of consciousness, but instead I was relegated to an introductory reading group. The weekly meetings, held in a small, rented room far away from the actual centre, consisted in reading a few pages from Ouspensky's *In Search of the Miraculous*, followed by a discussion. At the first meeting, we read chapter six, a chapter that had resonated with me the first time I read the book. Tom, the group leader, started reading.

"One of the next lectures began with a question asked by one of those present: *What was the aim of his teaching?*"

As soon as I heard the words, my heart pounded. I wanted to get up and run out of the room but I was frozen. My heart kept beating faster and faster until it no longer seemed a heartbeat but a fine vibration near my sternum. My body got hot. Two large beads of sweat formed in my armpits, growing and then dripping in slow motion. The vibrations hit a crescendo and started to subside. My body and mind shifted from contraction to spaciousness, giving rise to feelings of warmth and well-being.

That sense of well-being felt similar to how I'd felt in the aftermath of my spontaneous awakening. When I later told Tom about what had happened, he commended me on my courage for staying with my fear. I nodded modestly. Actually, it was not courage but fear itself that kept me rooted in my chair.

Following the second or third Gurdjieff group meeting, I became acquainted with Dino at the bus stop on the way home. It turned out we were neighbours in the West End. We started walking back home together after every meeting, Dino holding on to my arm, as he was legally blind and could see little in the dark.

Having read widely on the topic, Dino considered himself a Buddhist and we had frequent conversations on various aspects of the teachings. Sometimes we'd argue over our interpretations and when he couldn't get the last word in, he'd clamp his jaws and say through clenched teeth, "Noble silence!"

The Buddha had the habit of maintaining "noble silence" when someone asked an abstract question such as "Who created life?" or "When did life begin?"—matters that the Buddha considered irrelevant to the task at hand: achieving liberation from suffering.

Dino also liked to say, "*Dukkha, dukkha!*"[13] when talking about the hardships of his life. I told him that my understanding of the word had evolved from simple suffering to the conditioned nature of life. I could actually taste the unsatisfactory nature of life when I was in a contracted state of mind and discursive thoughts were taking up all the mental space.

He was constantly checking his blood pressure with a monitor and urged me to get one and do the same. Apparently, his readings went up during and after meditation. Knowing that he was strong-willed, I said, "Maybe you're trying too hard. Right effort is one of the steps in the meditation stage of the Noble Eightfold Path. Do you know the analogy the Buddha gave on this topic? He told a meditation practitioner to be like a musician tuning his instrument. The strings must not be too slack, but they shouldn't be too tight either."

As he seemed to be conflating concentration with mindfulness, I urged him to read the *Discourse on the Four Foundations of Mindfulness*. "It's so different from other Buddhist discourses. It has a direct, modern feel about it. I think it should be better known among the greater public."

Dino was the only person other than my doctor with whom I could talk about my anxiety and feelings of dread. He criticized my tendency to hunker down in my apartment.

"When you start doing less and less, you're on a downward spiral. The solution is to keep doing what you used to do."

He did so by jogging, hiking and playing tennis despite the onset of blindness, and by taking long, difficult trips to India and Pakistan despite his illnesses, real or imaginary. He urged me to go on long walks with him in Stanley Park. We'd walk deep into areas of the park that were more like a forest, where

---

13   One of the three characteristics of life according to Buddhism, commonly translated as suffering.

tall trees blocked out the sunlight. When I got home, I'd feel much better, with my mind in a more spacious state.

During one such walk the talk came around to the topic of death.

"Death terrifies me," I confessed. "Maybe it's because I'm afraid I'll die without doing what I have to do."

"I'm not afraid of dying," replied Dino, perhaps a tad too forcefully. "But I don't want to leave Catherine alone." Catherine was Dino's partner, a sweet woman devoted to him.

"You should give her some space so she can become more independent."

"You don't know Catherine," Dino waved dismissively. "She needs me. I have to stay alive for her sake."

During these walks I couldn't help thinking about how similar they felt to my walks with Antoine on Mount Royal. The similarities between Dino and Antoine were striking. Both were self-taught intellectuals with penetrative minds. Both of them had had difficult childhoods, and although Dino's story of growing up in an orphanage seemed more horrific, he mentioned it only once and nonchalantly at that, as if it had not affected his life in any way.

Paranoia was another characteristic they shared. For Dino, it was mostly personal, thinking that people were out to take advantage of him or scam him. For instance, after leaving Vancouver, I had ordered Eckhart Tolle's *The Power of Now* for Dino, but he twice refused to accept the delivery, thinking it was a scam. I had to call him and tell him it was a gift from me. Antoine, on the other hand, was more likely to rant about groups of people and global conspiracy theories.

I thought it was odd I had made two paranoid friends around the same time. In contrast, I had gone through life thinking the world was a safe and welcoming place I could explore at will, and that people everywhere would be well disposed toward me. I'd later discover that deep down I too was paranoid, extremely so, in specific situations.

~

The job search in Vancouver was frustrating, which didn't help my state of mind. Few in Vancouver were as enthusiastic as I was about sustainability, barring the people at the Vancity credit union who interviewed me for a job that never materialized. The previous year, Hong Kong had been handed back to China by the UK, sparking a recession in Vancouver, which had close economic and financial connections to the former British colony. I arrived in Vancouver a couple of months before the handover. My arrival in Montreal had coincided with the depths of an economic crisis, and I left just when things were turning around!

Job interviews were hard to come by in Vancouver, and even when I did get one, I might have come across as an anxious person and difficult to deal with, putting off interviewers. After several frustrating months of searching, and just before my bank balance went into the red, I found a temporary job with the same company I had worked for in Montreal, and in the same position. So much for my intention of getting away from what I considered wrong livelihood!

If I had thought that my anxiety would subside now that I had the comforting structure of employment, I was mistaken. Several times, feeling lightheaded and vulnerable, I rushed to the clinic thinking the end was nigh. I also kept waking up early with a fast heartbeat, so I'd go for a walk in Stanley Park and watch dawn lifting over English Bay before showering and heading off to work.

My office on Burrard Street was a fifteen-minute walk from

my place, and I'd take a shortcut with the harbour on my left, the sound of traffic on Robson Street coming from my right and downtown high-rises looming ahead. One day on my way back home, I saw, for the first time in my life, a double rainbow forming above. I sat on a bench to enjoy it. Initially, the colours were blurred but they soon became bolder with clearly defined borders. Meanwhile, people kept walking past me, briskly and purposefully, unaware of the spectacle above. I wanted to stand in front of them, throw my arms up in the air and yell, "Look, you normal people, I'm falling apart, but I can still appreciate this gift of nature! Why can't you?"

My job came to an end as scheduled, so I updated and sent out my resume, keeping a close eye on my bank balance. Mundane activities like buying groceries and preparing food became overwhelming. I also enrolled in job search workshops, but the response was poor, unlike during my first experience in Montreal.

With few options left, I decided to return to Sri Lanka. But soon after buying my ticket, I felt it was a mistake and didn't want to go. I put off my departure twice and each time, I felt a short-lived sense of relief. Sitting on English Bay beach, I watched Vancouverites frolicking in the silvery sand and agonized about my impending departure. *To go or not to go?* The indecision made my anxiety more excruciating. While I had previously felt anxiety as a contracted state of mind, now I felt something that could only be described as stickiness, in both mind and body, and the hot sun made it worse.

On the morning of my departure, I woke up feeling refreshed and relaxed. I sat on my balcony, enjoying my last Vancouver breakfast of cheddar on toasted sourdough rye and watching early risers strolling down Denman Street. Both body and mind had shifted from contraction to spaciousness. I felt a sense of well-being, similar to what I had experienced at my first Gurdjieff meeting but without the preliminary intensity and panic. Dave, another Vancouver friend, had offered to drive me to the airport, and after leaving some stuff in Dino's basement locker, I headed off in an upbeat mood, blissfully oblivious to what was awaiting me in Sri Lanka.

Chapter 11
Indian Ocean, Mount Lavinia

I always make sure to book an aisle seat on flights, so I don't know how I ended up in a middle seat, squeezed between two obese people on a non-stop twelve-hour flight to Hong Kong. And one of them happened to be Chinese—the first overweight Chinese woman I had ever seen! By the time I got off the plane in Hong Kong, the sense of well-being and expansion I'd felt the previous day in Vancouver had dissipated. I had planned to explore the city during the long transit but feeling the same stickiness in body and mind I had experienced at the end of my Vancouver stay, I returned to the airport. There I had a meal of sweet and sour soup followed by crispy yellow chow mein with stir-fried tofu and bok choy, whose bright green colour, juicy texture and slightly bitter taste soothed me somewhat.

Back in my family home in Mount Lavinia, a suburb of Colombo, things didn't get any better. In the morning, I'd make myself a cup of tea and sit in my favourite seat in the living room, a cane chair by the wall of louvres. I spent more and more time in that chair, gazing at my mother's red-and-white anthuriums and the green lawn beyond. I felt safe sitting there, especially when my mother sat in her favourite chair at the other end of the living room. But as the days turned into weeks and I found it increasingly difficult to get off my chair, I sensed my mother's increasing concern for me emanating from the back of the room.

~

The Indian Ocean was just two kilometres away, and one of my favourite pastimes during a vacation was walking on the beach in the late afternoon. After the tourists roll up their towels, pack up their tanning paraphernalia and retreat to their hotel rooms, the locals take over the beach. I'd take off my flip-flops and start walking, feeling my feet and toes sinking into the damp, shifting sand, with the fishy ocean smell wafting toward me. I'd nod to groups of senior citizens taking their evening constitutional, circumvent groups of boisterous bare-bodied boys playing beach cricket, and step aside to avoid fully dressed young girls squealing and playing tag with the foamy waves. As I walked along, with my old school on the left and the tall buildings in Colombo's business district behind me, the sun set on my right, its fading rays lighting up the Mount Lavinia Hotel, the former British governor's residence, rising ahead. Apparently, our suburb had got its name when the British governor of the country named his new official residence Mount Lavinia House in honour of his mistress, a dancer of mixed Portuguese descent named Lavinia. The mansion was built on a cliff, hence the "Mount" part.

After my walk I'd sit at a beach bar and treat myself to a tall bottle of chilled Lion Lager and a plate of devilled tuna, with my bare feet in the sand just a few feet from the waves gliding in and out. The evening ocean breeze would brush my face, and I'd gaze at the sky shifting from red to orange and then to deep violet and take a swig of the bitter lager to douse the fiery taste of the tuna. *Ah, the wonder of being alive!*

Later I'd walk up Beach Road to Galle Road—Sri Lanka's main road, snaking its way along the western coast from Colombo all the way to Galle in the south—and eat hoppers, a kind of savoury bowl-shaped crepe. Along with kottu roti, hoppers, or appa as they are called in Sinhala, are the most popular local street foods. I'd watch the hopper maker grease his pan with a piece of rag dipped in oil, take a ladleful of the hopper batter made of rice flour, coconut milk and water, pour it into the pan, swirl the batter around to distribute it evenly and then crack an egg into the middle. He'd then cover the pan, checking from time to time to make sure the batter and the egg were properly cooked. Satisfied, he'd use a flat spoon to slide the now crispy brown-and-white hopper onto a plate.

I'd usually go to the beach several evenings a week, but on that trip home, I went to the beach only a couple of times over the whole four-month period. The last time I went, the moon was full and the sea choppy. I felt extremely agitated, as had happened many times in Vancouver. I returned home quickly, leaving behind a half-full bottle of beer and a scarcely touched plate of devilled tuna on the table.

Damn this watery energy! I just can't get away from it!

No longer confident about navigating the chaotic streets of Colombo, I decided not to drive the family car, opting to hail a tuk-tuk, take the bus or simply walk. It also happened sometimes that I'd venture out, wait for a tuk-tuk or a bus and then turn back, feeling I couldn't go through with it.

I remembered a similar experience in my late teens, when I'd spent most of my time in my room reading my way through a pile of books borrowed from the British Council library and from friends or their fathers. One evening I started reading Nietzsche's *Thus Spake Zarathustra* after dinner and kept going until I finished it in the middle of the night. By then I was too wide awake, so I read a book of Chekhov's plays until I heard the usual chorus of birds chirping outside my bedroom window. The pile of unread books having dwindled, I decided to go to the British Council to replenish stocks. While waiting for the bus, I was overcome with an unusual feeling that I couldn't face the world. I rushed back home, threw the books I was carrying on my desk, sat on the bed, put my head in my hands and sobbed, not knowing why I was crying. My mother hurried into my room, sat next to me and tried to console me. In her great wisdom, she gave me a sort of ultimatum—see a psychiatrist or go stay with one of my brothers for a while.

"How can a psychiatrist understand what I'm going through?" I protested. Not that I understood it either.

I went to stay with my middle brother, who was the manager of a large tea and rubber plantation a couple of hours' drive from Mount Lavinia. There, I spent a lot of time playing with my two-year-old nephew and sitting on a large black rock, gazing at the lush greenery around me. After a couple of months, I came back home recovered, studied for an accounting exam and things went back to normal. About a year later, I went to Paris, leaving home for good.

~

A week or so after my return to Sri Lanka from Vancouver, I started feeling the sensation of needles falling through my brain. This disquieting perception steadily became stronger, heightening my sense of dread.

My mind is slipping away, but it's being held together with pins and needles!

The thought that I might be going insane crept its way into my mind only to snowball later. The previously delightful orchestra of bird calls that woke me up became an irritating cacophony. The shrill, piercing cry of a *koha*, an Asian koel, which makes its appearance in the skies at the time of the local New Year in April, was particularly annoying. More disconcerting was the sadistically cheerful sound of the musical horn of the ice cream truck that kept cruising through our neighbourhood.

I had a vivid dream during that time. The setting was two vast stretches of bare land with craggy outcroppings separated by a large body of water. A group of people on the other shore waved at me, which warmed my heart. But then I heard the piercing cry of the *koha* and the ice cream truck, and I saw that the people on the other side were actually making urgent signs for me to come over, as if there was an imminent danger lurking on my side. I hesitated, as my swimming ability was limited and the water on my side was covered with dark green slime. A young woman, smartly dressed in a dark business suit and high heels, appeared from nowhere and walked toward the water. Without turning around, she made a beckoning sign with her hand over her shoulder. I understood she wanted to me to lie on her back while she swam across. The next moment, I was on the other shore with the woman, now naked, resting on the sandy ground with her back to a tree. Her curly dark hair, intertwined with seaweed, was thrown over her face, covering her breasts as well but exposing a smooth shaved pubis. As I leaned forward to draw apart her hair and see her face, I woke up. I took the dream to be a good omen.

I sat in my favourite chair, trying to make sense of what had happened to me since I left Montreal. A line of reasoning that had been percolating at the back of my mind came to the forefront. As I had surmised before, the continual stream of thoughts in our minds serves to suppress deeply buried negative emotions. So my mental spaciousness had allowed unresolved fear and anxiety from the past to resurface. I thought about what could have caused such emotions in my life and concluded it was most likely my father's sudden death when I was just one and a half years old. It happened on Sri Lankan New Year, when my father was taking a nap after lunch. I was probably in my cot next to the bed. But it would take me another fifteen years or so to better understand that fateful day.

I remembered a quote attributed to Carl Jung: "Until you make the unconscious conscious, it will direct your life and you will call it fate,"[14] and consoled myself with the thought that my current troubles were an unexpected yet essential part of my path toward permanent awakening. I believed that in the enlightened state, all unresolved emotions are released and the unconscious becomes fully conscious.

My doctor in Vancouver had prescribed a tranquilizer that I didn't take. I saw a doctor in Colombo, who also prescribed a tranquilizer and multivitamins. I tried the multivitamins, which made me feel worse, so I stopped taking them. I knew I had to see this through on my own, without the help of chemicals.

I went to see a Buddhist monk in a local temple who taught meditation. I told him about my state of mind and my theory that it was at least partly the result of practising awareness of awareness. He was skeptical but told me to stop my sitting

---

14 While this quote is widely attributed to Jung, its exact source is unknown.

practice and take up walking meditation instead. I did so and found that sensing my feet on the ground served as an antidote to the anxiety. He also asked me to translate into French a small book on Buddhism he had written in Sinhala, which forced me to sit in front of the computer and concentrate. The concentration and the process of switching from one language to another were also soothing, which led me to another realization.

I had not stayed long enough in shamatha or the concentration phase of meditation, moving too fast into awareness and then into awareness of awareness without a solid foundation to keep me grounded!

Most meditation practitioners spend most of their lives in the concentration stage, so I put this theory to the Buddhist monk at our subsequent meeting, and he appeared to agreed with me.

I had signed up for a ten-day vipassana retreat near Kandy, in the central part of the country, but I kept agonizing over whether to go, given my state of mind. The indecision further fuelled my anxiety. The night before the start of the retreat, I remained undecided. I packed my bag just in case, but in the morning, I decided not to go. With that decision, I took a further step on my downward spiral.

A month went by in Sri Lanka, and then another. I put off the date of my departure again and again. I could hardly bring myself to take a bus; I couldn't see myself flying back to Vancouver with little money in the bank and having to start my job search all over again. One morning, while reading the newspaper, I learned about a young man in our neighbourhood who had killed his parents during an acute schizophrenic episode.

Could this kind of thing happen to me as well?

I tried to put that terrifying thought out of my mind but it kept popping back in. After that day I no longer felt safe sitting in my favourite chair. The feelings of dread that had come up occasionally in Vancouver became my default state and my mind slipped further into a downward spiral.

I'm going insane! Oh, the terror of being alive!

As an antidote, I took to walking inside the house and in the garden. Sometimes, I'd venture out into our neighbourhood, making sure to take my driver's licence with me just in case I forgot where home was. Preparing for the worst, I came up with a plan: if I felt that my mind was slipping away completely, I'd get into a cab, go to my sister's place and ask her to take me to a hospital. To be on the safe side, I wrote her address on a piece of paper and tucked it into my wallet, next to my driver's licence. I now realize that my plan had a serious flaw since it assumed I'd be able to walk along that razor edge between sanity and insanity. I'd have to be sane enough to know I was going insane but not too far gone to know that I had a sister whose address was in my wallet.

While walking around our neighbourhood, I remembered how I'd ride my bike through it as a kid, carefree and confident about my current and future place in the world. It would have been impossible for me to imagine then that a few decades later, I'd be walking the same streets in a desperate attempt to hang onto my sanity.

Until then, I had been more concerned that the contracted mental state created by anxiety would make me lose the mental spaciousness I had worked diligently to achieve. With the impending prospect of insanity, I saw spaciousness as my downfall and regretted having set out on this path. There was one positive outcome, though. I seemed to have lost my fear of death. Indeed, death was preferable to insanity.

While I was waging the mother of all battles in my mind, a real-life bloody war was being fought in the North of Sri

Lanka between an army made up of the majority Sinhalese and the LTTE, a group representing the minority Tamils that was seeking a separate state. Sitting in my chair, I'd hear the sirens of ambulances taking injured soldiers from the nearby domestic airport to the military hospital in Colombo. And if we had visitors when the ambulances passed by, the conversation would trail off into silence as the sirens got louder and when the sound faded in the distance, the chatting picked up again as if nothing untoward had happened.

I'm not sure how long I remained teetering on the edge of the abyss. Looking back, I can think of several events that reversed the downward spiral and set me on the path to recovery. The first happened when I heard a vegetable seller going down our road shouting, "Vegetables, fresh vegetables, cheap!"

My mother asked me to call out to him and I did. He opened the gate and came up the driveway, pushing his bicycle. He seemed normal, functional and perfectly sane. I envied him. At some point in my life, I had started considering myself different, with a special destiny, although I had no particular reason for thinking so. I remembered a discussion with Antoine in Montreal about the right- and left-hand paths in Tantra and how I had implied I was on a hero's journey. How arrogant I had been! I was being punished. I no longer wanted to be different. All I wanted was to be a normal, functioning member of society like everyone else. Like the humble vegetable seller. Remembering how Antoine had prayed to the Virgin Mary to deliver him from his addiction, I wanted to fall to my knees and beg forgiveness for my arrogance. But unlike Antoine, I had no one to petition for deliverance.

Some days were better than others. The second turning point happened on one of those better days, when I mustered enough mental resolve to go into town to cash in my return plane ticket. Going back to Vancouver was no longer an option. Canada was like the Garden of Eden I had been expelled from for committing the cardinal sin of pride. In the worst-case scenario, I'd be institutionalized. As terrifying as that prospect was, it was the pain and grief such an outcome would cause my mother that made it too unbearable even to contemplate. In the best-case scenario, I saw myself going to live with my sister—living at home was no longer a viable option—and working in my brother-in-law's clinic. I'd live out a humble and unpretentious life.

Having done the required paperwork at the airline office, I went to the bus stop nearby and waited, along with a woman who looked like a tourist. It turned out she was a Canadian working as a volunteer. The bus came along. We got in and kept chatting. I felt an energetic connection to her, which gave rise to feelings of warmth and well-being, dissipating the anxiety and dread.

All is not lost. Recovery is still possible!

The third turning point consisted in a saviour appearing in the form of my eldest brother, about twelve years my senior, who lived in London. Having changed jobs, he came on a surprise visit to Sri Lanka before starting in his new position. I saw a new exit path opening up but waited a couple of days for him to notice any difference in me. He didn't make any comment, so I went into his room one morning, shut the door and told him about the state I had gotten into. My brother's eyes widened as he listened and I knew what he was thinking. *This is so unlike my intrepid kid brother.* Unsympathetically, he said, "You've got to get your act together."

I could see it bothered him that I no longer corresponded to his image of me.

"I have to get away from here," I told him. "I need your

help." Perhaps for the first time in my life, I actually reached out to someone to ask for help. "I'm in no shape to go back to Canada."

"Come to London and stay with me," my brother said.

"I can't go alone. You have to take me with you."

Again, he looked at me as if he was looking at a stranger. But he put off the date for his new position by one week, changed his flight and bought me a one-way ticket to London.

Before we left, my brother wanted me to go with him to a party, saying it would do me good, and I reluctantly agreed. I had become sensitive to noise and thought my feeling of disorientation would be aggravated by having to interact with many people at the same time. But as soon as we got to the party, I felt less anxious. Being in a room full of other bodies was soothing, and the upbeat mood soon rubbed off on me. The smell of alcohol also had a surprisingly relaxing effect and I felt the energy shifting from my head to my body. I stood in a corner, sipping a gin and tonic with a smile.

A week later, I left my mother behind and went to London with my brother, who had been a kind of father figure to me. I felt the urge to fall on my knees at my mother's feet, a traditional way of taking leave of parents and elders, though more so in rural areas. But I didn't want to alarm her with unusual behaviour.

Chapter 12
Nowy Świat, Warsaw

I was well into my four-month stay in London when I met up with Sami in a pub on Kensington High Street. He was a close friend from school, then living in Warsaw, who I hadn't seen for about seven years. It intrigued me that he and Antoine shared the same birthday as well as incisive intellect. But while Antoine slowly descended into the abyss, Sami had steadily climbed up the corporate ladder. Over a pint of lager, I told him about the events that had led me from Montreal to Vancouver, to Sri Lanka, and then to London.

"I think I've overstayed my welcome here. My brother is fine with me staying at his place, but my sister-in-law thinks it's time for me to move on. I'm much better now, but you see, I've lost my confidence. I don't feel I can go back to Canada and start fending for myself again."

Sami responded in the same way my brother had some months earlier in Sri Lanka.

"Why don't you come and stay with me in Warsaw, then?"

I had started recovering in London by going for long daily walks on the Epsom Downs, not far from my brother's place, and later by venturing into the city to meet up with old friends. But it was in Warsaw that I began to put myself back together. Fittingly so, as during most of my stay in the city, I lived close to the Old Town, which had been destroyed by Germany at the end of WWII and was then meticulously rebuilt brick by brick after the war. It was also fitting because my recent downfall could be traced back to that momentous day in Paris when the walls of my mind disintegrated at about the same time the Berlin Wall crumbled. It's now clear that the fall of Poland's Communist government in June 1989 opened the first crack in that wall.

The first two weeks in Warsaw followed the same pattern. I'd take a cab from Sami's place in a small, gated community in the upscale suburb of Wilanów—home to the Wilanów Palace, also known as the Polish Versailles—and wander around town. I'd invariably end up on the aptly named Nowy Świat or New World Street, winding gracefully from Old Town with its broad sidewalks, antique lampposts, and chic boutiques, cafés and restaurants. It represented the modern face of Warsaw ten years into the post-Communist period, so unlike the dark and bleak Warsaw that friends in London had warned me against.

Although I had gained strength from my long walks in London, I'd feel exhausted with pain in my feet after just an hour or so of walking. So I'd shuffle into the elegant Blikle Café on Nowy Świat, sink into one of its plush couches and order a pot of Earl Grey tea with a piece of makowiec, a traditional Polish poppy seed cake.

Life on Nowy Świat had not always been uplifting; some of the bloodiest battles of the Warsaw Uprising[15] at the end of

---

15   Led by the Polish underground resistance to liberate the city from German occupation.

WWII were fought in the area. So I wondered whether I was channelling some of that pain and suffering. More likely, with my mind relaxing into a less contracted state, my body was releasing all the anxiety, fear and dread I had experienced during the preceding year.

One day at Blikle's, I saw a petite woman with long, straight, blond hair walking briskly past the glass front. She reminded me of Alexandra, the girl I dated in Paris, and her parting words to me, "I feel that your body is completely cut off from your mind."

I hadn't understood what she meant until I read about the importance of body awareness in Ouspensky's book a few years later. Gurdjieff talked about the existence of psychic centres in man, akin to the chakras in kundalini yoga, and the need for the balanced development of those centres to achieve a harmonious state of being. Since most of his followers had overdeveloped mental centres, he recommended hard physical labour, in addition to the practice of the "sacred dances" he taught, to develop body awareness.

It occurred to me, as I sipped tea at Blikle's, that my spontaneous awakening in Paris was a heightened embodied experience where my mind had synchronized with my body for the first time. So different from the "cosmic consciousness" that my friend Govinda claimed to have experienced in London at about the same time after isolating himself and fasting for several days. I also understood that while I was well established in three of the Buddha's four foundations of mindfulness—awareness of the mind, awareness of the contents of the mind, and awareness of the sensations received through the body—the same could not be said for awareness of the body. Had my awareness been more grounded in my body, I'd have been better equipped to withstand the onslaught of negative emotions during my stays in Vancouver and Sri Lanka. At Blikle's in Warsaw, I set myself the intention to work on developing body awareness.

After resting at Blikle's I'd take a cab back to Wilanów, have a long nap to further restore myself and then read a few chapters of a three-volume set on Poland's checkered history. Countless invasions, partitions and conquests had made Poland's boundaries fluid. I drew parallels with the Buddhist notion of impermanence and the illusory boundary between self and the world. During the entire nineteenth century, and for many years before and after, no independent Polish state existed. But the Polish identity and language had endured.

~

Just before leaving London for Warsaw, I was browsing in an independent bookstore on Charing Cross Road and came across a book on the Alexander Technique. Alexander, a Shakespearean actor, had developed a unique bodywork approach to cure himself after losing his voice. A few months into my stay in Warsaw, I attended sittings with an informal Zen group. After the first session Hannah came to speak to me and gave me her card, having noticed I had scoliosis. I looked at the card and saw she was a certified Alexander Technique teacher. Impressed by the synchronicity, I signed up for regular Alexander Technique sessions, the first of many bodywork practices I'd try in keeping with my intention to develop body awareness.

It was also the easiest of practices, since all I had to do was lie on my back on Hannah's treatment table with my knees drawn up as she made subtle adjustments. Sometimes I'd feel my spinal cord elongating, but more often I'd fall into a deep sleep. When I left Hannah's and walked to the tram stop, I'd feel disoriented, as if I were in a different body. An encouraging sign, according to Hannah.

Hannah had a grey tabby cat named Olaf, just like my nemesis at the Hôtel d'Alger. The first time he saw me, he gave me a baleful look and walked away disdainfully to sit sphinx-like in the farthest corner of the room, with his paws tucked under and an air of indifference. Several sessions later, Hannah was about halfway through when Olaf got up lazily from his usual seat, leaped softly on to the treatment table and sat on my stomach, still maintaining his aloofness as if he was doing nothing out of the ordinary.

"He has never done that before!" said Hannah. "Shall I chase him away?"

I said no. After that, at some point during each session, Olaf would take over by sitting on my belly.

~

I was hired for the first job I applied for, at the same firm I had worked at in Paris before leaving for Montreal. I had also walked away from that firm in Sri Lanka, convinced I was meant for bigger things. It felt good to be a normal, functioning member of society once again after a hiatus of over a year, but the first few weeks at work were a bit difficult as I kept dozing off.

I moved out of Sami's place and into a spacious apartment in a building just behind Blikle Café. It had high ceilings and its large windows opened onto a large, leafy courtyard. The location was ideal, at the corner of Nowy Świat and Chmielna, a pedestrian street lined with chic boutiques, restaurants, bars and cafés.

Every day, as I crossed the massive Plac Defilad, or Parade Square, on my way to work, I'd contemplate the monumental Palace of Culture and Science, a somewhat grotesque Gothic edifice dominating the Warsaw skyline. It was a gift from Stalin, and a replica of the Seven Sisters or "people's cathedrals" built in Moscow by gulag inmates after the end of WWII. One morning, I was cutting through the small park behind the massive building when I felt my shoes treading the pathway! Strangely enough, until then, I hadn't really experienced the sensation of my feet on ground. I continued walking, feeling elated, akin to how I had felt when I rode a bike on my own for the first time or finally mastered the headstand in yoga. The experience confirmed that my mental centre of gravity was shifting from my head to my body, probably as a result of my bodywork with Hannah and the tai chi practice I had recently taken up. Occasionally, I'd fleetingly feel that sensation again, but it would take twelve more years for it to become an integral part of my day-to-day awareness.

~

Early on during my Warsaw stay, through a friend of Sami's, I met Hermina, a party girl who introduced me to Warsaw's club scene. Hermina lived fully in the moment and had no use for plans. Setting up dates with her was quite pointless, but then she'd turn up when least expected. She also gave me my first taste of Polish hospitality, as she'd insist I eat something whenever I came to her place, even just to pick her up. Even if we were going out to dinner, she'd peel an orange for me and watch me eat it, showing a surprisingly nurturing side, or she'd make me a sandwich despite my protests that I didn't want to spoil my appetite.

One night after she had stood me up once again, I decided to go clubbing on my own, something I had rarely done before. As my taxi neared Scena, a popular club located on a side street off Nowy Świat, there was a flutter in the pit of my stomach.

But after I had been frisked by the dark-suited, heavily built bouncers, paid the cover charge, checked my coat and walked in, I felt both calm and exhilarated. I stood at the bar propped up by my right arm, feeling my feet firmly on the floor, the music vibrating in my torso and the coolness of the drink in my left hand. I tasted the bitter-sweetness of the vodka mixed with orange juice and surveyed the scene of gyrating nubile women as feminine fragrances wafted toward me.

I'm practising the Buddha's four foundations of mindfulness way better than I did sitting on my meditation cushion!

I also remembered how my energy had shifted when I had gone to the party with my brother just before leaving Sri Lanka. After that solitary night out, clubbing became an essential and entertaining part of the process of putting myself back together.

~

At the end of my first year in Warsaw, to celebrate the dawning of the new millennium, I signed up for a ten-day vipassana course in London, redeeming myself for backing out from attending the retreat in Sri Lanka the previous year. I also felt compelled to practise the Burmese vipassana technique as taught by S. N. Goenka, as I thought his book might have helped me integrate wakefulness into day-to-day life.

To my surprise, the meditation instructions were given not by the retreat's teacher but through taped recordings made by Goenka. I felt strong resistance to his voice, similar to my initial experience at the Shambhala centre. During the first three days we practised observing the breath, followed by the specific Burmese vipassana technique of sweeping the body with attention, scanning for sensations. The aim was to observe the sensations with equanimity or, in other words, without attachment or aversion. The use of the word *vipassana* or insight to describe the technique surprised me, as it seemed to me simply a different form of concentration or *shamatha*. But it worked well for me, as it was precisely the lack of *shamatha* that had led to my downfall, according to my self-diagnosis. This form of *shamatha* also helped me develop awareness of the body, the specific foundation of mindfulness I was lacking. I struggled, experiencing more pain than in previous retreats, but once I let go of my resistance, there arose unconditional joy.

There's absolutely nothing to worry about. Everything's fine with my life and the world.

I felt a sense of absolute freedom, even though my days were strictly regimented. Those feelings of joy and freedom came and went throughout the ten days and even afterwards.

During my stay in Warsaw, I attended a number of ten-day vipassana retreats, including a couple in Switzerland and several in Sri Lanka, at a custom-built centre on a mountaintop near Kandy.

At one such retreat in Sri Lanka, while waiting outside the spacious meditation hall with its high ceilings, wooden beams and tiled floors, I found myself standing next to a Buddhist monk. We were admiring the panoramic view of greenish-blue mountains and lush valleys all around us against the backdrop of the sky dotted with fluffy white clouds.

I was surprised to see a Buddhist monk there, as most Sri Lankan monks don't usually practise or teach meditation; instead they spend their time giving talks on Buddhist teachings and performing priestly functions, urging lay followers to give offerings to the temple to accumulate merit and ensure better conditions in the afterlife. This didn't make sense to me even as a teenager, as the whole point of becoming a monk was to liberate oneself from worldly obligations, and to focus on meditation so as to achieve liberation from suffering.

The monk pointed to the distant horizon. "On a clear day you can see Pidurutalagala from here." Pidurutalagala is the tallest mountain in Sri Lanka.

"I was surprised to hear the meditation teacher tell us not to gaze at the scenery," I said. "What's the point in building a centre in a place of stunning beauty like this, and then telling us not to appreciate it?"

He shrugged with the air of a man who had more important things on his mind. "I guess they want us to focus inward and not outward."

The monk moved closer to me. He looked around as if to make sure no one would hear him, and said in a conspiratorial tone, "You know, here in this centre, they talk about sensations as if you only feel them in the body." He wagged a finger at me. "That's wrong! The term *vedana* used in the *Satipatthana Sutta* refers not just to physical sensations but to all perceptions received through the five senses, that is, sights, sounds, smells, sensations and taste."

It all clicked for me. It was my turn to glance around and say in a low voice, "I know that Goenka had done a lot to spread Buddhist teachings around the world, but don't you think it's incorrect to call this technique *vipassana* when it's actually a form of *shamatha*?"

"Exactly!" The monk gave me a satisfied smile, seeing in me a kindred spirit.

~

It was also during my Warsaw period that I finally admitted to myself that I wanted to write—a dream that had been brewing below my conscious mind since reading Dostoevsky in my late teens. I remember telling my literary friend Siri, "The best thing a man can do is to write." Still, I couldn't bring myself to say that *I* wanted to write.

Every Sunday afternoon in Warsaw, I'd go for a long walk in Łazienki Park. Although not far from the city centre, it sprawled over an area of 76 hectares, boasting three types of gardens, a royal palace and the Chopin monument. One Sunday, walking past the monument, I saw the familiar spectacle of tourists being photographed next to the bronze Chopin sitting under a tree. Two boys were leaning over the adjacent pond and churning the water with twigs. A flock of pigeons soared high into the blue sky, turning into mere black specks and then flying in a large arc before swooping low over the pond. Seeing the birds' reflection in the greenish pond water, I had an epiphany.

I need to write, and I need to write about my experience of wakefulness.

I kept walking, immersed in my thoughts. It wasn't sufficient to wake up permanently; I also had to share my experience with others to give back what I'd received from books, teachings, life and the world, in keeping with the Bodhisattva[16] ideal in Mahayana Buddhism. I felt euphoric, boldly imagining myself writing a book that was personal yet universal, deep but not heavy, a book that would awaken the reader and inspire them to embark on their own quest toward wakefulness.

Later, in a saner state of mind, I had to admit to my crestfallen self that I might not have what it would take to pull off such an ambitious project. I'd never written anything creative in my

---

16   Unlike in the Hinayana, or the small vehicle of Buddhism—of which Theravada is one school—where the goal is individual liberation, in Mahayana, or the great vehicle of Buddhism, the aim is to become a Bodhisattva, someone who undertakes the journey to liberation not just for themselves but for all others as well. They delay achieving enlightenment out of compassion for the suffering of all sentient beings.

life! Except, perhaps, for the long poem I had written about five years earlier while grieving Aravind. So I took up the practice of doing one page of automatic writing every morning.

Around this time, I heard about a club that had opened in my neighbourhood, supposedly owned by the daughter of Polish filmmaker Andrzej Wajda, and went to check it out one Saturday night. The following Sunday, as I walked through Łazienki Park as usual, images of the previous night kept coming back to me. I remembered how the girl at the door looked guilty when she asked me to pay the cover charge of thirty-five zlotys. *Did I look as if I couldn't afford it? But I was wearing my smart Mexx jacket!* I climbed the marble staircase, went over to the bar and saw a number of white couches placed at two ends of the dance floor. *Surely, Wajda's daughter should have better taste than this.* The bartender put my vodka and orange on a white napkin but didn't give back my change. *Did she think I wanted her to keep the change? Should I ask her for it? No, I don't want to come across as cheap on my first visit.*

After the walk I took out my portable computer and wrote down my impressions of the club. I emailed it to the editor of the *Warsaw Insider*, a monthly English-language entertainment guide. She emailed back right away. "I want to buy your piece. Don't send it to anyone else."

~

Meanwhile, life in Warsaw was like a vacation that kept delighting. My job wasn't demanding but my salary was high, by local standards, which made me feel guilty. I told my Polish friends and colleagues that I wanted to "pump as much money as possible back into the local economy." I went out two, three or sometimes even four nights per week, ate often in trendy restaurants, and travelled around in taxis. I had the same feeling of abundance as in my early years in Paris, when I didn't even have a bank account and carried all my money in my pocket but spent "with no thought for the morrow."

I had always lived in fully furnished apartments, but for the first time, I did some redecorating by buying colourful cushions and a couple of potted plants. I hung a couple of Van Gogh prints on the bare walls and put fresh flowers on the kitchen and lounge tables every week.

With hindsight, I can see that the Warsaw years were a well-deserved vacation for me—a period of respite between my dark night of the soul experience in Mount Lavinia and the long, intense emotional work that was awaiting me when I'd eventually return to Montreal after my mini odyssey through Vancouver, Mount Lavinia, London, Warsaw and Moscow.

~

My three-year, three-month and three-day "vacation" in Poland came to an abrupt end when I went to a dinner at a restaurant organized by my friend Lena and found myself sitting next to Katerina, a former date. After a lengthy conversation with the person sitting to her left, she finally turned to me.

"Hey, you know what? I went to see a psychic. I asked her about you as well, and she told me, 'Forget about this guy. He'll be leaving Poland soon and will never come back.'"

I'd have liked to know why she asked a psychic about me, as we hadn't seen each other in a while, but instead I said, "C'mon, Katerina, how can anyone tell the future? My life here is great. I have no intention of leaving Poland."

A few days later, I had lunch at Ti Amo, across the street from my office. I cut a corner of the square naleśniki—a thick pancake filled with spinach and egg—dipped the piece into the creamy horseradish sauce and popped it into my mouth. As I savoured the heady mix of sweet, sharp and tangy flavours, I knew with certainty something I hadn't known before.

The psychic was right. It was time to move on.

~

I had met Katerina at one of Lena's many house parties during my first year in Warsaw. When I was introduced to her, she gave me an unfriendly look and moved away. So I was surprised when Lena called me the following day and invited me to a dinner party at Katerina's place the upcoming Friday. During the week Lena called me several times to confirm I'd be going, which puzzled me. On Friday evening she picked me up and we drove to Katerina's place, which turned out to be a penthouse apartment. Far too swanky for a Polish girl in her early twenties! So Katerina was rich.

It also turned out that the dinner party was made up of just the three of us. And the dinner in question was Chinese takeout she'd ordered beforehand. Katerina busied herself serving out the food, and I uncorked the bottle of red wine I had brought. In the background, Leonard Cohen mournfully sang *The Anthem* whose lyrics were possibly inspired by a quote attributed to Rumi.[17] To break the ice, and perhaps to impress Katerina, I said, "I used to practise Zen in Leonard Cohen's house in Montreal."

I hastened to add, "He wasn't there, of course. He was in a monastery in California at the time."

We sat down to a meal of warm egg rolls, followed by Cantonese fried rice with fiery Szechuan-style shrimps and a broccoli and carrot stir-fry. I picked up a broccoli floret with my

---

17   The wound is the place where the light enters you.

chopsticks and held it up, admiring its greenness before tasting its juicy texture. I was tempted to say that eating with chopsticks made the experience so much more sensual but decided against it, not wanting Katerina to think I was trying to impress her.

We had hardly finished eating when Lena stood up. "I've got to go. I have a report to finish for tomorrow morning."

I stood up too, assuming that since she had brought me there, she'd be taking me home as well.

But Lena said sharply, "Where are *you* going? You don't have a report to write. You can stay, and Katerina will call you a taxi when you're ready to go."

I sat down obediently. This Lena was quite different from the solicitous Lena who had brought me there.

About a week later, I took Katerina out to dinner at the Rabarbar, a bar-cum-restaurant and another of my favourite haunts. Zofia, one of the bartenders, with luxurious dark hair and girlish bangs, stood out in a land full of blondes. Initially, she was cold and distant, but soon she'd greet me with an extra-wide smile as soon as I walked in. One night, she even offered to give me Polish lessons in exchange for English conversation. But I never took her up on her offer.

On the dinner date I had smoked salmon on blinis and a salad of thinly sliced cucumber with fresh dill and sour cream. Katerina told me about her fancy car, a Jaguar I believe, her weekend shopping trips to Milan and her frequent jaunts to St. Moritz during the skiing season.

I guess I didn't look impressed enough, so to make things abundantly clear, Katerina laid her forearms across the table, leaned forward and said, bright-eyed, "You know, I'm very rich."

After dinner we went next door to the Barbados club. It was well past midnight when Katerina told me she wanted to go home. We stood outside waiting for a taxi when something inexplicable happened.

I saw myself saying goodbye to Katerina and abruptly walking away. I went home, made myself a snack of Polish white cheese on a slice of toast, ate it while watching *Fashion TV* and went to bed, feeling quite pleased with myself.

It was only when I woke up the next morning that it hit me.

How could I have left my young date stranded on a deserted Warsaw street in the middle of the night?

It took repeated abject apologies conveyed through Lena, emails and voice mail over a two-week period to convince Katerina to see me again. But I could sense she no longer trusted me. I felt genuine contrition for what had happened, but it surprises me now that I didn't seem particularly puzzled by my conduct.

~

Back at work, after the epiphany during the pancake lunch at Ti Amo, I moved quickly, giving notice to my boss and my landlord. Once these formalities were completed, I felt uneasy as if I had forgotten something. And then it occurred to me.

I don't know where I'm going next!

After a moment of existentialist panic, I figured I was now ready go back to Canada and start over. But I couldn't decide on which city. Should I return to Vancouver or to Montreal? Or maybe I'd have a better chance of finding work in Toronto. As I was mulling over these choices, a new option emerged.

Why not go to Moscow?

Given all the influence that Russia had had on my life, from Dostoevsky to Marx, to Gurdjieff and Ouspensky, it would be a missed opportunity to return to Canada without checking out neighbouring Moscow.

Chapter 13
People's Cathedral, Moscow

Thirteen years after the Berlin Wall fell, I flew into Moscow Sheremetyevo Airport. I arrived on April 13, which happened to be the Sri Lankan New Year, and the anniversary of my father's death. The border security agent scrutinized my business visa. Finally, she reluctantly stamped my passport and handed it back with a look that said, "I'm pretty sure you're not what you're making yourself out to be, but I've got nothing on you, so off you go."

I had studied a bit of Russian during my student days in Paris, planning to read Dostoevsky in the original Russian, but I tend to forget quickly what I learn. So I had booked two weeks of individual language lessons along with a room at Moscow State University, better known by its Russian acronym, MGU. I figured that at the least I had to learn the Cyrillic alphabet in order to find my way around Moscow.

Located in southwestern Moscow, almost on the city's outskirts, MGU's main building is one of the Seven Sisters dominating the Moscow skyline, replicated in Warsaw, and also built using Gulag inmates. For about fifty years since construction, it held the distinction of being the tallest building in Europe.

I got out of the van that had brought me from the airport and gazed at it. A monumental edifice, it combined Russian Baroque and Gothic styles with a wedding cake-like structure of stout bases and rising towers, topped off with a spire. As I'd discover later, it housed a small city teeming with life. Stalin's label for it, "the people's cathedral," seemed fitting. In the lobby, chandeliers hanging from high ceilings lit the incongruous spectacle of a vegetable seller with his produce spread on the marble floor. As I climbed the majestic staircase to the elevators, I had to step around a man on his knees cleaning the tiles with a dirty rag.

My room was on the seventh floor, reserved for foreigners studying Russian. I dropped my bags and looked around. The room was narrow and small but it shared an anteroom containing a fridge, toilet and shower with the adjoining room—comforts even a contemporary student in the West would be grateful for but which must have been unheard of luxuries in the postwar Soviet Union.

Exploring the seventh floor, I discovered a small cafeteria with a view of the Moskva River. A stocky man in a cheap grey suit sat near the entrance. I later learned he was the manager, an Armenian, who'd bring the day's supplies in his rickety old car in the morning and then sit at the same table staring silently into space. Someone told me that he suffered from PTSD, having fought with the Soviet Army in Afghanistan.

A young man with short-cropped black hair, sitting with his back straight at one of the tables, tucked into a large, flaky pastry that looked like feuilletés au fromage. Feeling hungry, I went up to him and asked what it was.

He gave me a wide grin. "Kachapuri."

I ordered one from the kitchen counter. The guy half swivelled in his chair, motioning me to come and sit with him with a wave of his arm. He introduced himself as Leo and told me he was a lawyer from Geneva.

"Since graduating seven years ago, I've been spending a couple of months every year in a different country learning its language. Last year I was in Brazil, learning Portuguese."

I'd have liked to know how he pulled that off professionally and financially, but decided that a Swiss lawyer might not appreciate such personal questions, especially from someone he'd just met.

Instead, I said, "I'd love to do something like that as well. Each time I learn a new language, I find it's a mind-blowing experience."

The young waitress, soon-to-become the ubiquitous Svetlana—except for periods when she went missing, on a drunken binge, according to an uncharitable few—served me the kachapuri straight from the oven. I cut off a piece of the warm oblong pastry, put it into my mouth and waited for the taste of melting cheese to hit my palate.

I brushed the flakes off my mouth. "This is better than feuilletés au fromage. The pastry has a different texture, and it's cheesier."

Leo nodded, again with a wide grin.

The next day I started my new routine. I hadn't thought that sitting from nine to twelve in the morning across from my language instructor Sonya, who only spoke Russian, would be so intense. I had to take a long nap afterwards to restore my energy. I'd then grab a quick bite at the cafeteria, do my homework, walk briskly around our building—which was so large it took me about twenty minutes—and go back to the cafeteria for dinner. This busy routine left me little or no time to look for suitable employment as I had planned.

At the cafeteria, I made two other friends. Georges, a serious-minded young man from Brussels, had a solid plan to learn Russian and then go on to do graduate studies at MGU. Thirty-something Paul, a gentle, gangly giant from London, didn't have any plan at all and was even somewhat surprised to find himself at MGU. He was quite jealous that my instructor Sonya was young and attractive. She had a likeness to a Hollywood star who had coincidentally played a Russian woman in a recent movie.

"Bloody hell, man, you got the hot movie star. They assigned me a bald commie!"

One day, at the cafeteria, I sat at the same table as Hoki, a Japanese student and long-time resident at MGU. To make room for me, he moved the voluminous dog-eared book he carried around everywhere. I looked at the book curiously and he turned it over to show me the title, *Ulysses*.

"I only read a page or two at a time," he said. "Joyce has to be savoured like a fine wine, you know. One sip at a time."

I had read *Ulysses* several times at different points in my life, or rather, I'd tried to. I must have skipped over a good part of it each time. "I can see why it's considered an important work in terms of style," I said, "but does it really say anything? All those innovations seemed quite contrived and gimmicky. All style, but no substance."

Was I a bit too frank? I added hastily, "I liked *A Portrait of the Artist as a Young Man*, though. Stephen Dedalus's search for identity resonated more with me."

Hoki gave me a pitying smile. "Joyce is so subtle that it takes a lifetime of study to get him."

Svetlana served me a kachapuri. Feeling a bit irritated, I tucked into it hurriedly, forgetting to savour it as usual. "My all-time favourite is Dostoevsky. He might not have been innovative, but he makes up for it with plenty of substance."

Hoki shook his head. "Dostoevsky is too in your face. It's a turn-off."

"Not for me," I replied. "I read Dostoevsky when I was about sixteen. His larger-than-life characters and their yearning for meaning brought to the surface all the existential questions buried in me. If not for Dostoevsky, I'd probably be in a middle-class suburb somewhere, leading a typical middle-class life, without thinking too much of what life is all about."

~

I had unwittingly timed my arrival in Moscow one week before Hitler's birthday, widely celebrated by the burgeoning local neo-Nazi movement. There was much talk about it at MGU, and we were warned not to go into central Moscow for a couple of days.

For my belated first outing in Moscow, I went to visit Red Square and the Dostoevsky museum. I went by metro, which is a tourist attraction in itself, with marble walls and chandeliers hanging from ceilings opulently decorated with mosaics. It was interesting to note that most commuters had a book in their hands. I got off at the Okhotny Ryad station, entered Red Square through the Resurrection Gate and was greeted with a sense of vastness. I walked over the historic cobblestones with the wall enclosing the Kremlin complex on my right, feeling tingling sensations working themselves up my legs and spreading to my torso. But soon my attention was taken up by the fairy tale-like Saint Basil's Cathedral rising into the sky at the other end of the square, with its riot of colours and distinctive cluster of turban-shaped domes. In undulating colours of green, white, red and blue, the domes gave Red Square a merry and playful look, belying its sometimes bloody history.

After wandering around Red Square, I took the metro to the Mendeleevskaya station and walked to the Dostoevsky museum, housed in his childhood home. It's located in the compound of the hospital for the poor, where Dostoevsky's father was a physician. As I walked through the house, looking at the now deserted hospital compound through the windows, I imagined young Fyodor looking out the same windows and seeing hospital patients in varying stages of illness and decay in the garden. I wondered whether this exposure to human suffering at an early age could have formed his character and influenced his writing. I later shared this insight with Sonya and she was visibly impressed.

Toward the end of my three-month stay in Moscow, I took the night train to Saint Petersburg and visited the apartment in which *The Brothers Karamazov* had been written, now another Dostoevsky museum. I emerged from the metro and then stood at a street crossing, not sure which way to go. I wanted to ask for directions from a young woman who was also waiting to cross, but I didn't. She walked ahead, and I took off in a different direction and went around in circles. When I got to the museum, the same girl was there.

The initially scheduled two weeks at MGU had passed quickly. The exhaustion I'd feel immediately after the Russian class subsequently gave way to a kind of high, similarly to how I felt when I had learned Polish about three years previously, and French about two decades before that. Learning a new language had sparked life into dormant neurons in my brain, making my mind more spacious and relaxed. I had also taken a liking to my new life at MGU, so I decided to extend my stay there indefinitely.

On Fridays Sonya didn't teach a formal class but instead took me out on field trips to various parts of Moscow. She was generous with her time, spending a good part of the day with me but only charging me for the usual three hours. During those trips she told me she had a young daughter and was living with her husband and father-in-law, a distinguished general, in a building once reserved for the Soviet elite. One day, she also confided in me that she wasn't happy with her life, but I didn't probe any further.

Early on in my Moscow stay, Leo, Georges, Paul and I went to visit the Kremlin complex. Among other historical structures, it enclosed four cathedrals built around a square, their golden cupolas glinting in the sun. We also visited the Armoury Chamber with its treasure trove of ancient Russian regalia, and several imposing palaces, all packed into a small area. Feeling a bit overwhelmed, we emerged from our tour into the refreshing vastness of Red Square and stood in line to visit the Lenin Mausoleum.

The talk turned to the failures of Marxism. I confessed to having been influenced by its ideals.

"Really?" asked Paul. "I thought that went out of fashion a long time ago."

"Well, I'm always a bit behind the times. I had a close friend back home who was involved in student politics, and he kept talking to me about Marxism. I resisted his arguments at first but was slowly seduced, becoming a kind of closet Marxist until I finally came out as a believer myself. I found the Marxist idea that man could be transformed by changing his material conditions compelling."

We never got to see Lenin's embalmed body since the doors closed before we got to the front of the line, so we decided to have a drink in a nearby bar before heading back to MGU. I had not had any wine since I left Warsaw, so I wanted to try a glass of the Georgian variety. Leo and the others ordered beers.

Leo turned to me and said with his customary wide grin, "Why are you drinking wine? You should be drinking beer."

"Who are you to tell me what to drink?"

Leo's grin faded and I took another sip of wine, surprised by my uncharacteristically aggressive reaction.

For a large and leading world city, official taxis are surprisingly rare in Moscow. To hail a ride one has to stick out a hand and negotiate a price with the driver of the first car that stops. Having succeeded in our negotiations, I settled into the back seat while Leo sat in front and chatted away with the driver.

I heard the driver saying, "I used to be a scientist working in the MIR space station's ground operations but lost my job after the Soviet Union fell apart. So now I'm driving a private taxi."

We sped past medieval churches with minaret-like onion domes twinkling in the bluish-black night sky. I marvelled at how magical Moscow looked at night, with the lights magnifying its past glory while the darkness masked its more recent shabbiness. At the same time, the unpleasant interaction with Leo played over and over at the back of my mind. He was right about the wine. It was awful.

But it wasn't the only time Leo triggered me. Another evening, Leo, Paul and I decided to go out to a club. When we came out of the MGU gates, I wanted to flag down a car, but Leo insisted on taking the metro. It just happened that we got off at the wrong station and had to take a private taxi anyway. I was livid.

Sitting in the front seat, I ranted, "You guys need to grow up. Who ever heard of adult men taking public transit to a club?"

For good measure, I refused to pay my share of the fare and neither Leo nor Paul dared to protest.

The cafeteria on our floor at MGU was mostly patronized by foreigners sprinkled with a few Russian men and a lone woman, Nina, who stood out with her angelic face, petite figure, wavy dark hair and flashing smile. I had noticed her but hadn't spoken to her until Leo introduced us. She seemed to wear the same clothes all the time—red jeans and a close-fitting black top. Except for this rather disconcerting fact, she was ultra-feminine, reminding me of Henry's comment on French women's femininity and my subsequently formulated theory on how language structure, more specifically inflection, can influence gender identity. As the Russian language also inflects for gender, and in fact, all parts of its grammar are inflected, Nina further confirmed my theory.

I ran into her one day in the cafeteria. She asked me for some milk to give to her cat, so we went back to my room together and I poured out some milk on a saucer. She sat on the corner of my bed, balancing the saucer in her hand, and kept chatting. After she left I thought it was a bit odd that MGU would allow students to keep pets in their rooms.

One Friday during lunch Leo told me he and Nina were going out to a club and invited me to come along. Later that evening we walked through the labyrinth of underground corridors to Nina's room. She was wearing her usual red jeans and black top. I made sure to look around for signs of a cat but didn't find any.

We stood at the bar with Nina perched on a stool between us. We had hardly started on our drinks when Leo took Nina's hand and led her to the dance floor, but before long she came back, looking flustered and quite unlike her usual poised self.

"What happened to Leo?"

"He's still in there. He tried to get fresh with me, but I don't like him in that way."

After a short while Leo joined us again with his customary wide grin, chatting as if nothing untoward had happened.

"Russia should become more European and eventually join the EU," he said.

I felt a surge of excessive anger. "Of course not. Russia should build on her history and forge her own path between Europe and Asia. Europe has only consumerism to offer, and the EU is a bureaucratic nightmare. Look at Switzerland—it's a country of robots. Russians are a people with passion. Do you want them to become like the Swiss?"

Leo took my outburst calmly. Nina looked uncomfortable, stuck between the two of us.

Leo was a likeable guy, and I enjoyed the feeling of male camaraderie I got from hanging out with him. But something about him didn't seem quite right, as if he was making himself out to be someone he wasn't. For instance, he liked to cultivate an image of himself as a hard-drinking man, organizing small vodka parties at MGU. But he didn't drink much, instead urging others to drink, including myself.

On one such occasion Leo said to one of the guys present, "You don't look Russian. You look like a European."

I pounced on him. "What do you mean? Is that supposed to be a compliment? Really? Haven't you seen how beautiful Russian women are? They're definitely way better looking than Swiss women."

It wasn't just Leo who caused me to react aggressively in Moscow. One day, during the Russian class, I was taking my time to respond to a question when Sonya said impatiently, "*Davai, davai!*"

"Don't talk to me like that," I snapped back.

Unlike Leo, who didn't show any hard feelings, Sonya cooled toward me after that incident. She had planned for us to see *The Seagull* as I had made the effort to reread Chekhov's play in Russian, but she called it off even though she had already bought the tickets. So, on a muggy June evening, I went alone to the Chekhov Moscow Art Theatre and saw the play alongside a packed and highly appreciative audience. I found that quite extraordinary, since the play had been showing there every day for a number of years.

I saw first-hand Russians' attachment and loyalty to their literary greats when Georges and I went to the Pushkin monument in central Moscow to attend the celebrations of Pushkin's birthday. They consisted of a literary marathon with his adoring fans stepping up to the foot of his statue one after another to recite his poems from morning till night. The highlight for me was when I heard and recognized a couple of lines from Pushkin's famous poem on love.

> *Silently and hopelessly I loved you,*
> *At times too jealous and at times too shy.*
> *God grant you find another who will love you*
> *As tenderly and truthfully as I* [18]

The vulnerability that came across in the poem and the magnanimous words hinting at unconditional love was at odds with Pushkin's persona as a Don Juan and his penchant for duels. As we walked back to the metro, a large block of concrete from an old building fell to the sidewalk just in front of us and shattered into pieces.

"Pushkin's poetry endures, but the same can't be said for Moscow's buildings," Georges said.

Later during my stay at MGU, Georges invited me on a day trip with two of his Russian friends to visit Yasnaya Polyana,

---

18   Translation by Babette Deutsch.

Tolstoy's estate museum located about 200 km from Moscow. On the way there in the bus, I ran out of things to say to one of the girls sitting next to me, and the talk I had with Hoki came to mind. It occurred to me that a similar comparison could be made of Dostoevsky and Tolstoy. Although Tolstoy was a sublime craftsman, I didn't think that anyone's life would have been changed by reading *War and Peace*, whereas I had come across a number of accounts of how *The Brothers Karamazov* had transformed readers. But it was Tolstoy, and not Dostoevsky, who seemed to have been on a quest for meaning throughout his turbulent life.

We explored Tolstoy's white-painted manor house with its green roof, where he wrote *War and Peace* and *Anna Karenina*. We dutifully looked at all the memorabilia and admired his vast library of some twenty-two thousand books, but it was only upon seeing his unmarked grave that Tolstoy came alive to me that day. According to his wishes, he'd been buried in the nearby forest under a green mound in the middle of an even greener, peaceful and idyllic clearing. Nature and the earth were the only testaments that Tolstoy needed.

During lunch the talk naturally turned to Tolstoy's works.

"I recently read the autobiographical trilogy he wrote in his twenties and found it had a special quality," I said. "So I'm quite surprised no one seems to know much about it. The first book starts when the narrator is ten, and he already has a lot of self-awareness. He seems to be quite aware of what's going on in his mind and around him."

Encouraged by the look of interest on my audience's faces, I continued, "For me it had a similar feel to Knut Hamsun's *Hunger*, which was widely acclaimed as one of the first modern works because of its psychological dimension. But Tolstoy wrote his trilogy about fifty years earlier!"

On the way back in the bus, the discussion, or rather, my monologue kept repeating in my mind and I wondered whether it was Tolstoy's self-awareness that made him a writer and later led to his spiritual awakening and becoming a born-again Christian. Self-awareness starts with becoming aware of thoughts in the mind and could eventually lead to *awareness of awareness*—awareness of the thinker thinking the thoughts.

Three months went by, and unlike my somewhat precipitous departure from Warsaw, the decision to leave Moscow was more of an inevitability. My feeble efforts at finding work had not yielded any appreciable results. Adapting to life in a large city was one of my strengths, but I didn't feel entirely comfortable in Moscow. I had always roamed city streets late at night without any thought for my safety, but in Moscow I was constantly on the alert for any potential danger, even in broad daylight. Everywhere I went, I felt an undercurrent of some harsh emotion, perhaps seething resentment. With hindsight, it could also have been my own emotions rising to the surface.

About a month into my stay in Moscow, Georges and I went to the Bolshoi Theatre to see a nineteenth-century Italian opera. We emerged from the metro with thoughts of nothing but spending a delightful evening of high culture. Instead, we came upon a scene of extreme violence: burning cars, smoke billowing in the air, shattered shop windows, broken glass on the sidewalks, and eerily empty streets, the silence broken only by the wailing of police sirens. Gangs of football hooligans had unleashed their anger and resentment after the Russian national team had lost an important game to Belgium.

Nothing of note actually happened to me, even though I

took risks by going out alone at night and flagging down cars in the early morning hours to get back to MGU. One Friday, Sonya and I were walking along the popular and artsy Arbat, a kilometre-long pedestrian street lined with historical buildings, when a young couple looking like neo-Nazis came up to us. The girl said something to Sonya, who was taken aback. I asked her what the girl said, but Sonya pretended she didn't understand.

Cured of the uncertainty I'd had in Warsaw over where in Canada to return to, I had no hesitation in booking a flight to Montreal. It pleased me to learn that the flight was transiting through Paris, which meant that I'd be repeating the same trip I had made about nine years earlier. It felt like I was starting afresh, even though I didn't know then that I had unfinished business to take care of in Montreal.

On the flight to Paris, I noticed a young mixed-race boy, about seven years old, sitting a couple of rows ahead of me. It was only after we disembarked that I realized he was travelling alone. In the labyrinth that is Charles de Gaulle Airport, we crossed paths several times, and although the boy seemed to want to give the impression he knew where he was going, I sensed he was lost and needed help. A boy so young shouldn't be travelling alone, I told myself, but I didn't offer to help.

Later, as I sat in the waiting lounge, the look on the boy's face kept appearing in my mind. I imagined myself taking him to where he needed to go, buying him a meal and asking him about his life before handing him over to the care of airline employees, and patting myself on the back for being such a great guy.

I remembered a similar incident in another airport. During my second year in Montreal, I went to the airport to meet Simone, a friend from Paris. Her flight was delayed, and while waiting, I noticed a little boy sitting on the edge of his seat. He kept looking around. Time went by and minutes turned into an hour, but no one came to pick up the boy, who hadn't budged. He was acting as if nothing was awry, except for his swivelling head, and I sensed his fear of being abandoned. I wanted to reach out, but each time I turned toward the boy, I choked up and had to look aside to brush away tears.

Chapter 14
Mount Royal Revisited

I landed at Montréal-Trudeau International Airport on a muggy Montreal summer evening. In the taxi on my way downtown, I thought about Antoine's hint five years earlier that I might be running away.

If he was right, am I now coming back to face the music?

So I felt like the prodigal son when I checked into a cheap hotel at the corner of Sainte-Catherine Street and Boulevard Saint-Laurent. The harried receptionist didn't seem too pleased to see me, clearly playing the role of the older brother who stayed at home and did the hard work.

Sainte-Catherine Street was bustling with tourists. I counted myself lucky to have found a hotel room for one night at relatively short notice. Partygoers bustled outside my window for most of the night. After a restless sleep I had an early breakfast and headed out on a quest for suitable housing. I climbed Boulevard Saint-Laurent, turned left on Sherbrooke Street, gravitated toward the McGill Ghetto and found myself in front of my old building on Durocher Street. Newly renovated, the building had a No Vacancy sign on the door. And it was pretty much the same everywhere I went, and so unlike the situation nearly ten years earlier when Montreal was a renter's paradise, especially for someone coming from Paris.

Discouraged by doors being shut and heads shaken in my face, I popped into The Word on Milton, just across the street from my old building, to cheer myself up. I had spent many hours browsing there during my earlier four-year stay in Montreal. This McGill Ghetto institution reminded me of the Shakespeare and Company bookshop in Paris.

I then headed back to the hotel to check out, passing by the café at the corner of Milton and Park where I used to go for a falafel sandwich and sip a cup of tea while reading the now sadly defunct *Montreal Mirror*, a free weekly alternative newspaper. The ubiquitous and tired-looking owner claimed he served the best falafel sandwich in town. I wouldn't have gone that far, but the sandwich was certainly filling, as it was made with a large pita bread and three falafel balls instead of the usual two. One day, I mentioned to the man that he seemed to be there all the time.

He looked at me wearily. "I can't find anyone to replace me. They all steal from me."

Looking up at me, he said, "You look like an honest man. Would you like to come and work for me?"

I declined.

Seeing the café, I felt like a falafel sandwich, something I hadn't eaten in several years. The same man was behind the counter, and the bags under his eyes were bigger. He didn't recognize me. I watched him pop three falafel balls into the microwave, toss a pita bread flat on the counter, slap some hummus in the middle and spread it with a knife. He then added the filling along a broad band in the middle of the pita, starting with lettuce and then piling on slices of tomatoes, onion rings, chopped parsley and a couple of pink marinated turnips cut like french fries. I asked him to add some grated carrots and coleslaw. He took the warm falafel balls from the microwave and pressed them flat on top of the vegetables, then drizzled it with some tahini from a plastic bottle.

He held up a similar bottle with red sauce. "Hot sauce?"

I nodded and he squirted some red sauce on the falafels, covered one end of the pita bread with the other, wrapped the sandwich with a piece of waxed paper and put it on the grill.

Still savouring the sweetness of the carrots and the coleslaw that balanced out the slightly bitter taste of other ingredients, I kept heading east on Milton. Despite the imminent prospect of becoming homeless, part of my mind was unconcerned, while another part berated me for my insouciance.

I then saw a Furnished Apartments Available sign on the door of a boxy white building at the corner of Milton and Saint Urbain. I pressed the button on the intercom. A smiling East Asian man opened the door and showed me a studio apartment on the seventh floor. It was smaller than my previous place on Durocher but furnished, excessively so. The rent was more than double. But seeing Mount Royal's green top through the floor-to-ceiling windows, I took it.

"I'll get my stuff from my hotel and be right back."

"What happened to you? Did your wife kick you out?" The man threw back his head and had a hearty laugh.

After plunking down my large duffle bag and laptop case in the apartment, I went for a walk up Mount Royal. I first headed west on Milton, then continued on Prince Arthur and turned north on Park Avenue. The busy street ahead opened up to spacious, rolling green fields on either side. I stopped at the traffic lights in front of the George-Étienne Cartier monument but was in no hurry to cross, lingering to take in the scene.

The winged Goddess of Liberty perched on top of the monument with her palm soaring into the blue sky, dwarfing the mountain which in turn peeked over the abundant dark green foliage of street-level trees. The sound of traffic quietened, went silent for a minute or so, then picked up again. In unison, the stream of discursive thoughts in my mind came to a standstill, but the inner silence wasn't deep enough for me to truly connect to the beauty of it all. The more I tried, the more elusive it became. I crossed Park Avenue, thinking about the Buddha's teaching on *tanha*, or grasping, which is the cause of *dukkha*, suffering, the essential human condition, and about William Blake who said something similar in "Eternity":

> *He who binds to himself a joy*
> *Does the winged life destroy*
> *But he who kisses the joy as it flies*
> *Lives in eternity's sunrise*

I crossed the open green space on the northern side of the monument, and went up the broad path past the first level of Chemin Olmsted, which winds up the mountain. As expected—unlike downtown Montreal that had prospered during my absence, with shiny new buildings coming up and others undergoing renovation—the park seemed somewhat the worse for wear. It had thinned on the slopes, with fallen trees replaced by mere saplings following the 1998 ice storm. I had moved to Vancouver about six months prior to that, and walking on balmy English Bay while Quebec was being battered by ice, I'd counted myself lucky. I hadn't known then that a more frightening storm was brewing in my mind.

I climbed the steps cut into the stone and took the footpath starting from the bend at the second level of the road. The footpath transformed itself into a wooden bridge over a trickling stream and then became a flight of dusty stairs and meandered up through the woods. Seeing a giant fallen tree in a large clearing of tall saplings on the right of the footpath, I walked over and laid my hand gently on it, thinking it might have fallen at the same time I was falling apart in Vancouver. I then lay down on the tree, Alexander Technique style, with my knees up and feet flat, crossed palms cradling my head and feeling the rough bark cutting into my back. Rays of sunshine filtered through the branches of the tall trees that rose into the hazy blue sky. I tried to distinguish between the loud and persistent bird calls. The sun shone directly on some leaves making them a translucent lime-green, while others shielded from the sun stayed dark green. Marvelling at the interplay of light and dark even on leaves of the same branch, I looked more closely and even spied a leaf that was part light and part dark. When I got off the fallen tree, I felt my awareness had descended into my body, giving rise to a sense of expansion and well-being.

Over the days that followed, that feeling of being in my body kept coming back, which seemed like a good omen. On the flight from Moscow, I had set two intentions for my second coming to Montreal: continue developing body awareness, one of the four foundations of mindfulness, and finally start writing my book.

~

During my stay in Warsaw, I had hosted a small vipassana group at my place, so I looked around for a group to sit with in Montreal. I found one at the Ashtanga yoga studio on Sainte-Catherine Street. As soon as I entered the large, empty, open space with hardwood floors and saw the setting sunlight pouring in through the floor-to-ceiling windows, I sensed my awareness shifting to my body.

I'm in the right place!

Although I hadn't necessarily planned to take up yoga again to develop body awareness, I went back to the studio the next morning to try out a class. I found that the sun salutation was different from what I had practised before—instead of flowing through down dog, we took five breaths in it. During the first down dog, I felt my hands and feet rooting to the mat and energy surging at the bottom of my spine, which formed the apex of a triangle.

As I walked out, I told the teacher, "I sweated a lot. I need to go back home and take another shower."

She nodded approvingly but with a tight-lipped smile that made me wonder whether I smelled foul.

"I usually don't sweat," I added, feeling the need to justify myself, "and I've practised yoga before, but I've never sweated like this."

"That's normal. This yoga series is very detoxifying, so in the beginning you sweat a lot."

I walked down the stairs, feeling soiled on the outside but cleansed inside. When I cut across the Place des Arts with my newly purchased purple yoga mat under my arm, I became aware of my feet on the ground. It had been a couple of years since I first felt that grounding sensation in Warsaw on my way to work. I went to the yoga studio every day for the next three months, and on my way back home, I'd feel my feet on the ground from time to time. But it would take another decade of efforts, both physical and psychological, before the sensation of feet on the ground became integrated into my day-to-day awareness.

After settling into my new life in Montreal, I looked up Antoine in the phone book and wrote him a letter in case he didn't want to see me for some reason. I had emailed him from Moscow to tell him about my upcoming return to Montreal, but hadn't gotten a response. Since parting ways at the main train station in Montreal about five years earlier, we had been in touch via email and phone. He'd even wanted to come to Sri Lanka to see me after he learned about the state I had gotten myself into. He was backpacking in Europe at the time, revisiting some of his youthful haunts.

"I need to do this kind of thing one more time before I'm too old," he'd told me.

My letter was returned undelivered, but I had a hunch I'd bump into Antoine sooner or later. So, when I heard someone call out my name while hurrying down Sainte-Catherine Street on my way to yoga, and Antoine appeared out of nowhere, I wasn't greatly surprised. But it was surprising that he didn't seem too pleased to see me. No hug, handshake or even a smile.

He came over to my place for lunch a few days later. When I took out the baked salmon from the oven to serve him, Antoine leaned back in his chair and put his hands in the air, palms outstretched toward me in a stop sign.

"Is this salmon wild or farmed?"

"I don't know," I said, sensing trouble. "It didn't say. But given the price, I'd say it's farmed."

He went on to make a long speech about the enormous harm done by salmon farms to fish stocks and the environment. Not that eating wild salmon was a solution either, he cautioned me, wagging a finger. He had broken up with a girlfriend because she wouldn't use phosphate-free detergent. It was a question of principles. He then picked up his knife and fork, tapped the top of the handles on the table, and said that out of respect for my hospitality, he'd eat the farmed salmon. He did so, with gusto.

Between mouthfuls, he asked me, "Are you still doing your Tantric practice of semen retention?"

"Yes, it became second nature for me quickly. It shifts your focus onto the now and your true needs instead of the wants created by society. If a critical mass of people did the same, perhaps it could bring about real transformation in the world. But like I said before, it's not for everyone."

He told me that he was no longer doing yoga. He had been kicked out of the Sivananda yoga ashram in Val-Morin after he criticized the centre's director for something she had said during a *satsang*, the twice-daily meetings consisting of chanting, readings and talks. He told me about the incident matter-of-factly, which surprised me. Antoine had never shied away from expressing his emotions and was quick to denounce anyone who appeared to be "in denial." I was also concerned, knowing that the ashram had become a surrogate family for him, the only family he had since leaving home as a teenager, barring perhaps the Montreal branches of Alcoholics Anonymous and Cocaine Anonymous.

Over a dessert of walnut cake accompanied by black tea, I told him, "I'm doing Ashtanga yoga now. It's a more vigorous form of yoga that develops both flexibility and strength. It's grounding, just what I need. In Sivananda yoga, it seems you work on the body in order to transcend it. That's the classical, outside-in approach, as set out in Patanjali's *Yoga Sutras*, where the purpose of hatha yoga is to prepare the body for meditation and eventually *samadhi*. Ashtanga is about embodiment, about being fully present in the world. It's more of an inside-out approach."

The Antoine I used to know had loved this kind of discussion, but now he responded with a sneer. "You're such a spiritual SOB."

"Not at all. If by spiritual you mean striving to achieve a transcendent state, that's not what I'm trying to do. What I'm seeking is a fully embodied awakened state. As the Buddha said, enlightenment cannot be achieved without a human body. So even the devas[19] have to incarnate themselves on Earth if they want to fully liberate themselves."

I could see he was waiting impatiently for me to finish.

"Whatever the word means," he said, "I'm no longer interested in those things. Mother Earth is bleeding. Sitting on your butt on a meditation cushion or doing yoga to improve the shape of it is not going to help."

"I think it depends on why and how you sit on a cushion or do yoga. If some internal transformation takes place, that change could be reflected in the outside world as well."

Antoine shook his head. "Only political power can bring about change in the world. But first of all, you have to understand what's actually going on. People believe mainstream media, so they don't really know. I get my news from the right sources."

Over the weeks, months and years that followed, we mostly talked about current affairs, but I couldn't pin down Antoine's place on the political spectrum. His politics seemed to be a toxic mix of extreme left- and right-wing views. He looked different when we bumped into each other in the street, but at closer quarters, I could see that something had changed in his face, as if a shadow was cast over it.

I remembered one of the Buddha's discourses in which he talked about four different types of people. Some are going from darkness to darkness, some from darkness to light, some from light to darkness and some from light to light. Of course, nothing is set in stone, and at any moment, the actions we take

---

19   Divine beings.

and the thoughts we think can alter the course of events. Antoine had known several twists and turns in his life, and when I first met him, he seemed to be moving towards light. Now it looked like his life was shifting towards darkness again. I brushed the thought away, but I soon saw that while Antoine had always been prone to bursts of fury, anger was now his default state.

~

After months of searching complicated by the lingering economic fallout of the September 11 attack on the World Trade Center in New York, I was hired by the same company I had worked for and walked away from in Sri Lanka, Paris and Warsaw. I eagerly accepted the job offer, motivated primarily by my tight cash flow situation. But after a week or two, I realized I had a big smile for no reason when sitting in my office, getting a cup of tea in the kitchen, walking over to the printer or talking to a colleague.

I'm in the right place!

Having stayed with the company since then, I wonder now whether this was what the psychic in the Cambodian restaurant in Paris was referring to.

I see you working in a large, structured organization, maybe a consulting company or something like a hospital. That place will be important for your development and your understanding of yourself.

Sitting in my office with the aroma of coffee wafting from the kitchen, I'd feel my feet on the ground, my buttocks on the chair, my torso erect in space and my hands on the laptop keyboard. I'd hear the grinding, percolating and hissing sounds of coffee being brewed in the nearby kitchen and the footsteps of my colleagues walking by. And if I looked through the window while tasting the bitter-sweetness of black tea laced with milk,

I'd see the St. Lawrence River shimmering in the distance to my left.

I'm practising the four foundations of mindfulness while working!

Soon after I joined, a colleague left for a bigger salary elsewhere and was replaced by Spence, who had impressive academic credentials. When he passed by my office, I was struck by how his upper torso tilted backwards when walking, as if he was avoiding meeting life head-on.

I got along well with him until one day, and I can't remember the actual context, he made a reference to excellence, implying I didn't give as much importance to excellence as he did.

Anger flooded my mind, taking up all the space. I forgot where I was.

"Excellence? Who do you think you are to talk about excellence? You're just a small, pathetic man full of repressed emotions, stuck in your ivory tower. You have no idea who I am. I've always pursued authentic meaning in the real world."

That was the gist of it. Later, anger subsided, freeing up sufficient mental space for me to look at what had happened with awareness. I had overreacted. Remembering how Leo had triggered anger in me in Moscow, I concluded that both Leo and Spence were my shadows[20] who were mirroring back to me non-integrated parts of myself. Impressed by my own psychological detective work, I emailed Spence to share my findings and apologise for my unprofessional conduct. He didn't reply and left the company not long afterwards.

---

20   "Everyone carries a shadow, and the less it is embodied in the individual's conscious life, the blacker and denser it is." Carl Jung, Psychology and Religion: West and East, *Collected Works of C.G. Jung*

I kept up my habit of going for walks on Mount Royal. I'd take the footpath to the fallen tree I had come to think of as "my tree," lie on it for a while, and then keep going up to the lookout on Camillien-Houde Way. After catching my breath while admiring the panoramic view of Montreal rooftops, church spires, high-rises and treetops, I'd take the footpath across the mountain, go down the stairs leading to the chalet and follow Chemin Olmsted back to the monument on Park Avenue.

On Boxing Day, about two years after returning to Montreal, I woke to the news that a powerful tsunami had hit several coastal countries in Southeast and South Asia, including Sri Lanka. The southern coast of Sri Lanka, the part of the country I am most familiar with, was the hardest hit. The death toll kept mounting to over twenty thousand. No one I knew was affected. Still, I was grieving, feeling vulnerable yet open. To get away from the news, I went for a walk up Mount Royal. On my way I saw a man with a white fox terrier that reminded me of Tintin's Snowy crossing the path ahead of me. Later, when sitting on my fallen tree, I heard boots crunching the snow behind me. I looked around and saw Tintin and Snowy coming up. Tintin stepped onto the fallen tree, said "Bonjour," jumped down and walked ahead. Snowy jumped lithely onto the fallen tree too, but instead of following his owner, he sat close to me on his hind legs, staring ahead. Tintin called out to Snowy several times, but he wouldn't budge, so finally Tintin came over with a half-irritated, half-amused look on his face and carried the dog away.

I thought about how Olaf the cat had sat on my stomach during Alexander Technique sessions in Warsaw. My mind then jumped back further in time to the date with Delphine in the Sri Lankan restaurant in Paris, when she responded to my reason for choosing to be single.

"No, it's with the right person at your side that you can

follow your dreams."

At the time I'd dismissed her words as romantic delusion. After steeping in my subconscious for over fifteen years, the same words re-emerged but with an aura of truth about them.

She was right!

I cut my walk short and headed back home, not really hearing the snow crunching under my boots or seeing squirrels scampering across the path. I stopped near the monument and remembered the epiphany I had experienced at the same spot almost ten years earlier.

I have a fear of intimacy. But I'm not ready to look at the issue, so I'm going to avoid relationships. Given the truth that had just emerged, I made a new resolution.

I'm now ready to look at the issue.

~

Realizing I had used the word *epiphany* several times without giving it much thought, I did some research on the topic. I found out that originally, *epiphany* referred to the manifestation of Jesus Christ's divinity, and it was James Joyce who first used the word in a secular context as a literary device. I also came across the related work of philosopher Martin Heidegger on Veritas and Aletheia, the Roman and Greek goddesses of truth. Veritas is considered to represent truths coming from the outside, while Aletheia is the incarnation of inner truth that reveals itself.

Not long after the encounter with Snowy and Aletheia's intervention, I met Pascale, a dancer and yoga teacher. The first time she saw me, an unfriendly look came over her face and she looked away. The second time, she gave me a broad smile, the kind of smile I'd see on my mother's face when she welcomed me after a long absence. The fluidity of Pascale's movements and the physical energy she projected drew me to her. She might have made a move toward me and I might not have reacted quickly enough. I tried to make amends, which she took as a cue to become aloof and distant. This push-pull dynamic went on for months, perhaps even a year, however, with some welcome breaks.

Through Pascale, I got to know about a bodywork approach called Hellerwork. Based on the better known Rolfing technique, it consisted of a series of ten deep-tissue massage sessions, each focusing on a specific part of the body. In keeping with my intention to develop body awareness, I signed up for a series of sessions with Jacques. I told Pascale about it as we walked along Sainte-Catherine Street.

She turned toward me. "It'll be interesting, you'll see. Things come up, you know."

I didn't know what she meant then, but I found out following the seventh session, when Jacques worked deep into my neck for an entire hour. I was taking a shower after coming home when Aletheia whispered in my ear.

My problem with intimacy comes from my relationship with my mother!

I stepped out of the shower with a feeling of palpable lightness, as if a weight I had been carrying all my life was finally off my back. In the days that followed, I felt an unusual and subtle energy flowing through me, making me feel alive and whole, as if all the energy I had been using to keep this truth from coming into my awareness was now flowing freely.

In a euphoric state, I called Antoine to tell him about my epiphany. He was unimpressed, even implying he had suspected so all along. But Jacques was impressed and took some credit for my transformation, albeit temporary.

"What exactly is the problem with your mother?" he asked.

"That's the thing, there's no problem at all. Maybe it's because we have such a close bond that there's no space for any other woman in my life."

I naively thought that my problems were all over.

Jacques recommended a book, *Keeping the Love You Find* by Harville Hendrix. Like Ouspensky's book, the title didn't inspire me, but its reading marked a pivotal moment in my awareness, this time of my psychological or shadow self.

What I gleaned from the book was that chronically single people, those who choose to be single and those who are single by default, are not fully matured adults. We're stuck in a childhood development stage because of unresolved wounds related to the parent or primary caregiver of the opposite sex. We have a mental imprint of the positive and negative traits of that caregiver, and when we meet a person with those same traits, there's a strong chemical attraction. Initially, we only see the positive traits that inspire romantic love, but later when the negative traits appear, our old childhood wounds are triggered, creating feelings of disillusionment, abandonment, betrayal, etc. The only real solution is to heal ourselves sufficiently on our own before engaging in a conscious relationship to complete the healing process and set the stage for authentic, unconditional love to arise.

Hendrix didn't really invent anything but simply synthesized various existing psychological approaches and applied them to relationships. I discussed the book with Solange, a friend who happened to be a psychologist.

"Don't you think that childhood wounding is the key issue for understanding relationship problems?"

"It's just one psychological approach among many," she said.

I wasn't too surprised by her response, as I knew that she hadn't worked through her own issues with her father but had simply learned to cope with or avoid them. Naturally, she wasn't too eager to look at her clients' childhood wounding.

I went even further, wondering whether all human behaviour, or misbehaviour, could be understood through the prism of childhood wounding. Inspired by Colin Wilson's thinking, I had reasoned that Antoine's apparent rejection of his own people and the West, and his idealization of authoritarian Russia and China, resulted from his alienated outsider status, namely lack of recognition for his abundant talents.

Instead, could his childhood wounding be at the root of his toxic political views?

I'd soon come to think of this phenomenon as political bypassing—that is, using politics to channel unresolved anger from the past.

I tried to get Antoine to read Hendrix's book but he waved his hand dismissively.

"I don't read those kinds of books."

I should have asked him what he meant by "those kinds of books," but I didn't. However, the next time we met, he brought me *The Wounded Woman* in which Linda Leonard, a Jungian analyst, delves into the childhood wounding of girls resulting from their unsatisfactory relationships with their fathers.

The book sets out the problem of the *puella aeterna* or the girl who never really grows up. In my view, Leonard didn't do justice to the subtitle of her book, *Healing the father-daughter relationship*, while Hendrix did provide a kind of blueprint for healing in his book. But I finally understood what Bibi meant when she cried out, "Woman-child, that's my problem!" And no wonder Bibi loved to talk about Antoine de Saint-Exupéry's *The Little Prince*, the quintessential *puer aeternus*.

I also understood why I hadn't wanted to find out more about her problem. As a closet *puer aeternus* or man-child, I wasn't at all ready then to wade into such deep waters.

Leonard also said that there were two modes of reacting to the father wound: the eternal girl and the armoured Amazon. That seemed like a false dichotomy to me.

Can't a woman be powerful but remain a little girl in some part of her psyche?

Such a woman could be irresistibly attractive, especially to a *puer aeternus*, inspiring both admiration and tenderness.

First featured in the Roman poet Ovid's epic work *Metamorphoses*, *puer aeternus* was later used to refer to one of Carl Jung's archetypes—universal images arising from our collective unconscious. Like other archetypes, the *puer* has both a dark and light side. The dark side is the man- or woman-child who refuses to grow up. The light symbolizes freshness, growth, hope for the future and the hero or heroine *they can become.*

~

I followed the deep-tissue massage experience with various other bodywork approaches, such as Alexander Lowen's bioenergetics exercises, Gabrielle Roth's 5Rhythms, Biodanza and the more well-established osteopathy. On my way to my first osteopathic appointment, while waiting in the metro for the train, I noticed a petite young woman coming toward me, with an alluring Barbie doll look and an open expression. She looked back at me and smiled.

The train came along and we both got in. As it took off, I noticed that the teenage boy sitting next to me was making strange movements with his arms. I pretended not to notice something was awry, as I'm wont to do in such situations. He then fell on the floor, writhing and foaming at the mouth, clearly having an epileptic fit. The young blond woman took charge of the situation, giving instructions to bystanders to hold the boy's legs and arms. I froze, unable to help, and looked on in admiration at the girl's ability to deal effectively with the emergency. At the next station, she and two men carried the boy out, leaving me still shaken.

I went to my appointment and told the osteopath the story of my life, starting with my father's traumatic, sudden death when he was having a siesta after lunch, very likely in the presence of my one-and-a-half-year-old self. I also told her what I had just witnessed in the metro. She put two and two together.

"What you saw was a re-enactment of your father's death. And the young woman clearly played the role of your mother. Your way of coping was to freeze up."

The osteopath's intuition and reasoning impressed me. I didn't know then that this re-enactment was just the first of several other powerful encounters to come with the same woman.

~

I hadn't had much contact with Dino since I left Vancouver, so soon after reconnecting with Antoine, I called him up to let him know I was back in Montreal. Since then, we'd spoken to each other regularly. Stubborn and paranoid, he refused to embrace the internet, citing privacy concerns. One day, he phoned to tell me that he had been diagnosed with a rare spinal disease and had maybe one and a half years left to live. Surgery was a possible solution, but it was risky and could leave him paralyzed. He told me all that in a matter-of-fact tone and even laughed at the unpronounceable name of his disease, in stark contrast to the hypochondriac who had freaked out over his imaginary ailments.

"What can I say? Life is *dukkha* after all," he added.

What could I have said? *Dukkha* indeed!

He called me again soon after, sounding like a man on a mission. He wanted to apologize to me for any harm he might have caused me. As a firm believer in karma and rebirth, he wanted to make sure his slate was as clean as possible when he moved on to his next life.

"Dino, I can't remember you causing any harm to me. We had plenty of arguments, but they were mostly philosophical. You've been a good friend to me. If anyone has to apologize, it's me. Remember when I told you I was broke, and you told me to go on welfare, and I said I've never received handouts and never will? You called me a stupid, high-minded idealist, and I called you a shameless scrounger. It was totally uncalled for, and I'm truly sorry."

And then it struck me.

Is Dino apologizing to me for imaginary harm he might have caused because it's easy to do and the stakes are low?

"Dino, have you asked for forgiveness from your children for any wounding you might have caused them?"

His first marriage had been disastrous and he had not been a good father.

"No," he said, "I don't think I need to ask for any forgiveness from them. I did my best under the circumstances. You should know better than me that karma is created by *cetana*, intention. I had no intention to harm anyone."

"Dino, you need to reach out to them. It's going to be healing for all of you."

I think he hung up on me, or almost.

The last time we spoke on the phone, I told him, "Dino, please keep calling me. I don't want to call you and catch you at a bad time."

I knew that Dino would call me when he was feeling physically and mentally good. He might have called me several times after that. And then the calls stopped.

I assumed the worst.

~

Not long after learning about the conditioning power of childhood wounding, and just a few months before my mother passed away, I connected with Sally, who turned out to be a *puella aeterna*. She was one of the many young, fit and attractive women I'd often see around the yoga studio. I hadn't paid any special attention to Sally until one day, I turned up at the studio and found out that she was teaching the class. She stood at the doorway, transfigured by the sunlight streaming into the studio and turning her lime-green outfit translucent.

As a teacher, she was omnipresent, straightening a back here, pulling up an arm there, flowing in and out of postures, cajoling, gently chastising, cracking jokes and spouting words of wisdom. I felt my energy connecting with her, then swirling around and enveloping the whole studio. After the class several women went up to Sally to thank her for such a great class. But I avoided her, feeling guilty about something I couldn't put my finger on. When I did get around to talking to her, the energy had dissipated, connection giving way to separation.

~

My mother had not been in the best of health for some months, yet when I was informed of her passing, my initial reaction was disbelief. I got the news as I was about to step over the threshold of the yoga studio. I went numb and felt the need to go home. A while later, I found myself at my place, not remembering how I'd gotten there. I called up Antoine to give him the news and tell him I was going back to Sri Lanka for the funeral, but I couldn't bring myself to say, "My mother has died." I kept choking up.

He was full of his characteristic tough love. "Oh, she was an old lady. You couldn't have expected her to live forever. Look on the bright side—you're free to grow up now."

During the flight home I did experience a feeling of freedom and unconditional joy a couple of times. In general, my emotional state fluctuated from numbness to pretending nothing had happened. When I arrived at our family home, where the funeral was going to take place, I didn't want to look at my mother's body in the customary open casket. A voice in my head kept saying, *That's not my mother, she's not dead.* It was only when I took my first shower in two days that I properly grieved for the first time. My tears mingled with the warm water streaming down my face.

Despite having spent two sleepless nights in the air, I kept vigil by the casket all night, as is the custom, but avoided looking at the body. The previous afternoon, the head monk of the neighbourhood Buddhist temple had come to perform a religious ceremony. He had known my mother longer than I had. On his way in he stopped near the casket, adjusted his saffron-coloured robe, gave the body a cursory glance and shrugged as if to say, "What's the big deal? Isn't life supposed to be impermanent?"

"Let the dead bury the dead." Christ's intriguing words kept coming up as I sat by my mother's casket. I remembered how I had been inspired by the life of Jesus when I first read the New Testament. It was Christ's refreshingly radical voice that I found appealing, so unlike the sad platitudes mouthed by official church representatives. To my sixteen-year-old self, the most powerful moment in the New Testament was when Jesus refused to pass judgement on a woman caught in the act of adultery. "He that is without sin among you, let him cast the first stone at her."

I brought my attention back to my mother. I always knew I'd had a close bond with her, but I had actually felt it only about six months earlier, when my mother was in hospital and I went to see her with my siblings. We were about to leave for the night when she waved in the direction of the extra bed in her room.

"This room is large enough for several people," she said. "Why don't you stay with me?"

My siblings and I exchanged surprised looks. Our mother was a fiercely independent person. We had hired a private nursing agency to look after her needs around the clock in addition to the regular hospital staff. But I was also pleased.

Over the next two or three days that I spent in her hospital room, I frequently found myself sitting alone with her at her bedside. We stayed mostly silent. She looked contented, and so was I. During those moments I understood that the bond between us was not just emotional but energetic. It was physical and palpable. I also understood why I had never really missed my mother after leaving home.

I didn't miss her because energetically, we were never really separated!

My thoughts went back further, to school. I saw my seven-year-old self coming home after our strenuous school schedule from eight in the morning to three in the afternoon. I'd kick off my shoes, peel off my socks and white school shirt and sit at the head of the dining table, reading a book I had borrowed from the library. My mother sat next to me and patiently fed me, mixing the red rice, yellow dahl and curries into tasty food balls with her fingers. Rice and curry never tasted better!

Mother was at her motherly best when I fell sick. She'd wake up several times during the night and hover over my bed with an anxious look on her face, even if all I had was the flu. She'd lay a cool hand on my hot forehead, then cover it with a cotton cloth soaked in eau de cologne, pop a thermometer into my mouth and give me an Aspirin dissolved in Orange Crush.

When I was about twelve years old, I contracted something a little more serious—a mild form of hepatitis—and my mother swung into action. She quarantined me from the rest of the household, drew up a special meal plan of rather bland food that would go easy on my liver and exposed herself fearlessly to the virus. Despite the drawbacks of prolonged confinement, I enjoyed the extra attention. My friends kept me supplied with books. And when I was fit enough to go back to school, my mother hired a taxi to take me to school and back so I wouldn't have to exert myself by taking the bus. While I was still quarantined, an uncle came to visit us and I overheard a conversation in the next room.

I heard my mother saying, "It's better he got this now than later in life."

"Ah yes, it could be more serious then," my uncle replied.

"No, it's not that. Missing a few weeks of school at his age is not a big deal. But if he got something like this when he's preparing for an important exam, that could really set him back."

Struck by mother's practical wisdom, I had a minor epiphany that has stayed with me since then.

Women make more sense than men!

The morning after my night of vigil, I took a shower and got dressed for the funeral, trying to remember which literary character kept admiring his own shoes during his mother's funeral. Was it Camus's Meursault in *The Stranger*? My mood was sombre as I greeted mourners at the door, but later when strolling around the garden and chatting with relatives I hadn't seen in a long time, I had a big smile and felt unconditional joy again.

Reality hit me when the dark-suited funeral director in dark glasses approached the casket to seal it. My siblings and I crowded around to get a last look at my mother.

Amma, I'll never see your so special smile again. I'll never again hear you say my name in the way only you do.

As the casket was being closed, a breeze from the garden lifted the white lace curtains and wafted the scent of fresh jasmine through our living room.

The day after the funeral, I went back to the cemetery to collect my mother's ashes. I stared numbly at the clay pot I was holding in my hands.

Ashes to ashes, dust to dust.

My mother had had a long life, brought up six children pretty much on her own, fulfilled her duties and obligations toward her family, relatives and neighbours, as she liked to remind me, and had lived through several momentous world events. Now all that was left of her life was a pile of ashes.

Anicca, dukkha, anatta.[21]

I kept the ashes in my room until everything was ready for internment in a family burial plot in my mother's hometown. The clay pot became a constant presence in my life, both comforting and disconcerting. If I woke up at night, my eyes searched it out in the darkness. At some point after the funeral, I started feeling some pain around my navel, possibly a phantom pain, which lasted about two weeks. I emailed Delta, my holistic massage therapist, to ask her about it.

She was unequivocal. "The umbilical cord is finally being cut."

---

21   Impermanence, conditioned nature of life, no-self: the three characteristics of the human condition, according to the Buddha.

I ended up staying four months in Sri Lanka. On the way back to Montreal, I spent a couple of days in Paris and caught up with Gord. I talked to him about the feeling of unconditional joy I had experienced. He told me he had felt the same during his own mother's funeral. He attributed it to reconnecting with old friends and family, but I wasn't convinced. I had experienced that feeling several times before and after the funeral. It was similar to how I felt following my epiphany after my neck massage from Jacques about three years earlier.

~

I'd emailed Sally to inform her of my sudden departure before leaving Montreal, but it took her a month to get back to me with her condolences. When I eventually returned to the yoga studio, she looked at me reproachfully.

"You disappeared for four months."

I grieved properly only upon my return to Montreal. Having spent most of my time in Sri Lanka with siblings, relatives and friends while taking care of family matters and also working online, I hadn't had the time or space to grieve.

Unfailingly, after yoga classes with Sally, feelings of sadness, depression and heaviness came up, usually on the way home. After a shower I felt better, and following a good night's sleep, I was back to normal. But after the next class, the same process would be repeated. It went on like that for several months, a never-ending process of grief. I felt like a Bodhisattva, taking on the collective unresolved grief of everyone separated from their loved ones throughout the ages.

It became experientially clear to me that the process of opening up the body during yoga facilitated the release of emotions trapped inside. I tried not to identify with the emotions but watched them come up and fade away with as much equanimity as possible, like how I had observed sensations during ten-day vipassana retreats. Had I shied away from the emotions—or to use the Buddha's terminology, had I reacted with *dvesha* or aversion—the negative emotions would have been strengthened and perpetuated, creating more *dukkha* or suffering.

I told Sally about what was coming up for me.

She was dismayed. "Oh no! You're supposed to feel good after yoga."

I don't think she believed what she said but was simply reacting to my comments. It's likely that the connection I felt with Sally and her own childhood wounding had triggered and accelerated my process of letting go.

During one of our conversations, she told me she had been abandoned by her father when she was two. "I saw him again at eighteen, but there was nothing, no connection. He was just a stranger to me."

I told her my father had died when I was a baby. "Isn't it a bit of a coincidence we both lost our fathers around the same age?"

Sally didn't seem to think so, or at least, she wanted to give me the impression she didn't, but she went on to tell me about her ex-boyfriend of seven years.

"I thought I was going to spend the rest of my life with him and make babies and all the rest. But he broke up with me. And I've been single since then. I'm fucked up." She nodded, as if hearing the words convinced her further. "Yes, I'm fucked up."

Sally seemed to be getting increasingly frustrated with me, possibly due to the lack of action on my part. So I invited her to have a cup of tea with me in the café downstairs from the studio with the intention of sorting things out. Not that I knew what things needed to be sorted out or how. I might have even hoped that she'd do the sorting out.

I admired her as she slunk down the stairs panther-like, dressed in blue jeans and a navy sweater. She sat in front of me. I asked her whether she wouldn't mind moving to a less crowded part of the café. She didn't at all, which I found encouraging. But after sitting again, she leaned back in her chair, crossing her arms.

"Soooo." She pouted.

Clearly, she had no intention of sorting anything out.

I remembered a similar scene with Bibi in the salon de thé on Rue Mouffetard. Her aloofness had drawn me in then. But the distance that had opened up between Sally and me had become an unbridgeable chasm. I floundered in that space and rambled on about Bibi, how exhausting the relationship had been and how relieved I was when it all ended. The expression on Sally's face shifted from puzzlement to bewilderment and then to anger.

To redeem myself for the café debacle, I called her up the next day and invited her to have dinner with me.

"I can't! I can't!" she said hysterically.

"Why can't you?"

"I can't! I can't!"

"Is it a question of timing?" I asked.

"Yes! Yes!"

I hung up quickly, relieved but also frustrated, as I hadn't asked her what this timing was all about and how long it was going to last. Later, I talked to Sally about Hendrix's and Leonard's books and offered to lend them to her, but she declined with a look that seemed to say, "I see no reason why I should read such books."

~

The topic of unresolved emotions arising during yoga and meditation is an important one but rarely discussed in "spiritual" circles, in my opinion. It came up when I had dinner at Shambhala, a Tibetan restaurant on Saint Denis Street, with Solange, my psychologist friend who also happened to be a long-time meditation practitioner.

"Generally speaking, when you start doing a practice, you feel good and get hooked. After a while you hit a plateau where you don't feel anything much but you keep going anyway in the hope that you'll get those good feelings again." I took a sip of kir. "And at some point, negative emotions might start to arise. Most people give up at this point, but that would be a real pity. It's a sign the practice is really working and getting into the deeper levels of the mind."

Solange looked dubious. "There are plenty of people out there who use meditation to cope with their emotions and calm themselves. So I can understand why people give up their practice when it becomes too difficult."

"That's true. Still, calming the mind is *shamatha*, the first stage of meditation, which prepares you for *vipashyana*, where you open up your mind and see things as they are. I don't think any real transformation can take place if you don't go beyond *shamatha*."

"Not everyone is ready to see things clearly, as you say."

Remembering how I had teetered at the edge of the abyss following my own *vipashyana* practice, I adopted a humbler tone.

"You're right. If your mind opens up before you're ready, it wouldn't be a good thing. I learned that the hard way. Still, I've come to believe that many people drawn to spiritual practices have unresolved emotional issues. So if they use a practice like *shamatha* or something similar to simply cope with life, it could lead to spiritual bypassing."

We were speaking French, but I said *spiritual bypassing* in English. Solange said she didn't know what I meant.

"It was one of your fellow psychologists who coined the term. It basically means using spiritual ideas and practices to bypass or avoid dealing with unresolved emotional issues."

She shrugged, tucking into her momos.

"It's a real dilemma," I mused. "How do you avoid spiritual bypassing and at the same time make sure you don't fall into the abyss? The answer may be to combine a contemplative practice with psychotherapy, bodywork and other healing approaches."

Solange nodded quickly, as if she wanted to change the subject.

~

As time went by, Antoine became angrier. A couple of times, I caught him muttering under his breath, "Sometimes, I feel like blowing up something."

I fully expected the police to turn up at my door one day, show me a picture of Antoine and ask, "Do you know this man?"

I developed a modus operandi for dealing with him. I stopped reaching out to him, but when he called or dropped by when he was in the neighbourhood, I always made myself available. And instead of letting him trigger me with his misogynistic and misanthropic comments, extreme political views or conspiracy theories, I just held the space for him.

Still, Antoine was a great friend, ever ready to go the extra mile for someone in need. When I moved from Montreal to Vancouver, he had helped clear out my apartment and pack my bag. He did the same when I left for Sri Lanka to attend my mother's funeral. I had wanted to leave behind stuff I had bought like bedding, cutlery, cooking utensils and so on, but he wouldn't hear of it.

"Why do you want to throw away money like that? I'll take the stuff and keep it for you."

I don't know how serious he was, but he opened the fridge, held up a half-full bottle of vodka and offered to keep it for me as well.

I didn't like his crafty smile, so I said, "No. Let's just leave it in the fridge for the janitor."

I didn't want to take the blame for Antoine falling off the wagon after all these years of sobriety.

One Christmas Day, Antoine called me. I asked him how he was, since I hadn't heard from him for about a month.

"Things are not good. I'm very ill." He sounded rueful.

He was waiting for the results of a biopsy of his liver but his doctor thought that he didn't have long to live. Knowing that Antoine tended to exaggerate, I might have been in denial. But when I went to see him and found him virtually immobile in his bed, the gravity of the situation dawned on me.

"I've been cheated of some good ten years," he told me. "I had projects, you know. Important projects."

That was news to me.

"I cried when I learned I was going to die, but it was a cleansing cry, and now I've come to terms with it."

I believed him. He no longer looked angry. I told him he should get in touch with his estranged sister, his only family member in Montreal. I offered to do so in case he was too proud to pick up the phone.

"No, I'll do it."

He might have been waiting for someone to tell him to do it. The end came quicker than we thought. I was the last person other than hospital staff to see him alive. I had visited him in the palliative care unit of Notre Dame Hospital on Sherbrooke

Street, about a twenty minutes' walk from my place. He was even more intense than usual, more alive than I'd ever seen him. He commented on an article on Putin's Russia that he had read in *The Economist*.

"They're saying Medvedev is a puppet, and Putin is the real power behind the throne. Western journalists don't know how things work in Russia. It's a collegial system of government they have over there."

He looked at me with a genuine expression of dismay at such stupidity. It was an odd discussion to have in a palliative care unit with a dying man, so to bring things back to the matter at hand, I asked him whether he was feeling any pain.

He tapped one of the tubes hanging over the bed.

"I'm getting a little bit of help from my friend, morphine. I can regulate the dosage myself." He had a gleam in his eye.

When I was leaving, he asked me to bring him a recent issue of *The Economist* the next time I came. Though I didn't want to touch him out of fear for passing on any germs, when he stuck his hand out I shook it, promising to be back soon. Walking back to my place on Saint Urbain, I couldn't help thinking that with his intelligence, curiosity and intensity, he could have done so much. I drew a parallel with Aravind's life and death. I felt I should have done more for Antoine.

I saw that my strategy of holding the space came from a place of passivity and a desire to avoid confrontation. The gleam in his eye when talking about morphine also troubled me.

Was that the gleam of an addict anticipating his next fix?

The next morning his sister called me at work to tell me that Antoine had passed away during the night.

"But I was with him until about nine. He was so full of life when I left. What time did it happen?"

"About ten, I'm told."

I felt numbness and sullen anger.

Another one from my immediate circle has been taken away.

While he was a difficult person to deal with, and we had drawn apart in recent years, he was still my closest friend in Montreal. But I felt some relief too, glad he had died before he got too attached to morphine.

The last image of Antoine's smiling face remained fresh in my mind, so different from the dark and brooding face I had encountered on Sainte-Catherine Street about seven years earlier.

Light had overcome darkness!

Part III
Pilgrimages

Chapter 15
Bodh Gaya, India

The day before I left for India, I attended the funeral of one of my brothers in Sri Lanka. His passing didn't come as a surprise, as I'd learned he was terminal six months earlier, around the time of Antoine's death. The oncologist having told us to prepare for the worst, the close family members were all gathered in my brother's hospital room. After a good part of the day had gone by, a couple of nurses walked in and unhooked all the tubes without saying a word to us. We looked at each other as if to say, "Is this it?"

It was.

To the nurses, death was a mundane, no-fuss affair.

A couple of days earlier, I had gone to see my brother at his home. He told another visitor with a mixture of admiration, incredulity and concern, "Can you believe that my brother's going on a pilgrimage to India on his own? Everyone I know who's done that has gone with a group. How's he going to find his way over there?"

Bodh Gaya, where the Buddha was supposed to have attained enlightenment over two and a half thousand years ago, is the Buddhists' Mecca, located in the northeastern state of Bihar. This pilgrimage had been on my bucket list for as long I could remember, so it might have been the new Zen practice I had taken up about six months earlier that made me finally get around to it. I had practised Zen with other groups, but it was only after joining the centre founded by Japanese monk Taisen Deshimaru in Montreal that I understood Zen, or at least, the Soto Zen variety. The largest of the three traditional schools of Zen, Soto advocates zazen or sitting meditation, with a strong focus on the posture. Soto Zen aims to literally do what the Buddha did, and realize the truth about ultimate reality for oneself simply through the sitting practice, without any dependence on meditation objects, teachings or any external agency. Zen originated from Chan Buddhism, one of the Chinese Buddhist schools, whose approach is epitomized in the following verse:

> *A special transmission outside the scriptures,*
> *Not depending on words or letters;*
> *Directly pointing to the mind*
> *Seeing into one's true nature and attaining*
> *Buddhahood.*[22]

My plan was to fly to New Delhi and then take an overnight train to Bodh Gaya. I booked a hotel in Paharganj, a neighbourhood popular with backpackers for its proximity to the main New Delhi railway station. My taxi from the airport snaked its way

---

[22] The source of this verse is unknown but it is attributed to Bodhidharma, the monk from South India who introduced Buddhism to China in the fifth or sixth century.

through narrow streets to my hotel. Paharganj was part slum, part rubble, with odd buildings housing mid-range hotels and restaurants thrown into the mix, as if by accident.

In the morning, I went out to get some breakfast. As I picked my way through the rubble a shoeshine boy grabbed my foot, without so much as a by-your-leave, and started shining my moccasins, which didn't need any shining. When he was done, the boy put on a poker face and asked for the exorbitant amount of three hundred rupees, probably the equivalent of a labourer's daily wage. Not wanting to mar the beginning of my pilgrimage with an inauspicious haggle over money, I handed over the money, expecting a look of delight and gratitude on the boy's face. Instead, he looked disappointed. Perhaps he thought he should have asked for even more, or maybe he missed the usual heady cut and thrust of a brisk bargain.

The sixteen-hour journey to Bodh Gaya was epic, reminding me of the scene from *Doctor Zhivago* in the train taking the family from Moscow to their country house. To start off, the train was late, not by minutes but by many hours. I went into the first-class waiting room, a large, dusty room with a creaky ceiling fan and rickety chairs lined up against the four walls. A short, chubby woman with dark skin, in a bright orange sari and bare feet, sat at a desk near the entrance. She stopped me by extending her arm imperiously in my direction, palm outward, then took my ticket, examined it, turned it around a couple of times and showed it to a passenger seated nearby who nodded. She didn't know how to read! And then she waved me in just as imperiously.

We waited and waited. Occasionally a crackling voice coming through the PA system unapologetically announced a further delay. No one was surprised, angry or even slightly upset. Three women sat stoically near me, clearly a mother with her two daughters, all three strikingly beautiful and colourfully dressed in elegant but simple clothes. They looked dignified yet vulnerable, making me think they could be aristocrats fallen on hard times. Since they had a number of packages with them, I wondered whether it would be culturally appropriate for me to offer them my help when the train finally arrived. To my relief, the mother eventually hired a porter.

I had taken a sleeping berth in the most expensive class available on the train from New Delhi to Bodh Gaya, expecting to travel in luxurious comfort in an empty compartment. But now it was June, when locals go on vacation, which meant that the train was overbooked and I had to fight off people trying to encroach on my territory. To get to the toilet, I had to step over passengers sleeping in the aisle. But I was pleasantly surprised to find the toilets' cleanliness beyond reproach each time I used them. I slept little on that sixteen-hour journey, and didn't eat much either, in an attempt to ward off the dreaded Delhi Belly.[23] I had to avert my eyes from the aromatic and delectable dishes served in hygienically packed containers to my fellow passengers by smartly uniformed train kitchen staff. But I couldn't resist the temptation to taste a couple of spicy, freshly fried samosas.

In Bodh Gaya I booked myself into a hotel, took a shower and walked over to the nearby Mahabodhi Temple,[24] dating back to 260 BC. The interior of the current temple, built in the seventh century, was smaller than I'd expected, but it had an imposing fifty-foot-tall, ornately sculpted tower. Behind the temple was the most famous tree in the world, the Bodhi, or sacred fig tree. With heart-shaped leaves, it's a direct descendant of the very tree under which the Buddha was supposed to have attained enlightenment. After circling the temple a couple of

---

23 Traveller's diarrhea.
24 Temple of the Great Awakening.

times, I went into the garden at the back, sat on a bench under a tree and gazed at the Bodhi tree with the temple tower rising behind it. The Bodhi tree wasn't tall. It looked more like a cluster of a trees with branches spreading laterally and some putting down thick prop roots.

I might have expected something special to happen at my long-awaited pilgrimage destination but I felt nothing. A little monk, dressed in the usual saffron-coloured robe, came toward me with his shaven head shining in the sun, carrying a large black umbrella almost as tall as he was. After making some initial small talk, he soon got to the main business on his mind.

He was learning English but lacked a good dictionary, which cost 500 rupees, so would I be kind enough to buy him one. I told him I had just arrived and didn't have enough Indian rupees on me but was going to be around for a few days and would buy him his dictionary another time. He then became very demanding, insisting that he couldn't wait for another time and that he had to have the dictionary right then.

Provoked by his sudden change in tone, I yelled at him. "What kind of Buddhist monk are you? You should be ashamed of yourself. You're a disgrace and totally unworthy of the robes you're wearing. Get away from me!"

The little monk trudged off, his shoulders drooping and his black umbrella now seemingly taller than he. My anger gave way to remorse. The brat was obnoxious, but he was still a member of the order of monks founded by the Buddha, and we were at the very spot where the Buddha was said to have attained his goal of liberation from suffering. To redeem myself, I vowed to buy him his damn dictionary the next time I saw him. And when I did, my intuition told me that the kid was actually a scam artist in cahoots with the bookshop owner, and I was not the first person to buy him a dictionary. But I let myself be scammed anyway, as

I had with the shoeshine boy.

During the three days I spent in Bodh Gaya, I visited the Mahabodhi Temple several times daily and walked around the complex. Since footwear had to be left at the entrance, and given the forty-degree temperature, walking in bare feet on the burning ground was uncomfortable at best and impossible when the sun hit its zenith. So I mostly sat on my favourite bench and gazed at the Bodhi tree. After his final awakening the Buddha had spent seven weeks at different spots in what is now the Mahabodhi Temple complex, including one whole week gazing at the Bodhi tree.

The little monk took me in a tuk-tuk to visit the nearby Sujata Stupa, a monument marking an important event just before Siddhartha, the future Buddha, reached his goal. Having renounced worldly life and left his sheltered home in his late twenties, Siddhartha studied with various yogic meditation teachers, quickly mastering their techniques. But he soon realized that achieving transcendent meditative states did not bring him closer to his goal of achieving liberation from suffering. He then took up the practice of extreme asceticism, which included eating virtually nothing, until he encountered Sujata, a milkmaid, at the very spot marked by the stupa in her name. She offered him milk rice, which he accepted. Immediately gaining strength, Siddhartha understood that the middle way between sensual indulgence and self-mortification was the true path to awakening. Soon after, he went to Bodh Gaya, sat under the Bodhi tree and finally achieved his goal of enlightenment.

The Gnostic centre I had frequented fifteen years earlier gave the story a Tantric spin—the future Buddha had a sexual encounter with Sujata, which eventually led to his awakening. While I had dismissed out of hand most of the centre's outlandish claims, I felt that some kind of energetic connection between

Sujata and Siddhartha could not be ruled out.

Sitting on my favourite bench and gazing at the Bodhi tree, I also wondered about what had actually happened under that tree on that iconic day. The traditional Buddhist texts say the Buddha attained enlightenment by practising concentration and reaching higher and higher levels of *jhana*. But these are transcendent states he had already attained and which he thought did not lead to the cessation of suffering. Subsequently, on various occasions during his forty-five-year ministry, the Buddha stated that mindfulness, an embodied state, was the only path to awakening.

I also went on a day trip from Bodh Gaya to Rajgir to visit Vulture Peak, a favourite mountain retreat of the Buddha where sixteen years after his enlightenment, he gave important teachings to a large gathering of followers. During one sermon the Buddha didn't say anything but simply held up a white flower, implying that the highest truth can only be transmitted wordlessly. Among his disciples, only Mahakasyapa reacted by smiling, signifying that he understood, thereby becoming recognized as the first patriarch of the Zen school of Buddhism.

We arrived at the bottom of Vulture Peak, and seeing that the way up was by ski lift, my fear of heights was triggered and I hesitated. The driver I had hired for the day leaned against the car, arms folded, looking scornfully at me as if he knew what was going through my mind. Encouraged by the sight of an overweight grandmother getting airborne, legs swinging and grinning broadly, I grabbed the next chair and sat down, clutching the sides grimly, my own legs frozen in mid-air. I made sure not to look down until I got to the top.

On the way back we stopped in Nalanda, the site of an ancient Buddhist university dating back to the fifth century and probably the world's first university. Under the scorching June sun, I walked around the vast, ruined complex of monasteries and temples with a growing sense of gloom. When I stood at the edge of the red brick foundations of what was originally a debating hall, my feelings turned into anger and frustration.

What's there to debate?

While India has a long tradition of thinkers and religious leaders debating philosophical ideas, Buddhism is different. It's a practice, a way of life, and not a philosophy. The eminently pragmatic Buddha had a laser focus on the problem of liberating oneself from suffering and refused to be dragged into academic debates. To illustrate his approach, the Buddha told the parable of a man shot by a poisoned arrow. Instead of having the arrow removed, the injured man insisted on knowing the name of the archer, where the archer was from, what was the status of his family, where the arrow was made, etc.

Standing in Nalanda, I tried to imagine what a resurrected Buddha would have done had he happened to wander in here in the fifth century. I saw him storming into the hall, breaking up a debate and chasing the monks away, like Christ chased away the money changers in the Jerusalem Temple.

On our way back the car broke down and it was late when we finally returned to Bodh Gaya. I was getting out of the car when a burly, angry-looking man yanked open the door.

"Give me the money!" he yelled.

I got out of the car with exaggerated vigour and yelled back. "Who the hell are you?"

Learning he was the owner of the car, I continued angrily, "I paid the money to the travel agent. And I paid for an air-conditioned car, but you sent me an old car which, by the way, broke down, so *you* owe *me* money!"

Travelling around the state of Bihar from my base in Bodh Gaya, I saw signs of poverty everywhere, reminding me of the conditions that would have existed around 600 BC, when urbanization sparked the *sramana* movement, which the Buddha was part of. *Sramanas* were seekers who renounced worldly life and adopted an ascetic lifestyle to liberate themselves from the cycle of life and death.

After spending seven weeks in Bodh Gaya, the Buddha went to Sarnath, where he met five former *sramanas* and preached his first ever sermon. In the *Dhammacakkappavattana Sutta*, translated as the *Setting in Motion of the Wheel of Dharma* discourse, he talked mainly about the Four Noble Truths—the truth of suffering, or the conditioned and unsatisfactory nature of life; the truth of the cause of suffering; the truth of the cessation of suffering; and the truth of the path that leads to the cessation of suffering. Sarnath is now considered the birthplace of both Buddhism and the Buddhist sangha, or community of monks.

To go to Sarnath in the neighbouring state of Uttar Pradesh, I took a train and then a long taxi ride. When we arrived at the Sri Lankan temple where I had booked a room, it was almost midnight—the train had been late by several hours. It also turned out that I didn't have any change to give the driver a tip. I thought I'd get some change from someone inside, but only the caretaker was still up so he went and explained the situation to the driver and closed the gate. Incensed, the driver then yelled, "*Baksheesh, baksheesh*," and kept kicking and banging on the gate for at least ten minutes.

I visited several historical Buddhist monuments or remnants thereof in the area, but unlike Bodh Gaya, a bustling place with many businesses thriving around the Mahabodhi Temple, Sarnath had a neglected air. I didn't see any other visitors around, most likely because it wasn't the pilgrimage season.

After a stay of just one night, I took a taxi to neighbouring Varanasi, also known as Benares, the oldest continuously inhabited city in the world. My taxi dropped me off on the outskirts, as anti-pollution regulations prevented cars from going any further. I switched to a rickshaw, which only took me part of the way, as my hotel was located on the banks of the Ganges and the streets were too narrow. No one knew how to get to my hotel, so I walked on blindly through a maze of cramped, winding streets, my red duffle bag slung over my left shoulder. When the hotel appeared in front of me, it felt like a miracle.

Later that evening, I stood for several hours on the riverbank and watched a number of funeral pyres burning while waiting to see the daily *agni pooja* or worship of fire performed by Hindu priests. When things finally got going with hundreds of people, both locals and tourists, thronging the area, the spectacle became more like Bollywood meets Benares.

My final pilgrimage destination in India was Kushinagar, a small town in the state of Uttar Pradesh, where the Buddha had died and was cremated. After more interminable waiting in an Indian Railways waiting room, I took a train from Varanasi to Gorakhpur and then travelled by taxi to Kushinagar. I left my bag in my room at the Sri Lankan temple and took a rickshaw to the Ramabhar Stupa, which marked the spot where the Buddha was cremated. I circled the ruined monument, mentally repeating what I remembered of the Buddha's final words.

"Work diligently. Component things are impermanent."

Thinking about how perennial and universal this 2,500-year-old message was, I then went to gaze at the reclining statue of the dying Buddha at the Parinirvana Stupa. Like in Sarnath, the sites were somewhat desolate and no one else was around. In one of the many stories about the Buddha's death, his disciples urged him not to die in a nondescript place like Kushinagar but rather to go to a grander place where he could be given a fitting funeral. I found myself agreeing with them.

To cheer myself up, I went to have a meal at Dr. Kumar's Restaurant, near my lodgings. I didn't have much choice, as it was to be the only game in town. It wasn't much of a restaurant either, just a couple of tables under the porch of Dr. Kumar's modest house. I sat at one of the tables and Dr. Kumar himself, a strapping man in glasses, came out and handed me a menu that seemed more like a brochure. The first few pages were dedicated to Dr. Kumar's academic achievements as a professor of philosophy. The menu was also surprisingly long for such a small operation and went on for several pages. Playing it safe, I chose a couple of simple dishes—vegetable fried rice with curried eggs. Dr. Kumar took my order, went in and came out soon after, donning a helmet.

"Now, I go buy eggs."

He straddled his motorbike and roared off, and was gone for almost an hour.

While waiting, among other things, I thought about the Buddha's encounter with Bahiya, which put his teaching in a nutshell. In brief, Bahiya was a *sramana* considered to be awakened by his followers, and he himself had come to believe so. One day, he realized he wasn't and decided to seek teachings from the Buddha and actually become enlightened. He caught up with the Buddha as he was about to enter a town to beg for alms and asked him for a teaching. The Buddha replied that the time was unsuitable, but Bahiya insisted, saying, "I don't know how long I will live or you will."

They went back and forth until finally, the Buddha relented.

> *Bahiya, you should train yourself thus. In the seen will be merely what is seen; in the heard will be merely what is heard; in the sensed will be merely what is sensed; in the cognized will be*

merely what is cognized. When, Bahiya, for you in the seen is merely what is seen, in the heard is merely what is heard, in the sensed is merely what is sensed, in the cognized is merely what is cognized, then, Bahiya, you will not be "with that." When, Bahiya, you are not "with that," then, Bahiya, you will not be "in that." When, Bahiya, you are not "in that," then, Bahiya, you will be neither here nor beyond nor in between the two. This is the end of suffering.[25]

Upon hearing this teaching, Bahiya immediately became enlightened. But the story does not end there. Soon after, Bahiya was attacked by a cow and gored to death, and the Buddha and his disciples came across Bahiya's body upon their return from the town. The Buddha then asked his disciples to take Bahiya's body and cremate it as if he were one of their fellow monks.

The last stop in my pilgrimage was Lumbini, across the border in Nepal, the birthplace of the future Buddha, where it all began. Not wanting to travel in a crowded bus, I hired a jeep driven by a man who was known to the Buddhist monk who ran the Sri Lankan temple. Up until then I had been driven around by uncommunicative men, so as we headed off, I felt good about leaving India in a comfortable vehicle driven by a friendly man who spoke good English. But halfway through the trip, he told me he was going to transfer me to a taxi and I ended up once again with a surly driver in a cramped car.

Not long before we got to the border, the man stopped for a meal but I stayed put in the car, preferring not to eat while travelling, out of an abundance of caution. The driver must have told the restaurant owner about me because the man came to

---

25 Bahiya Sutta, translated from the Pali by John D. Ireland.

check me out.

"How come you're travelling alone on a pilgrimage? Don't you have family or friends?" he asked in a half-angry, half-incredulous tone.

After driving for about another half hour, the driver stopped the car in the middle of nowhere. He took my bag from the boot, threw it on the muddy ground, raised his hands up in front of him and shouted, "Nepal!"

Then, with a mocking smirk on his face, he got into his car, slammed the door, turned around and drove off.

I picked up my bag, wondering what I had done to deserve such discourteous behaviour, and walked toward the border. But as I crossed into Nepal, I felt a shift in energy, as if a weight had been lifted off my back.

To get my passport stamped, I went over to the Nepalese border post, which was actually a medium-sized house, and saw several chubby men dressed in knee-length khaki shorts and white sleeveless undershirts lolling around on chairs. I wondered whether that was their usual attire or whether they were on their afternoon siesta. After one of the men stamped my passport, I asked him a question on currency regulations I had read about in the guide book.

He waved airily, as if to say, "What regulations? There's nothing to worry about."

From the border post, I walked across to the entrance to the Lumbini complex enclosing the main pilgrimage sites, monasteries and temples of the various Buddhist countries, but closed to any kind of business. The only way to get around is by bicycle or rickshaw. A large board at the entrance listed the regulated prices for rickshaw rides to various places in the zone. When we got to the Korean monastery where I was planning to stay, the rickshaw driver asked me for more than the regulated price, and we got into an ugly haggle.

I put down my duffle bag in the dormitory—which I had to myself, as it was not the pilgrimage season—rented a bicycle for fifty rupees and went for a ride. The zone had a long canal running through it. I noted with interest that all the temples from the Theravada Buddhist countries were located on one side of the canal, with the Mahayana and Vajrayana temples and monasteries on the other side.

According to legend, Maya Devi gave birth to the future Buddha in the Lumbini gardens while travelling to her own family home for the birth, as was (and sometimes still is) the custom. After visiting the various sites, including the actual spot where the birth took place, marked by the Maya Devi Temple, I went back to the Korean monastery, had dinner in their canteen, and lay on my bed, hands clasped behind my head.

All Buddhists know that Maya Devi died seven days after giving birth, and baby Siddhartha was brought up by his aunt, but strangely, I have never heard or come across any discussion of the psychological implications of this significant event on the future Buddha.

I remembered a conversation I'd had with my friend Sylvain on a park bench in Saint Louis Square, in Montreal, just before leaving on my pilgrimage.

"Don't you think Siddhartha's quest for liberation from suffering might have been triggered by the unresolved trauma arising from the tragic separation from his mother?" I asked.

"Absolutely." Having spent the first month of his life in a newborn intensive care unit, Sylvain knew a thing or two about separation. He also knew a thing or two about Buddhism, as he had delved deep into Eastern wisdom before becoming a born-again Christian.

"It's the same kind of thing with Jesus, you know. He was

basically an illegitimate child, and people in his village would have known about that," he continued.

I looked around, concerned that someone might have heard this blasphemous comment. "I hadn't thought about that but it makes sense. Assuming that their quests were triggered by their separation from the ultimate feminine or masculine archetype, it's a bit paradoxical that the Buddha's teachings were directed more towards the intellect, while Christ's message was essentially heart-based."

The next morning I left for Kathmandu, my final destination. One of the Korean monastery's employees had sold me the bus ticket, and I can't remember what the dispute was all about, but I rebuked him for trying to rip me off.

During the trip I couldn't enjoy the breathtaking views of rolling hills and lush valleys as the strapping young boy beside me kept taking up too much space, and I had to repeatedly reprimand him and push his thigh away with my knee. My hotel in Kathmandu was located in an area with no street names, so I got lost a number of times in the maze of narrow streets. Each time I knew it was nearby, but when I asked a rickshaw driver to take me to my hotel, they'd invariably quote an unreasonable amount, leading to more haggling and angry words.

From Kathmandu, I flew back to Sri Lanka. Throughout the trip, I had from time to time felt a tugging sensation in the pit of my stomach, but it was the day after I returned that Delhi Belly finally hit me with tremendous force. I lay in bed for three days, dehydrated and so weak that I couldn't even hold a phone to my ear. I had plenty of time to think about my pilgrimage. What kept coming up were all the squabbles throughout the trip. So much for starting off on an auspicious note by acting magnanimously with the shoeshine boy!

A few weeks later, back in Montreal, I caught up with Solange and gave her an account of my conflict-marred pilgrimage.

"I don't get it. I went on a pilgrimage to pay homage to the messenger of wisdom, equanimity and compassion, and all that came up was anger."

She put on her psychologist cap. "Just before you left, an older male sibling died. The trip might have brought up unresolved anger surrounding your father's death."

I then remembered seeing from my sick bed, straight ahead on the wall, a picture of my father that had appeared after my mother's death, and thinking how much he resembled the brother who had recently passed. He was also the brother I had stayed with for about three months after having an existentialist meltdown in my late teens.

Chapter 16
Boulevard Saint-Laurent Revisited

I had signed up to attend a ten-day Zen retreat in France at La Gendronnière, a monastery founded by Japanese monk Taisen Deshimaru, on my way back to Montreal. But three days before I left Sri Lanka, I was laid low again by a second delayed bout of Delhi Belly. Like about twelve years earlier in Sri Lanka, when I agonized over whether to attend a ten-day vipassana retreat, I vacillated. But unlike then, I decided to go. Gord met me at the Paris airport, took me to his place and later dropped me off at the Gare de Lyon. The train took me to Blois in central France, from where I was picked up and driven to the monastery.

I got off in front of the renovated eighteenth-century manor house. Its facade was patterned with red-and-white bricks and served as the administrative office. I made my way to the dormitory in the old servants' quarters. Inauspiciously, later that day during dinner, I passed out while having the beet salad starter. The next morning I lay in bed gazing at the heavy wooden beams above, not wanting to get up and disturb my neighbours who were still sound asleep. Some of them were heavy snorers, and I had been woken up several times by that orchestra, some playing high notes, others playing low notes and then all joining in for a rousing chorus!

After taking a shower I donned a black kimono and walked out into the cool morning air. The sound of the gong reverberated across the property. After strolling in the grounds, I entered the spacious meditation hall with heavy wooden columns, high ceilings and light beige wall-to-wall carpeting dotted with black meditation cushions. I felt glad about taking a chance and boarding my flight as scheduled. After the first session of zazen and the morning ceremony of chants, we all trooped off to the dining hall, sat across from each other on benches and ate the traditional breakfast of steaming rice porridge.

But things didn't go very smoothly over the days that followed. Anxiety kept coming up during the sitting sessions. I had been mostly anxiety-free since my move to Warsaw some ten years earlier, so it was disheartening that a problem I thought had been resolved was cropping up again. It didn't help that a sweltering heat wave was sweeping across France. The meditation hall's windows were shut, ostensibly to keep the heat out, creating suffocating conditions that heightened my impulse to rush out.

Sitting on my cushion, sweating and anxious, I remembered how many years earlier at the Shambhala centre someone had said, "I'm scared of my meditation cushion."

I'd scoffed. "What's there to be scared of? A cushion is just a cushion."

Still, outside of the sitting sessions, I enjoyed going for walks in the grounds and the adjoining woods, chopping vegetables and washing dishes in the spacious industrial-scale kitchen, and weeding and harvesting in the organic vegetable garden. I liked having coffee and chatting with fellow practitioners at the bar after breakfast and strolling back to my dormitory after the last zazen under a flickering dark blue sky.

As I sat in the vehicle about to take me to the train station, I turned around and surveyed the manor house, the meditation hall, the grounds, and the woods stretching all around me. I told myself, "I must come back here again."

A voice in my head replied, *You won't be coming back here again. You're going to die!*

I received this alarming prophecy with surprising sanguinity, given my already heightened state of anxiety.

As it turned out, I did go back the next year, and every year after that for a total of seven years. So I wonder now whether, had it not been for the letting go of powerful, dark emotions that took place during the year that followed the pilgrimage to India and the prophecy, I might well have succumbed to some psychosomatic disease.

~

I had hoped that the anxiety would go away once I got back to Montreal, but it didn't. A few days after my return, remembering how a party had soothed my anxiety in Sri Lanka, I walked over to the Samsara Lounge, just a block away from where I had attended Shambhala retreats. A favourite haunt of mine and located in the core of the Main's entertainment district, this lounge bar with its retro decor had become something of a Montreal institution. The wall behind the bar was plastered with fading smoke-stained black-and-white movie posters, and the retro theme carried through to every detail, with the cocktail menu printed on old vinyl records. What I liked most was that the bar attracted people of different age groups and backgrounds, unlike the more homogenous crowds at other places on the Main. Also, the type of crowd could change from one day to another.

Some partygoers would drop into the Samsara Lounge for a drink before heading off to a nearby club, while others would stop there for a final drink before going home. Those who chose to spend the whole evening there sensed a constant ebb and flow. At times, the place emptied itself only to fill up soon after. I also liked that the music travelled through the years as the evening progressed, starting with classic pop and rock and then moving through disco to R&B and rap.

When I walked up to the bar a few days after my return from France, one of the bartenders, a new girl in a black dress with a large, diamond-shaped silver buckle at the waist, stepped back as if startled. She then moved to the other end of the bar, seemingly to avoid me. But the next time I went there, she came to greet me with a wide smile.

"Vodka and orange?" she asked, her head bobbing.

She knows what I drink! Was she was pretending to ignore me the other day?

She scooped some ice into a glass with one hand and measured out a shot of vodka with the other. Then she poured in orange juice, stuck a slice of orange on the rim, slapped down a white napkin on the black counter and placed my drink on it. Magali and I got acquainted over my next few visits. In addition to bartending, she was a fitness instructor and an aspiring singer.

"I've never met anyone like you," she said one day. "You have an MBA, you're into yoga and meditation, and you hang around in bars."

Several months later, her final message to me in all caps would be much less complimentary: *YOU DON'T KNOW WHAT YOU WANT. I KNOW WHAT I WANT. I WANT TO*

BE HAPPY!

But on that day, I saw an opportunity to give my usual speech.

"Meditation is not just one thing, you know," I explained. "There are two main meditative approaches, concentration and awareness. To practise concentration, you need to sit in a quiet place and try to calm your mind and ultimately go inward. I practise awareness. That can be done anywhere and at any time. It's just being open to whatever comes up in the present moment. It requires stopping the flow of thoughts, grounding yourself and then actively receiving the impressions from the world outside. There are a lot of things going on in a bar, so it's a great place for awareness practice."

I looked forward to our weekly chats, but one Friday when I turned up at the bar, Magali wasn't there. Not wanting to ask the other bartenders about her, I waited a while, feeling a sense of panic rising in me. I remembered her mentioning another bar on Mont-Royal Avenue, so I rushed out. While waiting for a taxi, I ran into Sabrina, a nocturnal acquaintance, and asked her to come along with me.

In the taxi I told Sabrina about my recent travels and added, "Something disturbing happened today at work. One of my team members was rushed to hospital. She was diagnosed with advanced cervical cancer. It looks pretty bad. I feel she's not going to make it. And I don't know why, but I have a vague feeling of guilt."

I looked at the crowds of young people milling about on the sidewalks as we headed north on Saint-Laurent, sensing the energy coming from the street. "So I'm in a kind of strange mood, raw and vulnerable, but also open. It's not a bad feeling. Very authentic."

The other bar on Mont-Royal was a trendy place, so while waiting in line, I briefed Sabrina on our mission. She looked indignant and threatened to leave.

"What's wrong with you? Why are you rushing around town looking for a girl half your age? Plus, you hardly know her."

I hung my head in shame and pleaded with her to stay.

The place was dimly lit and filled with mostly young White women, in short black dresses, carrying tall and colourful drinks, taking selfies and shouting in each other's ears. We worked our way through to the bar, ordered a couple of normal-sized non-colourful drinks and downed them in silence. I saw no sign of Magali either behind or in front of the bar. So, after finishing our drinks, we headed back to the Samsara Lounge, which by then had gotten busy. The bouncer waved us in. Standing against the wall at the back of the bar, I saw someone who looked like Magali. I craned my neck to get a better look. Sabrina grinned.

"You're not even sure whether it's her, right?"

I nodded, and then confirmed rather sheepishly, "It's her."

Sabrina doubled up with laughter. "Do you realize what a crazy thing you did? You went rushing across town looking for a girl who was here the whole time."

I laughed too, mostly to hide my embarrassment. But walking back to my place, I had a flash of intuition about my strange behaviour. I don't know how I could have missed it before, but with her dark wavy hair and prominent forehead, Magali reminded me of my mother.

Did she trigger some anxiety from my childhood? Did I panic and overreact as a baby, thinking my mother was gone when she must have been somewhere in our house?

~

It took another six months for the pieces of the puzzle to fall into place. Feeling the need to develop abdominal strength as part of my intention to achieve body awareness, I signed up for a Pilates class at a studio on Boulevard Saint-Laurent, just a few doors from the Samsara Lounge. I buzzed the intercom and Alice, the instructor, wearing mauve leggings and a black T-shirt with "Fatal Mistake" in golden lettering, opened the door to the studio. Her hips swayed as she walked back to her little desk. She had a radiant smile and large, wide-set eyes whose colour changed depending on the light and angle. There was something vaguely familiar about her, and I felt an instant connection.

Though I was looking forward to seeing her again, a couple of hours before the next class, I felt anxious. It was hard to sit still at my desk. I got to the studio with a queasy feeling in my stomach and was sitting on the stairs, taking off my shoes, when Alice came out and put on her trainers. She explained to me she had switched classes just for that week. But her words didn't sink in. Bewildered, I watched her leave.

How can she be leaving?

I went into the studio like a zombie and lay on the mat, feeling the life force draining out of me. Somehow I got through the class, went back home and flopped onto my couch, a black cloud of grief and depression hanging over me.

The next day, refreshed by a ten-hour sleep, I was able to think more clearly about my grotesquely excessive reaction. My mind went back to a similar reaction triggered by Magali's absence. I had another flash of intuition.

Did the sight of Alice leaving also trigger some deep unresolved emotions from my childhood?

I put two and two together.

Did Goddess Aletheia concoct a mise en scène to make me relive what I had experienced during a life-defining event?

~

It's Sri Lankan New Year and my mother is busy in the kitchen preparing the traditional sweetmeats. I'm one and a half years old and cooing in my cot next to my parents' bed, where my father is having his usual after-lunch siesta. I hear screams, loud sobbing and panic-stricken voices, followed by a hushed silence. Now our house is full of people talking in low voices. Someone says, "Oh, the poor little fatherless baby." And Amma's not here! Amma, where are you? I need you!

Did I notice my mother leaving to take my father to the hospital on the day he died?

~

The next week I returned to Alice's class with trepidation. Nothing untoward took place, but as I left the studio, the black cloud of depression came over me again. I'd been planning to buy groceries afterwards, but instead I returned home and lay on my couch for several hours. I finally found the strength to get up and clean my apartment and felt much better after the physical activity.

The same pattern repeated every week for several months. The process was strikingly similar to what had happened with Sally three years earlier. But this time, the emotions that came up were so dark and overwhelming that I no longer wanted to be a Bodhisattva taking on collective suffering.

But as I did in Sri Lanka during my dark night of the soul, I took comfort from the extrapolation of Jung's quote that to awaken permanently, the unconscious must be made conscious.

Feeling the need to talk, I made an appointment with a shrink for the first time in my life. The man I saw seemed in need of help himself, far more than I. But talking about the emotions coming up had a soothing effect. The process might also have prepared the ground for Goddess Aletheia to do her work. One day, on my way home from the psychologist's office on Sherbrooke Street, I was walking in front of the Indian restaurant at the eastern end of Prince Arthur Street when I understood why I found Alice vaguely familiar.

I'd been having dinner in the same restaurant about a year earlier with a couple of friends when Alice came in, wearing her red Kanuk coat, to get some takeout. Upon seeing her, a sense of well-being had spread through my body and mind, so unlike what I experienced the third time I saw her.

The psychologist seemed averse to saying anything, preferring to listen and take notes. Occasionally, he'd come up with a long, convoluted question, making elliptical outlines in the air with his pen, which left me bewildered and made me wish he had remained silent. But with some persistent prodding on my part, I succeeded in extracting a cautious validation of my self-diagnosis.

"Would you agree that my perceived feeling of abandonment by my mother is the root cause of my PTSD symptoms and tendency to avoid intimacy?"

He responded in his usual elliptical style. "It's possible that one could say that, speculatively speaking, of course, keeping in mind that this is not in fact a diagnosis, since it's far too early to reach a conclusion, which I must say, in all frankness, would require much further analysis over many years to be scientifically valid."

Solange, on the other hand, was unequivocal, not letting any professional qualms hold her back. "You're spot on!"

She also agreed that it was probably my experience of wakefulness in daily life, coupled with bodywork practices, that had brought the unconscious emotions into the light of day.

Encouraged by her reaction, I ventured, "I think it's no

coincidence that this happened just nine months after my pilgrimage to India and the Zen retreat in France."

Solange seemed less sure.

Feeling I had at last gotten to the bottom of things, I thought once again that my problems were over, not knowing that much work still needed to be done.

Chapter 17
Eihei-ji, Japan

From the Skyliner train from Narita Airport, I watched the looming Tokyo skyline draw nearer. When we approached the Ueno station, the surroundings were strangely familiar, something I had not experienced before in my travels. I exited the train station and looked around. As if on cue, a black taxi stopped in front of me, the back door opening automatically. The driver, in a dark suit, white gloves and a black airline pilot's cap, greeted me with a knowing smile.

We drove through the streets of Tokyo as neon signs lit up and the sidewalks filled with dark-suited salary men carrying black briefcases and hurrying home. Around us and ahead of us, the traffic flowed almost noiselessly. A slight discordant note was struck when we stopped at a traffic light. I noticed a couple of young girls shouting and trying to shove leaflets into the hands of passers-by. The pedestrians were brushing past them as if they didn't exist. I'd have expected them to stop, take a leaflet with both hands and bow to each other a couple of times before carrying on.

The next morning, after a traditional Japanese breakfast of miso soup, steamed white rice, grilled fish, omelette and pickled onions, I checked out of my hotel and headed off to the Tokyo train station to catch the bullet train to Kyoto. While lining up to board the train, I noticed that the woman behind me had a lot of luggage. I stepped aside and motioned for her to get on ahead of me. The woman looked horrified and shook her head. I wondered what bothered her so much. Maybe she didn't want to breach Japanese train lining-up etiquette, or maybe it just wasn't done in Japan for a man to make way for a woman.

The main purpose of my trip to Japan was to visit Eihei-ji. The temple was founded by Dogen, who established the Soto school of Zen Buddhism in Japan in the thirteenth century after spending years studying and practising under Buddhist masters in China. I had wanted to visit Eihei-ji soon after I started practising zazen some three years earlier in Montreal. But I might have also been motivated by the mise en scène concocted by Goddess Aletheia following my pilgrimage to India.

At the Montreal dojo, I had sat warrior-like with my back straight, chin tucked in, tongue on the upper palate, knees on the floor forming a stable triangle with the cushion, one bare upturned foot on the opposite thigh in the half-lotus position, hands clasped together in front of the navel with thumbs touching slightly and eyes open but downcast. I felt the physicality of the posture and soon zazen represented for me the culmination of all the practices I had done in the previous seven years in Montreal to develop body awareness, the first foundation of mindfulness.

Nothing much happened on the cushion except for boredom, physical pain and the sensation of my spine seeking to unwind itself from its scoliosis. And off the cushion, the synchronization of the body with the mind during zazen led to anxiety coming up again. But instead of reacting with more anxiety as I had done previously, I felt raw, vulnerable and fully present.

When someone asked me how I was, instead of the customary "I'm fine, thank you," I'd say. "I'm feeling anxious." And they'd respond, "But you're saying that with a big smile on your face, as if you're enjoying it!"

Beginners in Zen usually start with the usual *shamatha* practice of following the breath, and while most might continue doing so their whole life, some gravitate toward *shikantaza*, which literally means "just sitting"—meditation with no object, simply being aware of what's coming up in their body, mind and the world outside. In my understanding, *shikantaza* could represent the union of *shamatha* and *vipashyana*, leading to awareness of awareness.

When teetering at the edge of the abyss in Sri Lanka, it became clear to me that my downfall stemmed from an extremely imbalanced union of *shamatha* and *vipashyana*, where *shamatha* was relatively underdeveloped. My practice of Burmese vipassana remedied this imbalance to some extent, but it was the practice of zazen that strengthened *shamatha*, brought about a more balanced union of concentration and awareness, and allowed me to mindfully withstand the powerful and dark emotions that came up subsequently through my interactions with Alice.

Soto Zen can be considered the purest form of Buddhism, given its focus on zazen and the expectation that the practitioners will realize the fundamental truth about ultimate reality simply by sitting like the Buddha did under the Bodhi tree. I didn't get that far, but less than a year into my Zen practice, I did get a glimpse into a fundamental psychological truth about myself through my strange behaviour at the Samsara Lounge. Another six months later, I discovered the whole psychological truth or, rather, fabrication, when Alice unwittingly enacted the fateful scene from my early childhood.

For my stay in Kyoto, I had booked a room in a temple in the walled Myoshin-ji complex, the leading temple of the Rinzai school of Zen Buddhism. Unlike Soto, which focuses on the practice of zazen or sitting meditation, the Rinzai school uses koans—paradoxical statements that are intended to paralyze logical reasoning and provoke enlightenment. Apparently, the Myoshin-ji school differed from the larger Rinzai school, as it used koans tailored to the student rather than the canon of established koans handed down over the generations. That made perfect sense to me.

Using a map given by the security guard at the entrance to the complex, I walked past magnificent but empty temples solidly built of wood. I found my way to Shojoin Temple and climbed the long wooden steps.

A man dressed in a dark blue cotton tunic and matching pants came rushing out and barked at me.

"No shoes up here. Can't you see the sign?"

He pointed to a sign at the bottom of the stairs I hadn't seen.

This turned out to be Reverend Kawasaki, the head of the temple with whom I had exchanged several cordial emails while still in Montreal, but who then showed me a whole new side to himself. Brisk and businesslike, he took me to my room, which was outside the actual temple, at the bottom of the garden. He gave me a sheet of paper with all the information I'd need and explained in detail where I could wear my shoes and where I needed to put on the slippers that came with the room. I got the distinct impression that Rev. Kawasaki found it rather distasteful to be in this business of renting rooms. I had naively imagined myself having lengthy discussions about Zen and the meaning of life with the good reverend over countless cups of tea! But to be fair, he did lead meditation sessions most mornings, serving us matcha tea and biscuits afterwards, both activities providing opportunities for discussion.

I settled into my spacious room scented with tea tree oil and sparsely furnished with a thin futon on the floor and a small desk in a corner. I then headed off to my first sightseeing destination, the nearby Ryoan-ji temple just outside Myoshin-ji's walls. I sat on the temple steps to quiet my mind and contemplate its famous garden of rocks in a sea of pebbles raked in straight lines. But all I could see was the scene with Rev. Kawasaki playing over and over again in front of my eyes.

The next morning I brewed a cup of tea in the adjacent tiny kitchen and sat on the heavy wooden bench in front of my room. Basking in the rays of the rising sun, I felt the warmth of the mug in my palms, the crisp October morning air on my face and the heavy wood against my back as the tea tree oil scent wafted from inside my room. The exquisite garden coloured in different shades of green lay before me. On my right were the wood-and-glass sliding doors of the entrance to Shojoin, and beyond the temple walls, the sloping and ornamented roofs of neighbouring temples rising into the sky.

Rev. Kawasaki came out, garbed in robes and other priestly paraphernalia, and drove away in his BMW, ostensibly to perform a ceremony. I remembered my state of my mind the previous day and wondered why his reprimand had affected me so much.

Did it trigger memories of another more significant reprimand from my past? Could this question be my own koan to contemplate during the trip, given to me unwittingly by the reverend?

Struck by the silence around me, I wondered how things had come to this. That Zen Buddhism was in steep decline in Japan wasn't news to me. But it was quite something else to be sipping tea in the midst of some fifty empty temples, which not too long ago had been filled with the hustle and bustle of monks engaged in the pursuit of *kensho*, or seeing one's own true nature. I could understand how Buddhism became virtually extinct in India. Since its beginnings in 500 BC, Buddhism had already begun to decline by the twelfth century when it was almost wiped out by the invading Muslim armies. In contrast, the Rinzai school was founded in Japan in the twelfth century and was thriving as late as the nineteenth century.

My interest in Zen had been sparked when I read D. T. Suzuki's books in my late teens, so I was thrilled to find out that Suzuki himself had been a frequent visitor to the neighbouring Shunkoin temple. The zany stories I'd read about spontaneous Zen monks contrasted refreshingly with the moralistic stories of scholarly Theravada Buddhist monks in Sri Lanka. I remembered reading with delight the Zen story of a "horse searcher" in search of the superlative horse who had gotten so good at his job that he didn't notice superficial characteristics like gender or colour.

I serendipitously stumbled upon the classical text of the story in J. D. Salinger's *Raise High the Roof Beam, Carpenters*:

> *Duke Mu of Ch'in said to [the famous judge of horses] Po Lo:*
>
> *"You are now advanced in years. Is there any member of your family whom I could employ to look for horses in your stead?"*
>
> *Po Lo replied: "A good horse can be picked out by its general build and appearance. But the superlative horse—one that raises no dust and leaves no tracks—is something evanescent and fleeting, elusive as thin air. The talent of my sons lies on a lower plane altogether: they can tell a good horse when they see one, but they cannot tell a superlative horse. I have a friend, however, one*

Chiu-fang Kao, a hawker of fuel and vegetables, who in things that pertain to horses is in no way my inferior. Pray see him."

Duke Mu did so, and subsequently despatched him on the quest for a steed. Three months later, he returned with the news that he had found one. "It is now in Sha-ch'iu," he added.

"What kind of a horse is it?" asked the Duke.

"Oh, it is a dun-coloured mare," was the reply.

However, on someone being sent to fetch it, the animal turned out to be a coal-black stallion! Much displeased, the Duke sent for Po Lo. "That friend of yours," he said, "whom I commissioned to look for a horse, has made a nice mess of it. Why, he cannot even distinguish a beast's colour or sex! What on earth can he know about horses?"

Po Lo heaved a sigh of satisfaction. "Has he really got as far as that?" he cried. "Ah, then he is worth a thousand of me put together. There is no comparison between us. What Kao keeps in view is the spiritual mechanism. In making sure of the essential, he forgets the homely details; intent on the inward qualities, he loses sight of the external. He sees what he wants to see, and not what he does not want to see. He looks at the things he ought to look at, and neglects those that need not be looked at. So clever a judge of horses is Kao, that he has it in him to judge something better than horses."

When the horse arrived, it turned out indeed to be a superlative horse.[26]

---

26   1912 translation by Lionel Giles.

Kyoto was not what I'd expected. I had pictured myself wandering around in a traditional Japanese city with a look of wonder. But my travel research must have been sloppy. What I saw instead was mostly a soulless modern city. The actual old part of the city, the Higashiyama district with its Gion neighbourhood, was a relatively small area. Its narrow streets were lined with tiny and charming but pricey restaurants, and filled with tourists and fake geishas-for-a-day. I might have seen a real geisha with a heavily powdered face glide out of a taxi and disappear in a flash into one of the restaurants.

And of course, there were temples, and more temples. But as they say in Asian tourist jargon, I was soon "templed out." The temples were all empty, looked pretty much the same and weren't really that old to boot. Most of them had been rebuilt after burning down accidentally, some more than once.

After a few days of wandering around Kyoto, I headed off to Eihei-ji, my main pilgrimage destination. I took the train to Fukui and went to the bus station to buy a ticket to Eihei-ji. The two girls behind the counter got quite flustered when they saw me and ran away. They came back with a man, presumably their boss, who figured out what I wanted in his halting English while the girls giggled behind him. I sat in the bus and when the driver started the engine, the "boss" came out, stood near the front of the bus and gave a deep bow. His torso kept going lower and lower until it became almost parallel to the ground. I was amused, then impressed, then inspired, recognizing this was a man doing the most ordinary of jobs in a superlative manner.

The bus dropped me off in front of the Eihei-ji gates. I walked up the temple driveway and through the Sammon gates. Two plaques on either side of them supposedly said, "Only those concerned with the problem of life and death should enter here. Those not completely concerned with this problem have no reason to pass this gate." I passed through with a clear conscience.

Unlike the temples I had seen in Kyoto that were like reconstructed museum pieces, the Eihei-ji complex blended seamlessly and organically with its natural surroundings. It consisted of a cluster of buildings all connected through long passages. The temple had been built into a hillside, with a stream bubbling nearby and tall pine trees growing from within its interior. And unlike the other temples, Eihei-ji was a hive of activity, with shaven-headed young monks in black kimonos running around. But I wasn't deceived, knowing that Eihei-ji ran a training program for about two hundred novice monks who'd later go their separate ways and take over the family business of running an empty temple and performing lucrative ceremonies.

After lingering in and strolling through the rooms that were open to the public, I ended back at the entrance. I enviously watched a few people, undoubtedly lay practitioners, going up to the reception and filling out forms before being admitted to the private areas of the temple. I too had wanted to spend a couple of days in Eihei-ji and follow the same routine as the monks, but I got an exceedingly polite fax from the temple authorities rejecting my request, as there were no English-speaking monks available to welcome me.

Like in Bodh Gaya, it felt quite anticlimactic, but I was loath to leave Eihei-ji just yet. Instead, I sat near the stream, basking in the warm sun that filtered through the pine trees and watching as the young monks went about their *samu*, the work required to run a Zen monastery and generate revenue through farming or other means. Unlike in the Theravada Buddhist tradition, where the monks are not expected to do any work, *samu* is a central aspect of Zen practice.

I thought about the Zen *sesshins* I'd done, which always had two periods of *samu* every day, ensuring that the practice of zazen is integrated into daily life. I remembered how I'd get goose bumps every evening at around ten, when the strident voice of the monitor keeping time in the dojo cut through the silence and stillness:

> *With utmost respect, I urge you*
> *Everyone of us must ponder the grave matter of*
> *life and death*
> *All things pass quickly*
> *We must be completely alert*
> *Never neglectful, never indulgent.*

Feeling pangs of hunger, I went out through Eihei-ji's immense gates, crossed the street and had a meal of miso soup, steamed white rice and fried tempura. I ate sitting cross-legged on a low wooden bench in a tiny restaurant run by three generations of the same family.

Since the bus had dropped me off in front of Eihei-ji's gates, I assumed it would pick me up from there as well. By the time I realized my mistake, the last bus to Fukui had already left. So I took a local bus and then a miniature train with just one small compartment. The conductor, a young woman in an eye-catching uniform that a flight attendant from a leading airline would have been proud to wear, walked down the aisle after each stop to collect fares, bowing to each passenger on both sides. I noticed that she did her bow-filled walk down the aisle even if no one got in at a particular station. She got off at the penultimate stop, presumably at the end of her shift. As she walked away, she projected a different energy with shoulders slumped and eyes downcast.

In the train back to Kyoto, I thought about how the day's experiences reminded me of traditional Japanese life depicted in master filmmaker Ozu's classic movies I had seen in a small independent cinema in the Paris Latin Quarter. I remembered walking out feeling uplifted by Ozu's quintessential Japanese ability to see the sacred in the ordinary. A funeral scene transfigured by the golden sunlight streaming in through the windows is still vivid in my mind.

As I gazed at the Japanese countryside rolling by, the story of Hui-neng popped into my mind. The sixth patriarch of Buddhism in seventh-century China, Hui-neng was an illiterate peasant working in the monastery kitchen when the fifth patriarch decided to have a poetry contest to choose his successor. The apparent heir, Shen-hsiu wrote:

> *The body is the tree of enlightenment*
> *The mind is like a bright mirror's stand*
> *Time after time polish it diligently*
> *So that no dust can collect*

Hui-neng heard about the poem and as he was illiterate, asked someone else to write down his own poem:

> *Enlightenment is not a tree,*
> *The bright mirror has no stand;*
> *Originally there is not one thing—*
> *What place could there be for dust?*[27]

The two poems represent the two paths to awakening, namely gradual and sudden, an issue I'd grapple with in subsequent

---

27   Hui Neng: Addiss, Stephen; Lombardo, Stanley; Roitman, Judith (2008), *Zen sourcebook : traditional documents from China, Korea, and Japan*

years. To cut a long and complicated story short, Hui-neng was ultimately recognized for his realization of the view and appointed the sixth patriarch.

After being turned down by Eihei-ji, I had booked a night at a temple in Koyasan. Koyasan is a Shingon Buddhist community at the top of Mount Koya, founded by the Japanese monk Kukai in the eighth century. I took the Nankai Electric Railway from Osaka. As we snaked up the lush green mountains, the scenery became increasingly rarefied, making it feel like we were arriving at a kind of Shangri-la. The sky was overcast, but on the last leg of the journey, the cable car I took broke through the low hanging clouds, exposing a brilliant blue canopy above.

What a metaphor for the sky-like nature of the mind obscured by the continual stream of discursive thoughts!

It felt like a good omen.

Koyasan turned out to be more prosaic than the Shangri-la I'd anticipated. The community's hundred or so temples were spread out over a relatively large area. They had a less traditional Japanese structure than those in Kyoto. Almost all the temples had burned down in the devastating fire of 1888 and been reconstructed.

I found my way to Muryoko-in Temple, founded over a thousand years ago, and a monk showed me to my room. I put down my red duffle bag and looked around appreciatively. Its furnishings were sparse but tasteful, and it had a lovely garden view. A young monk came in with a pot of tea and a tray of colourful sweets in different shapes. After tea I got to know Philippe, my next-door neighbour, a young Frenchman who had come to Japan on a whim.

"I was on vacation at home without any plans in particular, and one morning I got up and decided to buy a plane ticket to Osaka. So here I am."

Philippe was one of those easygoing, curious Frenchmen I immediately feel comfortable with, so together we visited Kukai's mausoleum in the massive Oku-no-in cemetery with its winding paths and giant cedar trees.

Dinner was served in my room at six by a platoon of black-robed monks carrying small, lacquered tables of varying heights. They set out little bowls of broth, fried tempura, green tea, and an array of intriguing food morsels in different shapes, textures and colours, then left as swiftly as they'd arrived.

I felt quite alone with that magnificent spread of *shojin ryori* in front of me. Most of the dishes in this vegetarian feast looked like desserts to me, and the tastes, like Japanese aesthetics in general, were subtle and clearly had to be acquired. But I ate everything out of respect for the time and effort that must have gone into preparing them. A rather shamefaced Philippe told me he hadn't been able to do justice to the meal, having unwisely eaten a large lunch earlier in the day. I had wisely skipped lunch in anticipation of the spread.

The next morning I was woken up at five by a monk ringing a bell in the corridor. One of the guests turned out to be a champion snorer and the shuddering of the beautifully decorated but paper-thin walls of my room had disturbed my sleep several times during the night. At six, the guests, about ten of us, were all huddled outside the small shrine room where the daily fire ceremony was to be performed, bleary-eyed, stealing glances at each other and trying to figure out who the snorer was. The inside of the shrine room was dark, the shadowy, black-robed figures within lit only by the fire. I smelled sandalwood incense and heard the reverberating sounds of drums, gongs and the Heart Sutra's familiar refrain—*shiki fu i ku ku fu i shiki*—stating the fundamental truth of the universe: "Form is emptiness, emptiness is form."

Shingon Buddhism is a form of Tantric Buddhism that offers a fast-tracked path to enlightenment and which spread through northern India around about the eighth century, consisting of practices such as *mantras*, or chants, *mudras*, or ritual gestures, and visualizations. Watching the fire ceremony in Koyasan, I wondered how these superficial Tantric techniques could replace the traditional Buddhist practice of sitting meditation, especially zazen. Over time with zazen, as I experienced it, the body synchronizes with the mind and becomes a *mudra* itself—the mother of all *mudras*.

I left Koyasan with Philippe, but we parted ways in Osaka. In the train to Tokyo, I felt that my stay in Koyasan had been more important for me than visiting Eihei-ji, my main destination. But I couldn't explain why.

Another koan to ponder!

After spending a few days in Tokyo, carefully avoiding temples, I took the Skyliner train back to Narita Airport, feeling somewhat disheartened. Japan had felt strangely familiar, but I didn't really get to know it during my two-week stay. I decided to apply for a leave of absence the next year and come back for an extended stay of six months, learn Japanese, and experience Japan properly.

Chapter 18
Sherbrooke Street

From Tokyo, I went to Sri Lanka and met up with my old friends Sami and Piyal, who were also vacationing there. The day before I left, we went to the Mount Lavinia beach, picking our way over the hot sand to my favourite beach restaurant for a lunch of rice and curry. We tucked into our red rice, dhal, mallung,[28] tempered okra, beetroot salad and prawn curry. The blazing sun cast a bluish haze over the ocean.

"I think I should buy a condo," I heard myself saying during a lull in the conversation.

My friends were dismissive. "Terrible idea. It's crazy to saddle yourself with a mortgage at your age."

I had been toying with the idea of buying a condo since around the same time I had an epiphany that I should look at my intimacy issues. But I was surprised by the words that had popped out of my mouth, especially since I'd planned to go back to Japan. My friends' opinion had a contrarian effect,

---

28   Finely chopped greens cooked with coconut and spices.

convincing me I should buy a condo.

On my way back I stopped in England to spend a few days with my brother in Epsom, and he decided to come with me to Montreal. I told him about my plans to buy a condo. He thought it was a good idea. I didn't tell him about my other plan of going back to Japan, expecting him to be much less supportive. Together, we went to see just one apartment in a building on Sherbrooke Street, which is the second-longest street in Montreal, running past the Olympic Stadium and the Botanical Gardens in the East to the stately historic Westmount mansions in the West. I had passed the building numerous times but expected it to be priced beyond my budget, so I went there simply out of curiosity.

In the elevator, the real estate agent explained that the price was discounted as the developer was facing a cash crunch. She opened the door to the apartment and I walked into a spacious living room with sunlight flooding in through the floor-to-ceiling windows. Outside, a street sloped away between two heritage buildings. Leafy trees cast well-defined shadows across Sherbrooke Street while a church spire rose high in the distance. I knew with absolute certainty that I had finally found my home—my superlative home!

All my adult life, I had moved from one furnished apartment to another with all my belongings in one bag. I liked to boast that all I needed was a couple of hours to leave a place for good, and had left several cities and countries quickly, for no particular reason. Even a one-year apartment lease was too much of a commitment to me, so for the previous seven years I had been living on Saint Urbain Street with a six-month lease. I timed the leases such that I'd leave on a month-long vacation when the lease ended and sign a new one upon my return. I had a good relationship with Julie, our building manager, who indulged my idiosyncrasies and kept my apartment rent-free for me during my vacations.

She told me once, "You're one of my best tenants. You always pay on the first day of the month, you don't make any trouble and you keep your place so well."

I returned the favour by giving her standing permission her to show my clean and uncluttered apartment as a model to prospective tenants. Whereas most tenants living in furnished apartments tend to ask for more furniture, I asked Julie to take away some large items, like the TV, to free up space in keeping with my minimalist style. Visitors commented that I lived like a monk.

Paradoxically, my life as an itinerant monk came to an end soon after hanging around temples and actual monks in Japan!

Soon after I signed the purchase agreement, feelings of euphoria and lightness came up, like almost ten years earlier when I had my epiphany in the shower regarding the root cause of my intimacy issues. Like then, it felt as if I had broken through some kind of psychological barrier. But the euphoria soon gave way to heaviness after I negotiated a mortgage loan at the bank. I could almost feel the loan's weight on my back. Later, after signing the mortgage deed at the lawyer's office, I was in no hurry to move into my new condo. All I had to do was pack my clothes and walk a few blocks, but I started feeling apprehensive. I put off the moving date several times, which meant I had to pay rent and make mortgage payments at the same time.

By the time I moved in, it was the middle of December. However much I cranked up the heating, the apartment remained cold, humid, and mostly empty, since the Canadian-made furniture I had ordered was still on the way. I had great hopes for my couch, having pictured myself snuggling in it. When it arrived two months later, I didn't like it. It looked different from what I had seen in the showroom. So in the morning, on the way to the washroom, I'd avert my eyes just to avoid seeing it.

Solange came to see my new place. Impressed and somewhat envious, she said, "I guess you bought this place because it's a good investment."

I looked at her blankly.

"I didn't think of it as an investment at all. I bought it because I sensed the energy was perfect for me and I wanted to live in a place where no one had lived before. I felt euphoric when I signed on the dotted line, which makes me think there was also an underlying psychological motivation. It might have marked my passage to adulthood, finally. I'm now a responsible adult who pays property taxes!"

A memory arose as I was talking. "A couple of years before my mother passed, when I was in Sri Lanka, I told her I was planning to buy a condo, thinking she'd be pleased, but she wasn't. She spread her arms wide and said, 'Why do you want to buy a place? This is your home.'"

"You see, that was my childhood home." I looked around at my apartment. This is my adult home."

But adulthood is not easy. With a feeling of heaviness, I went about buying everything I needed to make my new place functional. It was a long, drawn-out process since I couldn't operate at my usual level of efficiency. I'd walk up Boulevard Saint-Laurent, buy a few things, come back feeling exhausted and lie on my bed or couch to recover. The heaviness stayed with me for about six months and then faded away, until one day I realized it was gone.

But amid the initial gloom, one silver lining emerged. The first day on my way to work from the condo, I crossed Sherbrooke Street, went down Sanguinet Street, and cut across the open area between De Maisonneuve Boulevard and President

Kennedy Avenue. A flock of pigeons took off in a furious flutter of wings, soaring into the sky in a perfect spiralling formation. As I walked toward the Place des Festivals, hearing the ebb and flow of traffic, I realized I was continuously feeling the sensation of my boots on the ground.

I felt elated. Since the initial experience about twelve years earlier in Warsaw, the sensation of my feet on the ground had come back sporadically, especially after yoga or some other bodywork practice. So it was telling that the experience became quasi-permanent just a couple of days after moving into my condo.

I took it to mean that I had accomplished an intention I had set for my second coming to Montreal—develop body awareness, one of the four foundations of mindfulness, rounding off the other three foundations I believed I was already well established in.

With hindsight, this ordinary but momentous event also marked the end of a stage of my journey from the time I had started practising awareness meditation, relying on the Buddha's *Discourse on the Four Foundations of Mindfulness*.

~

Not long afterwards, when I wasn't particularly looking for anything, I came across the teachings of Jean Klein. A Berlin-born doctor living in France, he had experienced an awakening at the age of seventeen and was feeling a lack of fulfillment in his otherwise happy life when he responded to a "certain call to go to India."

Like me, Klein had been influenced by Dostoevsky, Nietzsche, Krishnamurti and, above all, René Guénon. While he did not go to India to look for a guru, he did meet and spend much time with a teacher who introduced him to Advaita Vedanta. Three years later, he had a permanent awakening:

> *One morning, between deep sleep and awakening, there was a sudden vanishing of all the residues of "my persons," each having believed themselves hitherto to be a doer, a sufferer, an enjoyer. All this vanished completely, and I was seized in full consciousness by an all-penetrating light, without inside or outside. This was the awakening in Reality, in the I am . . . I knew myself in the actual happening, not as a concept, but as a being without localisation in time or space. In this non-state, there was a freedom, full and objectless joy.*[29]

He also gave a more concrete example. Previously, when looking at and admiring birds flying in the sky, there was a "looker" looking at the birds but after that morning, the "looker" disappeared, leaving only pure perception.

I believe this is also what the Buddha taught Bahiya. "When, Bahiya, you are not 'with that,' then, Bahiya, you will not be 'in that.' When, Bahiya, you are not 'in that,' then, Bahiya, you will be neither here nor beyond nor in between the two. This is the end of suffering."

Jean Klein also had a teacher from the Kashmir Shaivism tradition, a form of non-dual Tantra, who taught him a yoga where the postures are done with as little effort as possible, giving priority to the energy body over the physical body. Going home after my first weekend workshop of non-dual yoga, I felt my feet solidly on the ground and my physical body expanding, which

---

[29] Jean Klein, *Neither This Nor That I am.*

made me think I was sensing my energy body. During my period of academic research in Paris I had learned that, depending on the tradition in India, we have different numbers of *koshas*[30] or bodies that interpenetrate each other. The simplest typology is four—the physical body, the mental body, the emotional body and the energy body.

Also during my Paris research period, I had learned that Advaita Vedanta and non-dual Tantra hold the same view—the empirical world and consciousness are one, or more correctly, not two. The main theoretical difference is that in Advaita Vedanta, the world is considered an illusion, whereas non-dual Tantra considers that the outward reality is a manifestation of awareness or consciousness. To achieve non-duality, Advaita Vedanta practitioners turn inward to realize the illusory nature of the world, while non-dual Tantra practitioners go outward and understand the fictitious nature of the separate self. Concretely, Advaita Vedanta can be considered a world-renouncing approach while non-dual Tantra advocates embracing the body and sensory experiences. When an Advaita Vedanta practitioner says, "I am not that," referring to the outside reality, the non-dual Tantric practitioner would respond, "I am all that."

Similarly to how Gurdjieff's teaching on self-remembering and waking up from sleep helped me understand mindfulness, the non-dual Tantric view that the empirical world and awareness are one helped me grasp the concept of no-self in Buddhism. When a practitioner internalizes that view, they realize no-self.

No-self is the third of the Buddha's three core characteristics of life: *anicca, dukkha, anatta*—impermanence, unsatisfactory nature of life, no-self. For me, impermanence was the easiest characteristic to grasp, especially as I had been exposed to the deaths of several loved ones from a young age. As for *dukkha*, I'd

---

30   Sheaths

understood suffering in the ordinary sense of the word, but later, after tasting wakefulness, I took it to mean the conditioned and unsatisfactory nature of life that arises from identifying with discursive thoughts and not being truly present.

Coming back to *anatta* or no-self, intellectually understanding what it meant did not necessarily mean I wanted to let go of my attachment to my fictitious, individual self. My experience of awareness of awareness was rooted in the existence of an observer. My state of wakefulness might have even strengthened the sense of an observer receiving perceptions from the world. So, now that I was well established in all four foundations of mindfulness, I set myself a new intention—*Let go of the observer.*

But it would take another seven years before another life-defining encounter inspired me to want to let go of the observer and realize the illusory nature of the separate self.

Chapter 19
Avon, France

A visit to Gurdjieff's grave at the Avon cemetery just outside Paris was long overdue. Considering the impact that his core teaching on self-remembering had had on my life, it's surprising that I didn't take the time to go there during my years in Paris.

A couple of years after my pilgrimage to Eihei-ji, I decided to make amends after becoming a member of the Gurdjieff Foundation of Montreal, housed in a three-storey heritage building in the Lionel-Groulx neighbourhood, not far from the Gnostic centre I'd frequented a couple of decades earlier. The walls of the centre's numerous rooms were adorned with pictures and paintings. I often found myself pausing in front of a photograph of Le Prieuré, the French manor house in Fontainebleau where Gurdjieff had set up shop in the 1920s. I vowed to visit Gurdjieff's grave on my next visit to Paris.

I stayed at my friend Marcelle's place in Belleville, in the heart of the North African quarter in Paris, near the trendy Ménilmontant district and not far from Rue Oberkampf where Bibi had lived. I told Marcelle about my plans to visit the Avon cemetery while having breakfast, as the din from the open-air market on Boulevard de Belleville came in through the open windows. Marcelle offered to come along, although she had never heard of Gurdjieff. That evening we had dinner at a restaurant on Boulevard Voltaire close to the Bataclan theatre, not knowing that in just a few months it was going to be the scene of a massacre that would shock France and the world. We were joined at the restaurant by Mathieu and Daniel, two old friends who had heard me talk about Gurdjieff many years earlier. They too decided to join us on our short trip to Avon.

We met outside the Porte d'Orléans metro station, piled into Daniel's car and off we went. It was quite the jolly expedition, unlike the lonely trek I had imagined. Avon is adjacent to Fontainebleau, well known for the historic Château de Fontainebleau, and surrounded by one of the largest forests in France. No one was around to give directions at the cemetery, so I led the way as if I knew where we were going, and sure enough, we were soon at Gurdjieff's graveside. As in life, Gurdjieff stood out in death. Unlike the other tombs with ornate headstones and long inscriptions vaunting the many accomplishments of the deceased, Gurdjieff's grave was marked by two rugged and massive obelisk-like stones at each end of a large, grassy plot.

A snail hung on for dear life to one of the stones under the scorching July sun. Marcelle and Daniel busied themselves getting water to save it. Hands clasped behind his back and neck craning, Mathieu was studying the inscriptions on some of the nearby headstones. I might have expected to feel something special, but I didn't, so I sat on the stone bench beside the plot and looked around. It took me some effort to dispel the fog in my mind and maintain the state of presence that Gurdjieff always talked about.

Someone, I think it was Daniel, said, "Tell us something about Gurdjieff's teachings."

"For me," I replied, "the most important thing he taught is that we're all living in a state of sleep and we need to wake up. It was after reading about that in Ouspensky's book that I understood the Buddha's teaching on mindfulness. After all, the word *Buddha* means the awakened one. His teaching might have been somewhat obscured over the centuries, so it's my theory that Gurdjieff's mission was to renew the Buddha's message and give it fresh impetus."

Feeling my audience was receptive, I warmed up. "This message of waking up is important not only for us as individuals, but also for our world. If a sufficient number of us wake up, many of our pressing global problems could well resolve themselves naturally. Of course, we need to be clear about what we mean by waking up. For me, it's awareness's ability to constantly break through the stream of discursive thoughts and become aware of itself without any conscious effort."

French people like to argue about this kind of didactic statement—or any kind of statement, for that matter—but to my surprise, my friends meekly accepted my long speech. I was relieved, as I didn't feel like getting into an intellectual discussion, the kind which I had relished during my pre-Gurdjieff days.

We bought some provisions at a nearby grocery store and drove to the nearby Le Prieuré. The renovated three-storey mansion is now a seniors' residence. I imagined Le Prieuré in Gurdjieff's heyday, bustling with students going around their duties, like the young monks at Eihei-ji. I saw people performing the complex movements or sacred dances to the haunting music composed by Gurdjieff himself.

We strolled around the grounds and picnicked under the shade of a massive tree, passing around baguette, cheese, smoked salmon and red wine. As we ate, we began to reminisce. I broke off a piece of bread and made myself a sandwich of cheese and smoked salmon, then stretched out my legs and propped myself up on one hand, Roman style. Sunlight laced through the tall shade trees lining the path to Le Prieuré. Under the cloudless sky, the scene looked idyllic. It didn't seem to matter that my friends had no idea of the path I had taken since we were students.

I remembered what I had said during a meeting at a café on Rue du Bac following the fall of the Berlin Wall and my own awakening. "True freedom is inner freedom."

I'd had only a vague idea of what I was saying, but since then I had tasted relative freedom, which arises when awareness breaks through the stream of discursive thoughts. For true freedom, awareness also has to shatter the belief in an observer perceiving that awareness, giving rise to *objective* or *pure* awareness of awareness.

The morning after visiting the Avon cemetery, I took the RER to Charles de Gaulle. Surprisingly, considering the number of times I had departed from the same terminal, I got lost. When I finally made it to the right gate, my flight to Montreal was already boarding. The line was long so I sat down to wait. Then I saw a young woman wearing baggy, pink Indian-style pants almost bursting through the crowd and walking purposefully in my general direction, her long blond hair streaming behind her.

Looks like Shakti, I thought casually. Oddly, she was walking fast and slowly at the same time. I looked at her more closely as she swept past me, headed for the washrooms.

I had seen Shakti at my yoga studio in Montreal about a year earlier. She was standing at the reception desk in a pair of black short shorts and a sleeveless green tank top and twirling a lock of long blond hair between her fingers. When I walked past her on my way out, my body jerked back as if I were in some kind of danger. I found that odd, since she had an alluring Barbie doll look. Later, thinking about the incident, my reaction reminded me of how Magali had seemed startled when she first saw me at the Samsara Lounge.

A week later, I found myself practising yoga beside Shakti and felt the energy flowing between us throughout the class. Afterwards, I was seated in the lobby putting on my shoes and she walked past, looking straight ahead but with a slight smile. When I went out into the street, she was standing next to her bike on the sidewalk, checking her phone. She looked up as I walked by and smiled, more widely this time.

"How did you find that class?" I asked.

"Loved it," she said, smiling even more broadly.

I moved closer and we began to chat. She introduced herself as Shakti. "My spiritual name," she added shyly.

I nodded approvingly. Shakti means power—more specifically, feminine energy. In non-dual Tantra, she represents the manifestation of the material world and is the consort of Shiva, who represents awareness. In union, Shiva and Shakti are not two but different aspects of the same ultimate reality. Coincidentally, I had been reading the *Vijnana Bhairava Tantra*, a text from the Kashmiri Shaivism tradition. Essentially a dialogue between Shiva and Shakti, it's an eminently practical and straightforward text, like the Buddha's *Discourse on the Four Foundations of Mindfulness*, and proposes 112 different practices for recognizing the true nature of reality.

Shakti was from Sherbrooke, a city about an hour and a

half's drive away, but living temporarily in Montreal as part of her residency in emergency medicine. I liked that she kept smiling for no particular reason. I also liked that she asked me right away where I was from. Canadians are usually hesitant to ask non-White people where they are from.

Shakti kept firing off questions. "Were you affected by the war in Sri Lanka?"

"No. At least, not directly, but you know, it was always at the back of my mind. What a relief it's all over! I never thought I'd be able to say that in my lifetime."

Leaning slightly toward me, she asked, "How long have you been in Quebec?" This seemed an important question for her, for some reason.

"About fifteen years."

She nodded, clearly approving.

"I guess you've been trying different kinds of yoga." It was half question, half statement, as if she already knew me.

"Yes," I said and felt irritated with myself for not asking her how she'd know that.

Instead, I continued, "I also do Kashmiri yoga, which is a more effortless or non-dual form of yoga. It's more about engaging the energy body than the physical body."

After a while the conversation, which had been flowing, came to an ebb. A police car sped by behind her on Sainte-Catherine Street, red lights flashing and sirens screeching.

"I'll see you next time," she said once it had passed.

"Yes, see you next time."

But as I turned around and walked away, I saw the smile give way to a look of disappointment. I hesitated, torn between turning back and continuing, but it was much easier to keep going.

The next week, on my way up the stairs to the yoga studio,

I saw Shakti sitting in the café downstairs near the entrance. I went into the studio and laid out my yoga mat and when she came in, I saw that she was accompanied by a guy. I looked at them as if I couldn't comprehend this unexpected turn of events. She gave me her usual wide smile and nodded. During the class she smiled and nodded to me a couple of times, but her companion didn't look as happy to be there. After the class the two of them were standing on the sidewalk. When I went by, they both smiled and we greeted each other, but I kept walking.

Several weeks went by and I couldn't help wondering whether the guy was Shakti's boyfriend or a friend she had brought along for support. But each time I pushed through the doors of the building housing the yoga studio, I got a queasy feeling in the pit of my stomach, similarly to how I had felt ahead of my Pilates class with Alice about three years earlier. And when I laid out my yoga mat and saw that Shakti wasn't there, I felt relieved and my body relaxed.

One evening the yoga class had already started when I saw a petite, pony-tailed blond woman dressed in black from neck to ankles standing by the glass doors, hugging a purple yoga mat to her chest. She came in, and after inspecting her for some minutes from the corners of my eyes, I concluded she was Shakti. Immediately, I felt a strong and inexplicable urge to throw up and sensed my body going limp. I considered leaving the class several times but struggled on despite persistent nausea. At the end of the class, she walked past me and said hello. I couldn't manage anything more than a hoarse "hi" in return.

My body was burning and I had a parched throat. I badly needed to drink some ice-cold water. By the time I'd gotten changed, she was gone. The next morning I woke physically refreshed but despondent. Some three years earlier I had released dark and heavy energy over a period of some six months during classes with Alice. At the end of that period, I concluded that all the unresolved emotions from the trauma around my mother's absence had been released and I was fully healed. Clearly, that conclusion was premature.

~

The line to board my flight to Montreal was getting shorter, but there was still no sign of the Shakti look-alike returning from the washrooms, so I made my way to the gate. When I got there, I saw Shakti's companion from the yoga class sitting on the floor surrounded by several pieces of baggage, confirming that the woman I had seen was her. On the plane they were seated just a few rows ahead of me.

I felt nonchalant and patted myself on my back for my apparent lack of any PTSD symptoms, considering what had happened the last time I saw Shakti. When I went to collect my luggage in Montreal, she was standing near the conveyor belt checking her phone. I didn't have long to wait. I slung my red duffle bag over my left shoulder and walked away. She looked up and craned her neck in my direction, reminding me of how my mother tried to get a last look at me at the airport in Sri Lanka when I first left.

I went to bed that evening again congratulating myself for not being triggered by Shakti. The next morning I woke up with a feeling of heaviness, just like after moving into my new condo. But as the day went on, it became clear to me that this heaviness was not in the body but just outside and around it. My body was enveloped by a field of energy so dense it was almost palpable. Days turned into weeks, and the sensation of carrying this field of dense energy stayed with me. From time to time I'd forget about it, talk and laugh with my colleagues, and enjoy a meal with a friend. But then it would come back and I'd feel the same kind of sullen anger I had felt when I heard about the deaths of Aravind and Antoine, and of my brother's terminal illness.

I kept thinking about the synchronicity of my encounter with Shakti and, knowing that Jung had written extensively on the topic, I tracked down one of his quotes.

"Synchronicity is the coming together of inner and outer events in a way that cannot be explained by cause and effect and that is meaningful to the observer."[31]

After about three or four weeks of lugging around this field of dense energy, I felt the need for a massage. I set up an appointment with Delta, my regular massage therapist. She had confided in me about being abandoned by her mother when she was two. That night I was woken up by a wave of energy passing over my body from toe to head several times. When I woke up the next morning, my body felt light. The heaviness was gone, hopefully for good, this time.

During the days that followed, I couldn't help speculating about what happened.

Did the visit to Gurdjieff's grave lead to the synchronistic encounter with Shakti and perhaps to the completion of my healing process? Was it the awareness of my energy body developed through the practice of non-dual yoga over the past couple of years that helped me bring to light the dark and heavy energetic baggage I've been carrying around, unbeknownst to me?

A few years later, while writing this chapter, my understanding of the synchronistic encounters with Shakti came full circle when Goddess Aletheia made another cameo appearance and whispered in my ear.

"The girl I saw in the metro on the way to my first appointment with an osteopath was Shakti."

---

31   C.G.Jung, *Synchronocity: An Acausal Connecting Principle.*

My mind flashed back to the scene some nine years before the airport encounter.

A boy writhing on the floor at my feet, foaming at the mouth. Shakti appearing from nowhere and taking charge. I'm frozen and no help to her.

Later, I tell the osteopath about the scene I just witnessed.

She responds, "What you saw was a re-enactment of your father's death. The young woman was clearly playing the role of your mother. Your way of coping was to freeze up."

Chapter 20
Gyumri, Armenia

I can't remember exactly when I got the idea to visit Gyumri in Armenia, Gurdjieff's birthplace. It must have been prompted by the synchronistic sequel to my pilgrimage to Gurdjieff's grave in Avon.

The plan was to fly through Istanbul to Tbilisi, hang out there for a couple of days to acclimatize to the region's energy, and then travel to Gyumri in a private taxi. This might seem like a roundabout way of getting there, but the border between Turkey and Armenia was closed due to festering wounds dating back to World War I. But I didn't mind it at all, as Gurdjieff had lived in Tbilisi, or Tiflis as it was then called, for two years after fleeing post-Revolution Russia.

On the twelve-hour Turkish Airlines flight from Montreal to Istanbul, I noticed a woman with long reddish-brown hair sitting in the front row just ahead of me. I discovered that she was a doctor when she responded to a call for medical help from the airline crew. What seemed like an insignificant observation then would turn out to be highly meaningful a year and a half later.

To someone coming off a long-haul transatlantic flight without getting much sleep, the Atatürk Airport in Istanbul can be a shock. Hordes of travellers rushing off in different directions. People sleeping on the floor. Food courts occupying most of the central space. Groups of men scantily covered in one piece of flimsy white cotton cloth, wearing leather sandals and carrying hardly anything—fellow pilgrims no doubt, but to a different destination than mine—contrasting with women covered in heavy black clothing from head to toe, dragging heavy luggage.

I wasn't sure if I was hungry, but I gravitated toward the food court, feeling the need to secure a stable space for myself in the chaos and prepare myself for a tedious nine-hour wait. I went into an Italian place, thinking I couldn't go wrong with Italian. I studied the menu at length and ordered a Niçoise salad, but when the waiter put the salad on the table, I knew right away I had made the wrong choice. It looked insipid. I had pictured a bowl exploding with colours—green lettuce, red tomatoes, yellow-and-white egg, pale pink tuna, black olives, onion rings purple on the outside and white inside. It also tasted insipid, mainly because the lettuce used was iceberg, a poor choice for a Niçoise salad. A man came by and sat at the table next to mine, waved away the menu offered by the waiter and ordered a risotto.

Why didn't I think of it myself? A warm, unctuous risotto was the perfect comfort food for a weary long-distance traveller.

I cheered up over a glass of Turkish tea served in a distinctive little vase-shaped glass with a gold rim. A Turkish tea glass has no handle, so you have to hold it delicately with your thumb, forefinger and middle finger. I had to tilt my elbow upwards and give my wrist a twirl when I brought the glass to my lips. The last time I'd held this kind of glass in my hand must have been some thirty years earlier, on my first trip to Istanbul. I remembered sitting in a teahouse in the gardens of the Topkapi Palace overlooking the Bosphorus. The waiter went by holding a tray full of freshly brewed glasses of reddish-brown tea at shoulder-level on his horizontal upturned palm, putting one down on each table with a little matching saucer as soon as he saw a glass was empty.

That had been quite an epic trip. I'd hitchhiked from Paris with Gord, and then taken the inaptly named Istanbul Express, which took three days and nights to chug its way from Venice through Eastern Europe to the shores of Asia.

During the trip I struck up a friendship with a Turkish medical student named Nadia, and she showed me the sights of Istanbul. After I went back to Paris, she wrote to me and we corresponded, mostly about literature and philosophy. One day she sent me a wedding photograph of herself and a fellow student she had introduced to me as a friend, and her letters stopped since then. She told me once that I reminded her of Diogenes going around with a lamp during the day looking for an honest man. Coincidentally, while I was planning my second trip to Istanbul, Nadia contacted me through social media, telling me she still remembered our conversation in the train about Herman Hesse's *Steppenwolf*.

That trip was also memorable for what happened when the train crossed into Bulgaria on the way back. A number of us, all young people, mostly Italian—I believe there was some geopolitical tension between Bulgaria and Italy—were thrown off the train for the flimsiest of reasons. My "offence" was that I had little money on me. Since I was going back to Paris, where I lived, I couldn't see how throwing me out of the train could have done anyone any good. As I stood on the train platform wondering what was going to happen next, my body trembled. A tall Bulgarian soldier standing close by waved his machine gun in my direction and said, "You, frightened." This observation gave him great delight.

"No, no, I'm cold," I protested, holding up a bit of my light cotton shirt between my thumb and forefinger for corroboration.

"No, not cold," he said, laughing aloud and pointing his machine gun toward the dark sky. True, it was a warm summer night. In my mind, I didn't feel terribly concerned, convinced that sanity would prevail and this Kafkaesque situation would be soon resolved. I wonder now whether my body knew something my discursive mind didn't, and that deep down I was worried about being stranded on the wrong side of the Iron Curtain.

~

The nine-hour wait at the Istanbul airport dragged by and I arrived at Tbilisi airport around four in the morning. Not knowing if I'd be able to find a taxi at such an early hour, I had requested an airport pick-up from my hotel, but when I got to the airport lobby and scanned the waiting crowd, I didn't see anyone holding a sign with my name or the hotel's name. My brain froze, unable to deal with this unexpected turn of events.

As I stood there somewhat dazed, a tall, pleasant-looking young man came up to me, said his name was Giorgi and asked if I needed a taxi. He said he knew where my hotel was located and could take me there, but when I asked him for the cost, he became evasive, telling me it would depend on the distance. A part of my mind saw a big red flag with SCAM written all over it but I followed Giorgi anyway.

When we exited the airport, I saw a number of taxis waiting and waved my arm in their direction, as if to say, "Plenty of taxis here. Why am I following this guy?"

Having cleverly foreseen such a train of thought, Giorgi had grabbed my bag before we got to the door and was now striding ahead, so I had no choice but to follow him. When I caught up with him, he was putting my red duffle bag into the boot of his car, which, unsurprisingly, was not a taxi. I pointed it out to Giorgi. He smiled rather condescendingly, as if he pitied me for raising such an absurd objection. "It's the same thing. You pay according to the distance."

The door clicked shut and I sat next to Giorgi, who now had the look of a man sitting down to a delicious meal. My shoulders slumped.

Why didn't I just grab my bag and walk to the taxi rank? Why did I let myself be scammed so easily?

Like the time I had let myself be pranked by the *Just for Laughs* crew in Montreal a few years earlier. I was crossing Phillips Square in front of The Bay on my way home after work when a woman standing next to a kiosk displaying ceramic plates and vases called out to me, "*Monsieur, monsieur!*"

She wanted me to look after her kiosk while she went to use the washroom in the nearby Burger King. Part of my mind thought it was fishy that she didn't ask someone from an adjoining kiosk, but I heard myself saying yes. The woman ran away with a big smile. Needless to say, my stint as a kiosk watcher was an unmitigated disaster, with the ceramics being smashed into smithereens all around me. Or maybe a mitigated disaster, because I managed to hold onto the two large vases on the counter—the only pranked victim to do so, or so I was told by the pranksters when they emerged grinning from their hiding places.

On the way to my hotel in Tbilisi, we drove past an astoundingly futuristic construction consisting of two huge steel tube-like structures lying on their sides at about a thirty-degree angle to each other. I remembered reading that the city had become known for its innovative architecture and later learned that this was the Rhike Park, Music Theatre and Exhibition Hall. I wanted to ask Giorgi about it but decided we weren't on speaking terms. Then a nagging undercurrent thought broke through to the surface. Giorgi reminded me of Jorge from Venezuela, another scammer from my past! They even had the same name!

~

It had happened several decades earlier, during a two-week trip to Italy during my Easter holidays in Paris. I was wandering around the streets of Rome on my first evening when a tall young man came toward me. He smiled and said he was going to a club, and he invited me to join him. I readily agreed but when we got there, I balked, seeing it was a strip club. I started having doubts about Jorge, yet I followed him. We were shown to a table. Two young women came and sat with us, and things became surreal. I watched helplessly as champagne, cigarettes, canapés and other snacks flowed to our table. It all ended when a man in a suit, presumably the manager, came to our table, holding a piece of paper in his hand, presumably our bill, flashed a light on it and asked, "Can you pay?"

Jorge paid up his share, and staying in character, gave me the card of his hotel and told me to come and look him up. I protested. The manager threatened to call the police. I told him to go ahead. We negotiated and settled on a price.

The next morning I woke up in my cheap *pensione* with a knot in the pit of my stomach. I had let myself be scammed of a good portion of my two-week budget on my first evening.

~

We finally arrived at my hotel in downtown Tbilisi, and Giorgi quoted an outrageous amount. We negotiated and I ended paying him about twenty Canadian dollars more than I'd have paid the hotel driver. I told the hotel receptionist that the driver had not turned up at the airport. Anna, a petite girl with large green eyes, short blond hair and a blue silk shawl around her shoulders, came out from behind her desk. She whirled her arms around like a pair of windmills and pointed with both hands at the floor in front of me, saying, "But the boy was here!"

She was referring to the hotel driver, and I later learned that he had indeed come to the hotel to pick up the sign with my name. But I kept looking at her wide-eyed, impressed by her flamboyant gesticulation. Thinking I hadn't understood, she swung her arms back and forth again, pushing back the ends of her shawl, and repeated, "But the boy was here!"

I went to my room, chuckling to myself, the unpleasantness of the incident swept away by the magical wave of the elf-like Anna's arms. I even felt compassion for Giorgi.

Couldn't such a personable and apparently intelligent young man who spoke good English do something better with his life than petty scams?

A few hours later, after a shower and a short nap, I breakfasted on toast, hard-boiled eggs, various types of local cheese, sliced tomatoes and cucumbers, and black olives. I'd have pretty much the same meal every morning over the next ten days of my trip. Refreshed, I walked up Pushkin Street, tugging my hood over my head to ward off the late November Tbilisi chill. I arrived at Freedom Square and resisted the temptation to board the warm and inviting bright red double-decker hop-on, hop-off bus.

I'm a pilgrim, not a tourist!

I walked down Rustaveli Avenue, the main thoroughfare in Tbilisi, and had a look at the Georgian National Opera and

Ballet Theatre of Tbilisi, where Gurdjieff and his students staged the first public performance of sacred dances. The sacred dances, or the movements, were inspired by various temple dances that Gurdjieff had seen or participated in during his travels in central Asia and Tibet. They played an important role in Gurdjieff's teaching and were aimed at harmonizing the centres and achieving self-remembering.

At first glance, Tbilisi was like any European city with its stately avenues, neoclassical architecture and chic women going about their business. Then I saw its crumbling sidewalks, shabby buildings, children and old people panhandling in the street, roaming packs of stray dogs with tagged ears, and underpasses converted into dingy mini shopping malls as I had seen elsewhere in former Soviet Union countries. I had to keep jumping out of the way when bright orange minivans packed with commuters screeched to a halt pretty much anywhere to disgorge and pick up passengers.

Tbilisi is the capital of Georgia, once part of the Soviet Union. Georgia's most famous son is Stalin, but apparently he did no special favours for his motherland during his reign. Stalin and Gurdjieff were supposed to have been fellow students at a seminary in Tiflis, as the city was then called, and even roommates in Gurdjieff's uncle's home. As the story goes, Stalin left without paying his bills!

Old Tbilisi was just a few minutes' walk from Freedom Square. Strolling through the labyrinth of its winding cobbled streets, I noticed that some parts had been renovated and transformed into cafés, bars and restaurants, albeit too exuberantly in some cases, with other parts on the verge of crumbling and falling apart. Although the sun was out, the cold penetrated my bones. The streets were deserted except for a few forlorn girls marking time on the sidewalks and clutching at their parkas while trying to entice the few passers-by into their empty restaurants.

I stepped into the Sioni Cathedral, founded in the seventh century and renovated in the seventeenth. Orthodox churches have a special feel to them, with their icons, standing congregations and the absence of pews. The silent piety of the black-clad worshippers shuffling around lighting candles made me feel like a shameless intruder, so I left as unobtrusively as I could.

My main mission in Tbilisi was to eat kachapuri, a Georgian specialty and a staple of my diet during my stay in Moscow about fifteen years earlier. I chose a restaurant specializing in Georgian pastries for its glass front, and ordered kachapuri with a cucumber and tomato salad, and a glass of Georgian red wine made using the thousand-year-old kvevri method. When my order arrived, the kachapuri turned out to be a sort of pizza and nothing like the flaky oblong pastry filled with cheese that had melted in my mouth in Moscow.

The next morning Alik came to drive me to Armenia as arranged by the hotel receptionist. I ran down the three flights of stairs, crossed Pushkin Street, threw my red duffle bag onto the back seat of the waiting steel blue Mercedes and got in. Alik took off without a word of greeting. Clearly, he was not a man to spend time on idle pleasantries. He spoke aggressively in what sounded like Russian, mentioning Yerevan, the capital of Armenia, several times. The lines of communication might have got crossed at some point, so I told him my destination was Gyumri and not Yerevan. Alik, who seemed an excitable man under normal circumstances, went ballistic, screaming into his cell phone and hitting the dashboard with his hand. I looked out of the window as if nothing untoward was happening inside.

He eventually calmed down and offered to take me to Gyumri for two hundred Georgian lari, just over a hundred Canadian dollars—quite the bargain considering the transborder trip would take about six hours. The deal done to his satisfaction, he introduced himself and informed me he was Kurdish, putting his hand over his heart, and even offered to get me a coffee. But this lull in our relations was short-lived. As we approached the Georgia-Armenia border, he said, "*Davai, davai,*" and motioned me to hand over the money. I crossed my arms and refused, saying I'd pay him when we got to Gyumri. But he kept insisting, so I handed over the 200 lari, suspecting another scam—and a more serious one at that, since I had to get out of the car and walk to the border control post while Alik drove through with my belongings.

When I told the two young Armenian border guards who looked like twin brothers that I had already obtained an electronic visa, they grudgingly stamped my passport. One of the twins asked me, "What's your nationality?"

I pointed with my chin to my Canadian passport in his hands but he repeated, "But where are you *really* from?"

To my relief Alik was waiting for me on the other side. He introduced me to another man, Garik, who'd be taking me on the next leg of my journey. The economics and logistics of cross-border transportation in the Caucasus became clear. Alik assured me that Garik's car was a blue Mercedes just like his, but when I got into it, I realized it was at least thirty years older and the seat belt didn't work. Garik told me to hold it across my chest with my hand if I saw a police cruiser coming along, making it sound as if it was the normal thing to do. Unlike the excitable Alik, Garik was a calm and dignified-looking man. But I still hadn't ruled out the possibility of a scam masterminded by Alik.

So I couldn't fully enjoy the trip through the northern Armenian countryside, as part of my mind was obsessing over what I'd do if Garik asked me for more money when we got to Gyumri. The other part of my mind was surprised by how quickly the landscape changed. Haunting, pockmarked brown mountains gave way to shimmering snow-capped peaks in the distance and to scenes of abandoned factories and rusting vehicles—images of a deindustrialized dystopia triggered by the Soviet Union's collapse.

Before too long, Gyumri loomed ahead. The city was built almost exclusively of black stone, projecting a bleak and dark energy, fittingly so, as it had been devastated by an earthquake in 1988. My fears of another scam turned out to be unfounded as Garik carried my bag to the Berlin Art Hotel's front desk. We concluded a deal for him to pick me up from Yerevan in a few days and take me back to the Tbilisi airport.

After checking in I headed off to find a place to eat. The large town square had a black stone church and a cathedral at either end, flanking an official-looking building on one side. There was a brightly lit restaurant with a glass front and diner booths in bright red, blue and orange, contrasting with the bleakness of the external surroundings. I sat in a red booth, noticing with some irritation that there was a wider than usual gap between the seat and the table.

The restaurant manager, a young blond woman in a leather jacket and boots, strode around with a smart phone tucked into the pocket of her crimson jeans. She kindly sat down with me and translated the menu for me. I ordered an Armenian yogurt soup, a kachapuri and a salad. Since the manager of the restaurant in which I'd eaten kachapuri in Moscow was Armenian, I had high hopes for the kachapuri but it turned out to a kind of pizza as well, this time with a thinner crust.

The next morning I had breakfast in the hotel dining room, with floor-to-ceiling windows opening out to the garden while watching fluffy snowflakes wafting down and covering the bare branches of the trees. I spread out the square-shaped sheet-like Armenian bread on my plate and filled it with stringy cheese, tomato and cucumber slices and olives and made myself a sandwich.

After breakfast I headed out to see Gurdjieff's house, just a ten-minute walk from the hotel. The fluffy snow was still falling when I started out. The wide streets were laid out in a grid and deserted, with few signs of life from the houses on either side. I must have taken a wrong turn as after walking for forty minutes, I still hadn't found the place.

A friendly gentleman, the first person I'd seen that morning, gave me directions and I finally stood in front of Gurdjieff's family home at No. 222 Matnishyan Street. The house, a one-storey stone structure, got a mention in *In Search for the Miraculous* when Ouspensky visited Gurdjieff in Alexandropol, as Gyumri was then called, following the Russian Revolution in 1917.

Arriving at my destination was much more anticlimactic than in my previous pilgrimages, as I could do nothing more than turn around and go back, after all the efforts I had made to get there. An unfriendly-looking older man peered over the wall of the house in front and gave me suspicious looks. I didn't feel comfortable hanging around or taking pictures.

I went back to the Berlin Art Hotel, which by then had become a comforting haven for me, and had an excellent lunch of cauliflower soup, cabbage salad, broiled fish, broccoli and rice prepared and tastefully presented by Ani, the hotel's chef. I then met with Alex, the hotel manager and a follower of Gurdjieff, and Arthur, a local Gurdjieff scholar. They took me to see the grave of Gurdjieff's father. Gurdjieff himself had never been able to visit his father's grave so he had asked his followers to do so in his stead. We came back to the hotel, sat at the large table in the library, drank vodka while munching on canapés with black olive tapenade, and talked about Gurdjieff. I wanted to tell them my theory that Gurdjieff's mission was to renew the Buddha's message of waking up. But I didn't want to risk disrupting the cordial and harmonious discussion.

~

A few days later, the Armenia leg of the pilgrimage completed, I went to Konya in south-central Turkey to visit the tomb of thirteenth-century Sufi poet Rumi, ticking off another item on my bucket list of pilgrimages. I'm not sure when I first heard of it, but ever since, I've been fascinated with the story of Rumi's transformation from eminent Islamic scholar to mystic poet of love after meeting his friend and teacher Shams, a wandering dervish.[32] One of the versions of their first meeting goes like this:

> *One day, Rumi was reading, seated next to a large stack of books. Shams, who was passing by, asked him, "What are you doing?" Rumi scoffingly replied, "Something you cannot understand." (This is knowledge that cannot be understood by the unlearned.) On hearing this, Shams threw the stack of books into a nearby pool of water. Rumi hastily rescued the books and to his surprise they were all dry. Rumi then asked Shams, "What is this?" Shams replied, "This is what you cannot understand." (This is knowledge that cannot be understood by the learned.)*[33]

---

32   A member of the Sufi order who has taken a vow of poverty and austerity.
33   Franklin Lewis, *Rumi, Past and Present, East and West*

I walked from my hotel in central Konya to the Mevlana Museum complex. It was located in an open area adjacent to a large pedestrian quarter. I went through the main gate and crossed the marble courtyard, entering the mausoleum through the ornate, heavy silver doors with the inscription, "Those who enter here incomplete will come out perfect."

Rumi's tomb was flanked by those of his son and other renowned dervishes, all covered by heavy shrouds with gold embroidery. A large turban protruded above Rumi's tomb, symbolizing his spiritual authority. A framed inscription of verse hung on the wall above the tomb and I later read with delight in the museum brochure that it was one I knew.

> *Come, come, whoever you are.*
> *Wanderer, worshipper, lover of leaving—it doesn't matter,*
> *Ours is not a caravan of despair.*
> *Come, even if you have broken your vow a thousand times,*
> *Come, come again, come.*[34]

I found the verse inspiring for its compassion and intriguing for its enigmatic expression, "lover of leaving." On the flight from Konya back to Istanbul, it occurred to me that, similarly to Koyasan and Eihei-ji in Japan, visiting Konya might have been as meaningful as going to Gyumri or even more.

But I couldn't explain why.

~

---

34   Translation of unknown origin

Back in Istanbul the next afternoon, my mission accomplished, I sipped Turkish tea in the café in the Topkapi Palace gardens overlooking the blue waters of the Bosphorus Strait, which splits Istanbul and Turkey into its European and Asian parts. I sat pretty much in the same spot as I had on my first trip to Istanbul. Large boats ferried passengers from Europe to Asia and from East to West, the waters reflecting the early December sun.

I thought about my own travels between the East and West, both literal and symbolic. Growing up in the East, I'd looked to the West for the possibilities it offered me to grow as an individual and figure out what I needed to do with my life. Living in the West, I had woken up momentarily to my true self and looked to the East for the means to awaken fully, and in the process, discovered that my individual identity was largely based on false perceptions.

Looking back at my pilgrimage to Gyumri, it was all about scams—about letting myself be scammed, recalling past scams and then fretting about being scammed when everything was above board.

Why such a preoccupation with scams? Was it to put the spotlight on the only scam that mattered—the scam that my sixteen-month-old brain perpetrated on itself that I had been abandoned by my mother?

The image of Ana the elf waving her magical arms flashed in my mind. This time, I heard her say, "But your mother was there!"

It struck me then that the movement of Ana's arms and their final position reminded me of one of Gurdjieff's sacred dances which I had practised in Montreal. When asked about the purpose of the sacred dances, Gurdjieff is supposed to have said, "To make sure the past does not influence the future."

I made the connection with the quote attributed to Jung:

"Until you make the unconscious conscious, it will direct your life and you will call it fate."

~

From Istanbul, I flew to Sri Lanka. Back in Mount Lavinia, I sat in my favourite chair overlooking the garden and thought some more about the pilgrimage. When I'd first decided to visit Gyumri, I expected something out of the ordinary to happen, as it had after my pilgrimages to Bodh Gaya, Eihei-ji and the Avon cemetery. But as I made my final preparations, I knew that this trip was going to be more about closure.

In *In Search of the Miraculous*, Gurdjieff says, "Awakening is possible only for those who seek it and want it, for those who are ready to struggle with themselves and work on themselves for a very long time and very persistently in order to attain it."[35]

I felt I no longer needed to struggle with myself. My long journey, triggered by the reading of Gurdjieff's teachings on that fateful Christmas Eve in Paris, had come full circle.

On my return to Montreal, I discussed my trip with Solange and told her about my conclusion. "I've been thinking about it for a while. I'm now dropping all of my so-called spiritual pursuits and embracing the Advaita Vedanta approach of non-doing. As Krishnamurti said, truth is a pathless land."

Solange looked dubious. "I don't see myself giving up my meditation practice."

"It's not a question of giving up. It's about letting go when you're ready. Have you heard about the Buddha's parable about the raft? It basically says that you make a raft to cross the river. Once you get to the other shore, you don't carry it on your head just because it has served you in the past. You leave it behind.

---

[35] P.D.Ouspensky, *In Search of the Miraculous*.

Without all these practices I've done over the past twenty-five years, I wouldn't have been able to establish myself in the four foundations of mindfulness, integrate wakefulness into my daily life, bring to light my emotional wounds and heal myself. But my quest now is to let go of the observer. Formalized practices could end up bolstering the sense of a doer and a separate self."

Solange continued to look dubious, so I continued, "Talking of scams, my self-perpetrated scam no doubt heightened and nourished my sense of separation. Clearly, our sense of separation from others and the world is rooted in the belief in a separate self, which, after all, is the most universal of all scams!"

Chapter 21
Saint Louis Square

It all started, or at least that's what I thought, when I found myself in my family doctor's office for the mandatory annual checkup. She swivelled around in her seat and peered at me above her glasses.

"Some of your test results are borderline. I want you to see a nephrologist."

Since that bout of hypochondria in Vancouver, I had reverted to my default attitude of avoiding doctors and hoping any ailments would go away on their own. So I put on my doubtful face, which in the past had worked to get my doctor to backtrack. But this time, she didn't budge.

So, about a year after my pilgrimage to Gyumri, I found myself in the waiting room of another clinic. I heard my name called out over the PA system, but I wasn't sure where the voice was coming from, since the clinic was large and offered various services. Confused, I stood up and looked around. A few minutes later, I heard the voice calling my name again. It was coming from a woman with long, reddish-brown hair standing in one of the doorways wearing a short dark brown skirt, long-sleeved light beige top, and high heels. She had a sheet of paper in her hand and looked irritated.

"Are you married or single?"

That was one of Dr. KK's first questions for me as we settled down in her office. She fired off a few more of the personal questions that doctors should ask but none had in my many medical consultations across the world.

She ended up with, "How long have you been in Quebec?"

Similarly to the conversation with Shakti a few years earlier, the question seemed important to the doctor.

Dr. KK moved on to the medical part of the consultation. Her manner was brisk and professional but chatty and friendly at the same time. Soon, I felt a wave of energy coming from her and enveloping me, making me feel contented to just be sitting there. Thinking about it later, it was as if I was back in my mother's womb, wanting for nothing. The flow of energy seemed similar to what I experienced during my first yoga class with Sally, except this time I was playing a more passive role and simply receiving. And while Sally had been running around, Dr. KK was simply sitting and emitting energy like a dynamo.

At one point, she uncoiled herself and leaped out of her chair, raising her forearm and giving a ladylike fist pump. "I'm going to take your blood pressure."

I might have glanced at the street through the floor-to-ceiling windows of her office. She waved her hand toward the street.

"Don't worry," she said. "The glass is tinted, so no one outside can see us."

I wasn't worried but I liked that she said no one could see us. She went back to her desk and asked me how much I weighed. I wasn't sure. She leaped out of her chair again with another gentle fist pump.

"I'm going to weigh you."

When she told me my weight, I blurted out in a panicky voice, "I've gained weight!"

She responded with a suppressed smile. Dr. KK had something intriguingly familiar about her and I remembered that Bibi used to give me the same little smile whenever I said or did something that amused her.

Come to think of it, Bibi was dressed almost exactly the same the first time I saw her except that her dark brown skirt was *longer and she* wasn't *wearing high heels. I don't think I ever saw Bibi wearing high heels. I wonder why. Did I ever ask her about it? If I did, I can't remember what she said.*

I caught my mind straying, broke through the internal dialogue and brought my focus back to the doctor, who was now back at her desk.

She took a sheet of paper, tore off a small piece, scribbled something and handed it to me. "Here's my email address. You can write to me if you have any problems."

I went out looking at the piece of paper in my hand, still enveloped in a cozy bubble of energy and feeling unsure of what had just taken place.

A couple of hours later, she called me at work to discuss a few things regarding my medical file. Again, her tone was professional but chatty.

At one point she said wistfully, "How fast the years go by."

I told her I'd be going on vacation soon and she responded with interest.

"Ah, are you going to Sri Lanka?"

Later in the day, the bubble of energy was ruptured when I got involved in an unpleasant email exchange with a colleague.

But when my thoughts returned to Dr. KK, the anger dissipated instead of ruminating, and the bubble was repaired.

I waited about a week and then sent Dr. KK a businesslike message on a pretext. She promptly responded with an equally businesslike message, not leaving any wriggle room for me to write back with something more personal.

I went to Sri Lanka and spent a month there, still basking in the warmth of the bubble of energy created by Dr. KK. Sami had coordinated his vacation with mine and we met up at the Mount Lavinia Hotel terrace for drinks and dinner. As we sat by the pool, with the sun disappearing below the horizon and waves pounding the rocks below, I told him about Dr. KK. Large black crows circled above, poised to swoop down and grab a morsel of food, under the watchful gaze of the uniformed security guard who took aim at them with a catapult. The crows scattered, squawking, their large black wings flapping furiously. The security guard reassured us that he was just trying to scare the crows away and not to kill them.

"My mind feels like a lake," I told Sami. "Calm and peaceful, so unlike the sea." We gazed out at the frothy ocean waves. "Maybe it's because I'm still feeling connection and not separation. I'm tempted to write to her, but I don't want to jeopardize our professional relationship. After all, I'll be seeing her again in a couple of months' time. And even if my imagination has blown things out of proportion, it would still be great to have her as a doctor."

"Why don't you write to her about a medical issue and then say a few things about what you're doing here? That would be an opportunity for her to respond in a more personal way if she wants."

"That's an excellent idea!" I said. "Why didn't I think of it myself?" But I didn't follow through.

The bubble of warm and fuzzy energy stayed with me during the wintry Montreal months while I waited for my second appointment with Dr. KK. A couple of days before the appointment, I got my hair cut. When the day finally arrived, I waited for her to call me, wearing a freshly laundered white shirt and thinking I wasn't even sure what she looked like. I opened the door to her office with a big smile and saw her sitting behind her desk, looking pretty and demure in a sky blue sweater, at least, that's what I thought. She responded with a curt nod. When I sat down I realized that she was actually looking stern and trying to give the impression she had things well under control. She acted cold and distant, so unlike the person I had seen three months earlier. The bubble of energy finally burst and I no longer felt connection, only separation.

She cut to the chase. "I looked at your test results. They're fine. I don't need to see you anymore."

This can't be happening!

I made an effort to gather my thoughts and protested. "But not all the results are fine."

"Ah, you've seen the results as well? But you're on the right track, so I don't need to see you again."

My sense of disbelief gave way to resentment.

When she stood up to take my blood pressure, she didn't jump out or pump her fist like the previous time. I noticed she was wearing black pants and black boots.

But when she got closer to me, she softened. She spread her arms wide, palms toward me, her head tilted to one side. A lock of hair fell away, revealing a gold-studded earlobe. "*You* don't need *me*," she said almost pleadingly.

I thought I heard a little girl's voice.

It was the perfect opportunity to say "No, no, of course, I

need you."

But I didn't. I just smiled passively, contentedly, forgetting I was supposed to look resentful.

She sat again and asked, "Do you have any questions for me?"

I stopped berating myself for the missed opportunity and searched in my mind for a medical question to gain more time. Men don't notice such things, or at least I don't, so before the second appointment, I had set myself the intention to check whether she had a ring on her finger. I remembered my intention and stared at her hands. An apprehensive look came over her face, and she took her left hand off the table and hid it underneath.

She repeated, "Do you have any other questions for me?"

I didn't. Our eyes locked defiantly for what seemed like a long time. She then reminded me of my mother. I finally broke the gaze, grabbed my jacket and walked out.

I've been thrust out of the womb!

The next day or two were filled with darkness, as I was overwhelmed by residual traumatic memories. But then light broke through and my mind became spacious again.

All is not lost. I do have some agency now. I can still write to her.

It was my turn to cut to the chase. I told her I was taken aback by how our doctor-patient relationship had ended so abruptly, but since we no longer had a professional relationship, I invited her to have lunch with me.

She didn't reply. I waited about ten days and wrote to her again. I started off with a caveat that if she thought my earlier invitation was inappropriate, she shouldn't read any further but simply delete my message. I explained in some detail my feelings over the past few months and invited her to meet me again, this time for a coffee near her clinic. I read the message before sending it off. It was focused, forthright and fearless. So unlike the rambling, beating-about-the-bush messages I had sent off to various women in the past. For instance, when a guarded Alice had asked me to express myself in writing, I complied, but she emailed me back saying something like, "I didn't read anything of much interest to me in your message." Naturally.

Karine didn't reply, at least not right away. Except for those initial two days of darkness, no unresolved emotions came up as they had in the past. This supported my conclusion that a critical phase of my healing journey had ended with the palpable letting go of heavy energy in the aftermath of my encounter with Shakti at the Paris airport.

That conclusion was tested some months after the airport encounter when I walked away from Annick with my emotional equanimity intact. I had met Annick when she gave me a ride to a mutual friend's place in the Laurentian mountains. I had hardly clipped on my seat belt when she mentioned, in an offhand way, that her biological clock was ticking and she wanted to have a child soon. As if it were one of those things that one typically says on meeting someone else for the first time. She followed it with a series of personal questions, including whether I rented or owned my place. But we hit it off so well that I didn't notice the landscape changing from dense city to suburban and then to open nature and rolling mountains.

Back in Montreal after the weekend, we kept in touch through email, text messages and phone calls. Since we connected so well, I thought about Harville Hendrix's imago theory and wondered whether she had any Daddy issues. I dug a little deeper to find out, but it appeared she didn't. I did learn that she had an autistic twin sister who had been institutionalized. The amateur psychologist in me went into overdrive.

Separation from a twin is like being separated from yourself. Being separated, or the perception of being separated from your mother before you develop a separate identity is like being separated from yourself! We have a similar wound, so no wonder we connected so well!

On our first proper date, she came to my place, looked around and said, "This is really nice."

She walked over to the floor-to-ceiling windows and pointed at Sherbrooke Street outside.

"But it's right in the middle of downtown. Don't you want to sell it and buy a duplex with me in a quieter part of town? We could live on the second floor and rent out the ground floor."

I was speechless. She changed the subject. The prematurity of the question was all the more astounding because I knew she had led a promiscuous life during her time as an actress on a local soap opera. We went out, and later when she dropped me off at my place, we brushed cheeks as we had done before. As I drew away, she looked disappointed.

After that Annick became distant, but I didn't let her pull me in. I simply moved on.

Moving on from Karine, however, was not an option. As she drew away from me, I moved toward her, inexorably, like a snowball rolling downhill, like what had happened with Bibi.

Separation from Karine was accompanied by a deep yearning to reconnect with her. Along with this longing came a shift in my energy. I started waking up early, around four, or sometimes even earlier.

One morning, for the first time since I had moved into my condo some seven years earlier, I felt a compelling need to see the sunrise so I went up to our rooftop. Having grown up on Sri Lanka's West Coast and having lived near Vancouver's English Bay, I've seen plenty of sunsets, but I don't think I had ever seen a proper sunrise.

I climbed the stairs to the rooftop, steaming mug of tea in

hand. The plaintive cry of a lone seagull pierced the muffled humming of the building ventilation system. Feeling the bracing breeze on my face, I pulled my hood over my head, sipped some tea and looked around, sensing the soles of my feet spreading in my flip-flops.

To the west, the darkened Mount Royal topped by its illuminated cross seemed at hand. Nearby, the larger-than-life purple mural of a sad, stern Leonard Cohen sporting a fedora looked toward the east where the rising sun heralded itself with a rosy-pink line above a broad expanse of dark land studded with flickering lights. In the foreground, the twin iron peaks of the Jacques Cartier Bridge spanned the still waters of the Saint Lawrence River. To the north, a flock of birds flew in front of a church dome with a rising spire beyond the green treetops of Saint Louis Square, while sleek steel, glass and concrete towers jostled for prominence downtown.

The sun appeared as a bright crimson dot, then as an arc that swelled into a semicircle before ballooning into a red circle just above the horizon. I marvelled at how quickly it all happened. Soon the sun was a glowing golden orb, pulsating with luminous energy, transforming the sky into a hazy blue and lighting up the mountain and the tops of the towers downtown.

I lingered, loath to leave the radiant light. A Chogyam Trungpa quote about the vision of the Great Eastern Sun surfaced in my mind, but I couldn't remember the actual words, so I went down to my place and thumbed through my worse-for-wear copy of *Shambhala: The Sacred Path of the Warrior*. I read, "The way of the Great Eastern Sun is based on seeing that there is a natural source of radiance and brilliance in the world—the innate wakefulness of human beings."

After that, weather permitting, I started going up to our rooftop regularly. With dawn breaking around me, I'd sip my tea, feeling the mug in my hand, my feet on the wooden deck, my back and buttocks against the aluminum chair, my T-shirt against my skin and the cool air caressing my face. As discursive thoughts subsided, I'd feel fully present, yet I still couldn't truly connect with the rising sun.

I'm still an observer and everything is being perceived through the filter of a separate self!

On some days I'd wake just after three, my energy level high, almost manic. I'd feel like running down the street, singing. At work, I'd get the urge to stand on my desk and shout out something like, "Wake up, guys! There's no time to lose!"

I was never a big fan of *kirtans*—the devotional chants sung in yoga centres—thinking that people tended to get carried away by the emotions and become detached from reality. But I felt the need to hear the chanting of the *Shiva Shiva Mahadeva* mantra and listened to it over and over again. I then moved on to other genres, typically inspirational or simply joyful music laced with longing or melancholy. When my energy level was high, listening to music that matched my mood became an essential need. Conversely, when my energy took a dip, music gave me a boost.

I had pretty much let go of any expectations of hearing back from Karine when, more than two months after my first message, she wrote back. Again, she cut to the chase. She thanked me for my invitations but had to decline as her code of professional ethics prohibited her from meeting with me in a social setting. However, if ever I needed any medical references, she'd be more than happy to help.

It pleased me to note that she had made a point to say "invitations" in the plural, which meant she had disregarded my caveat and read through to the end of my long second message. Her timing was baffling, but the message was unambiguous.

To mark a solar eclipse, I went for a walk on Mount Royal. When I approached my fallen tree, I saw a long-haired First Nations man in traditional clothing strolling back and forth nearby, playing a flute. I lay on the tree with my knees up and was listening to the haunting music when Goddess Aletheia revealed herself to me again.

This time, she took on the form of an alluring young girl with short, reddish-brown hair wearing a white summer dress and sitting languidly in a chair, thighs crossed and a red slipper dangling from her small foot. Even though it was over twenty years ago and I had not thought about her since then, I recognized the girl immediately. I had seen her a few times at the Gnostic centre.

The young girl was Karine!

I had no doubt in my mind as I swung my feet down and sat on the tree, no longer hearing the flute music played by the indigenous man.

The last personal question Dr. KK asked me, "How long have you been in Quebec?" made perfect sense now. Had she recognized me?

This latest epiphany gave a whole new dimension to my connection with Karine. I remembered that I'd had a vivid erotic dream involving her the day I saw her, and how easily I'd been able to practise the transmutation of sexual energy since then.

Did the connection to the young Karine help me in that process?

I also remembered how, fuelled by the new-found source of energy in myself, I'd get up early and walk to the reservoir on McGill campus to get a better view of the rising sun, and how I had bought a CD of *kirtans* and listened over and over to the *Shiva Shiva Mahadeva* chant. The energy I had been feeling since my recent separation from Karine was very similar to my experience of some twenty years earlier.

Did the connection to Karine give me another boost of energy?

I fast forwarded a couple of years from that time to my year in Vancouver and the nightmare of a trip back to Sri Lanka.

Was my dark night of the soul experience triggered by the separation from the young Karine?

I also remembered the doctor sitting a couple of rows ahead of me on the flight from Montreal to Istanbul a year earlier.

That might have been Karine too!

Still, after making all these momentous connections, I didn't think of writing to her again.

~

In the summer, on my way back home from work, I usually sit for a while in Saint Louis Square, my favourite urban space in Montreal. Located near the corner of Saint Denis and Sherbrooke Streets, Saint Louis Square is a park with a distinct European feel, a smaller version of a square in Rome with teeming local life I remembered from a trip to Italy during my stay in Paris.

I like to think of the square as a mandala—a geometric configuration with an inner circle and four outer gates. The inner circle is made up of a ring of benches with the intricately carved cast-iron fountain with its two basins and the surrounding large pool as its centrepiece. It's protected by a hedge of bushes splashed with red, orange, yellow and violet flowers. Beyond the hedge, a square made up of a low metal fence and four irregular, unkempt lawns on either side separate the inner circle from the rest of the mandala.

The outer square is made up of broad footpaths including two lengthwise paths facilitating the flow of foot traffic between Saint Denis Street and the western outer gate leading to Prince Arthur Street and onwards to Boulevard Saint-Laurent. The space between the inner and outer squares is made up of criss-crossing pathways, more unkempt triangular lawn areas and benches placed in the shade of tall maple trees, some nearly a hundred years old.

An octagon-shaped kiosk café at the western end forms a small mandala of its own. The entire mandala is protected by the Victorian-style residences, some with colourful rooftops matching the inner circle flowers, lining three sides of the square.

About three weeks after my latest epiphany, I sat on a bench in Saint Louis Square near the kiosk café, thinking that the steady stream of pedestrians along the footpaths gave the mandala a dynamic energy. In contrast, the sturdy and solemn trees brought stillness to the scene along with groups of youths sprawling on the green lawn, couples chatting on benches, and solitary seated people reading or simply contemplating.

I watched with amusement as two squirrels scampered through the large, oval-shaped bed of unruly plants and wilted flowers, taking turns chasing after each other. Two little girls did the same along the small pathway under the irate eyes of their stubbled father, who called them to order from time to time, quite unnecessarily, in my opinion.

The patter of falling water from the fountain was at the back of my mind when someone who looked like Karine made an apparition in front of the bed of plants. She had a large dog on a leash and wore a light summer dress like the one worn by the younger Karine, and a suppressed smile. I froze and the entire mandala in front of my eyes disappeared.

Is it her? No, it can't be. This person seems taller and her skin is too tanned. No, it's definitely not Karine.

A few minutes later, I stood up to leave and saw the Karine look-alike coming up the path with a bigger smile this time. That's all I remember. I might have even blacked out while still conscious. It was only on waking up the next morning that I thought it might have been her after all. It took me about a week to fully accept it was Karine who I had seen.

It was then I wrote to ask her whether she had attended the Gnostic centre some twenty years earlier, adding as a postscript that I might also have seen her on a flight to Istanbul a year earlier and very recently at Saint Louis Square.

She did not reply. But moving on was still not an option. In fact, I yearned even more to connect with her. One day, which I distinctly remember as a Saturday, my thoughts and feelings about Karine got so intense I thought I might even pass out, so I lay on my couch. I then felt a palpable shift of energy and I knew with certainty something I didn't know before. *We're connected energetically!*

Not long after, something shifted in my heart as well, and I felt unconditional love. The experience was not as dramatic as what had happened when Bibi opened my heart, but like then, it no longer mattered that Karine was not by my side.

My yearning turned inward, and for the first time on my journey, I truly wanted to let go of the observer and experience *anatta* or no-self, the third characteristic of life according to the Buddha.

Around the same time, I came across one of Rumi's poems, which expressed an identical sentiment. After spending several years in Konya with Rumi, Shams was forced to leave by Rumi's jealous disciples. Rumi then went to Damascus to look for his beloved friend and teacher, and upon returning alone to

Konya, wrote many lyric poems, pouring out his love, including the following:

> *Why should I seek?*
> *I'm the same as he.*
> *His essence speaks through me.*
> *I've been looking for myself.*[36]

~

I told Solange about Karine over dinner at the small Mexican restaurant on the pedestrian stretch of Prince Arthur Street, between Saint Louis Square and Boulevard Saint-Laurent. This stretch, which had had its heyday in the sixties, was revitalized more recently with restaurant seating in the middle of the street and large green hubs in between.

Hearing the first part of my story, Solange muttered something under her breath. Her words were drowned out by the water gushing from the small fountain next to us and the clattering high heels of the flamenco dancer busking nearby, a familiar sight on Prince Arthur in the summer.

I told her about seeing and connecting with a younger Karine, and how I'd walked away from her in Saint Louis Square.

"I'm not surprised you saw her there. She knows your address, so she must have come there on purpose." Solange had it in for Karine, for some reason.

"I don't see how you could jump to a conclusion like that. It was one of those synchronistic events that Jung talked about. I've already lived through a few of those."

I reminded her about the extraordinary synchronicity involving Shakti.

---

36   Coleman Barks, *Book of Love: Poems of Ecstasy and Longing.*

"It can't be just a coincidence that Shakti happened to be a doctor as well," I said. "What a healer she was for me! Unwittingly, of course. But maybe that's how true healing happens, spontaneously, when you're not trying to heal anyone. Coming back to healer Karine, I feel so terrible about not having recognized or acknowledged her. Plus, it was such a missed opportunity. I did write to her, but I don't know whether what I said was enough. Anyway, she hasn't replied, and I won't be too surprised if she doesn't."

Solange complained about the breeze and left to get a sweater from her car. I picked up my large margarita, looked at the lime-green liquid and leaned back in my chair. Its padding happened to match the colour of my drink. I brought the glass close to my lips, inhaled the tangy smell and took a sip, savouring the blend of sweet and sour tastes as I watched the flamenco dancer's swirling red-and-black skirt.

I thought about the long healing process that had paralleled my journey to wakefulness, and the image of Sisyphus pushing his heavy boulder up the mountain flashed into my mind. I first learned about the myth of Sisyphus when reading the complete works of Albert Camus gifted to me by Mademoiselle during my Hôtel d'Alger days. As a punishment for various crimes, Sisyphus had been condemned to push a heavy boulder up a mountain for eternity. As soon as he reached the top of the hill, the boulder rolled downhill and Sisyphus had to start all over again. Camus's solution to the problem was that we should imagine Sisyphus happy.

I felt that, like Sisyphus, I too had been condemned to carry heavy emotional baggage, and each time I thought the work was done, I had to start all over again. But while I might have not felt it, my baggage had gotten lighter and lighter. I'd like to think that the boulder got smaller and smaller each time it rolled down.

So I like to imagine Sisyphus as a truly free man, standing on the top of the hill, arms wide and face turned to the sky. A man who has done the work and fully atoned for his misdeeds.

A sweatered Solange came back and sat down. I gave her the gist of what I had been thinking.

"You know, there can't be light without darkness. Trauma can be a double-edged sword. If not for the trauma arising from the perceived sense of separation, I wouldn't have been driven to go on this journey toward wakefulness. On the other hand, I think unresolved emotional baggage makes the sense of separation more real and forces us to cling to our belief in a separate self. Buddhists, Advaita Vedantists and various other people will not agree with me, but as long as we're not healed emotionally and haven't made the unconscious conscious, I doubt it's possible to let go of the attachment to a separate body-mind identity and achieve no-self."

After finishing off our quesadillas and margaritas, we parted company. I went and sat on a bench in Saint Louis Square, which looked different at night, bathed in the soft light diffused from the lamps hanging like lanterns from dark trees. Star-studded patches of dark blue sky peeked through gaps in branches and the sound of the fountain seemed louder in the now dominant stillness.

I thought of something else I should have told Solange. "Thanks to Karine, I now have this longing to finally let go of my belief in a separate self. But there's nothing I can do to make that happen. It's in the hands of the universe!"

I also realized that I didn't know what Sisyphus's crimes were and googled it on my phone. According to Wikipedia, Sisyphus was punished for self-aggrandizement and deceitfulness. I couldn't help smiling.

Aren't we all guilty of the same offences? Don't we all give an exaggerated importance to our limited separate self and carry on living as if there's nothing more? And don't we all deceive ourselves, thinking that we know ourselves when we really don't? That we're separated from the world, others and our true selves when we're really not?

All separation, every kind of estrangement and alienation is false. All is one . . .[37]

---

37   Nisargadatta Maharaj, *I am That*. Nisargadatta (1897–1981) is one of the best-known modern teachers of non-duality, a man with no formal education and owner of a small shop in a Mumbai slum.

A Note from the Author

If you enjoyed this book, I would be very grateful if you could write a review and publish it at your point of purchase. Your review, even a brief one, will help other readers to decide if they'll enjoy my work.

If you want to be notified of new releases from myself and other AIA Publishing authors, please sign up to the AIA Publishing email list. You'll find the sign-up button on the right-hand side under the photo at www.aiapublishing.com. Of course, your information will never be shared, and the publisher won't inundate you with emails, just let you know of new releases.

www.ingramcontent.com/pod-product-compliance
Lightning Source LLC
Chambersburg PA
CBHW021139080526
44588CB00008B/135